BODY POSITIVE POWER

MEGAN JAYNE CRABBE

9 10 8

Vermilion, an imprint of Ebury Publishing,
20 Vauxhall Bridge Road,
London SW1V 2SA

Vermilion is part of the Penguin Random House group of companies
whose addresses can be found at global.penguinrandomhouse.com

First published in the United Kingdom by Vermilion in 2017

www.penguin.co.uk

A CIP catalogue record for this book is available from the British Library

ISBN 9781785041327

Typeset in India by Integra Software Services Pvt. Ltd, Pondicherry

Printed and bound in Great Britain by Clays Ltd, Elcograf S.p.A.

Penguin Random House is committed to a sustainable future for
our business, our readers and our planet. This book is made
from Forest Stewardship Council® certified paper.

CONTENTS

INTRODUCTION

Three years ago, I sat across from my dad, tracing patterns in the dark wood table between us. We'd come out for some lunch and a chance to catch up on each other's lives, and I had something big that I was anxiously waiting to tell him about. I braced myself, looked up from the table, and began.

'Hey, Dad ...'

'Yes, Megan?'

'You know those body-image issues that I've always had?'

In that moment, my dad could have been remembering any number of things. He could have thought back to when I was five years old and came home from school one day in my little blue check dress, clutching my stomach and asking him to tell me why it was so much bigger than the other girls'. He might have remembered a time 10 years later, standing beside my hospital bed, hoping for that day to be the one when I'd finally start my recovery. He could have pictured me at any point in the years that had passed since then, at any of the nine different dress sizes and hundreds of pounds up and down that my body had spanned since then.

Of course, he didn't mention any of those times. Instead, he replied with an ever so cautious 'yes ...'

'I've fixed them now,' I said, waiting to see the disbelief spread across his face. I'm sure he was expecting me to launch into the details of the new diet plan I'd found and how it was the one that was finally going to make everything better (nothing like all the ones before). I'm sure by now he knew not to get his hopes up.

I started to explain that I'd found something, something that in just a few short months had changed my life. Something called body positivity.

One day in the summer of 2014 I was having a perfectly ordinary Thursday. I'd woken up in the morning, taken my two diet pills, washed them down with a smoothie of apple, berries and kale, and forced myself to start the usual full body workout. Two hours later, I was slumped on the living-room floor getting my breath back, and beginning my daily routine of searching through Instagram for pictures of washboard abs and toned thighs to remind myself why all the pain, sweat and ignored hunger pangs were worth it.

Except that day, by some social-media miracle, I stumbled across something different. A woman wearing a bright red bikini and writing about loving her body as it was. In her own words, she was fat, she was body positive, and she was daring to be visibly happy in a body that I never thought people were allowed to be happy in. There she was embracing all the parts of herself that I'd spent my whole life hating myself for – her soft stomach that rolled when she sat, the cellulite that covered the thickness of her thighs, the jiggle and sway of her arms as she moved.

Seeing her happiness felt as if a sudden crack had been placed in the very foundation of how I believed that the world worked. Here, for the first time in my life, was someone saying that you don't have to spend your days starving, sweating, and hating yourself. That it's possible to accept, and even love, your body just as it is.

I had never even realised that was an option. Nobody had ever told me that shrinking my body didn't have to be my ultimate goal in life. I'd only ever been taught that self-love would come once the hand hit the right number on the scale.

I clicked away from her page and went back to my usual fitspo images to try and erase the thought of that red bikini, and everything that it might mean. But something in my mind had shifted.

As the days went by I started to question my daily routine more and more. Could I really do this for ever? Could I really keep dieting and exercising until I passed out every day for the rest of my life? Because that's what it was going to take to get the 'perfect' body that I'd been striving for since I could remember.

The idea of body positivity kept chipping away at me until a few weeks later that crack in my foundations had turned into a canyon. And there I was precariously balanced with a leg on each side, desperately trying to decide which way to jump.

I remember standing in the garden with my brother and asking for his advice. Did he think that I could do it? Could I really give up everything that I'd ever believed about weight and worth and beauty and learn a whole new way of seeing myself? I can't remember exactly what he said in response, but it was something along the lines of supporting whatever was going to make me truly happy.

At that point I knew, deep down, that if I hadn't found happiness hiding in my bathroom scales after all this time, I was never going to.

So I decided to take a leap. I let myself dive into the online body positive community. I searched out all the information that I could find. A couple of weeks later I borrowed a copy of *The Beauty Myth* from a friend, and the rest is history ...

Actually, the rest is in this book. Everything I've learned in the last three years about why we're at war with our bodies, and how we can make peace with them instead is in these pages. I hope that it helps every single one of you to make that leap, to reclaim your happiness, and to take your power back. Because life really is too short to spend hungry and hating your body.

P.S. Dad, I told you so.

GET THIN OR DIE TRYING

How Striving for the Ideal Body is Destroying Us

'We do not need to change our bodies, we need to change the rules'

– Naomi Wolf, *The Beauty Myth*

Obsession

We are obsessed with our bodies. Or rather, we are obsessed with everything that's wrong with our bodies. We are obsessed with shrinking our bodies, toning our bodies, sculpting our bodies, getting lean and perking up, burning fat and slimming down, flattering our figures and flattening our stomachs, accentuating curves and disguising flaws, battling the bulge, beating the scale, dropping dress sizes, becoming the best version of ourselves that we can be!

And for what? What are we in pursuit of when we do those things? It must be something good, because those things are not fun. Ask anyone on day five of the cabbage soup diet how much fun they're having, and let me know if you get out alive. Of course, we're not supposed to admit how not-fun it all is, we even go as far as lying to ourselves – I really am enjoying living off cayenne pepper and maple syrup cocktails, it's the best thing I've ever done for myself! The facade begins to crack when we start crying over our friend's pizza and wondering if tissue paper is edible, and if so, how many calories? Why do we keep lying to ourselves? Why do we willingly inflict so much discomfort, even pain, on our bodies? What for?

We do it to get the perfect body – flawless, unblemished, ideal. Some of us spend our entire lives chasing the ideal body. The one that will finally make us beautiful; the one that we're told will finally make us happy. We picture that body while we run desperately on the treadmill and our knees feel like they're about to buckle. Just one more mile. We imagine that body when we say no, yet again, to our favourite dessert. That'll go straight to our thighs. We have visions of that body when we step on to our scales and the numbers flash frantically in front of our eyes before they settle on our fate. Please, just two more pounds this week, we've worked so hard. And we have worked so hard. We starve, we sweat, we cry standing over those scales and fall to pieces at the sight of our naked reflection. We vow to be better next week.

Everywhere we go we carry around our feelings of not being good enough. They weigh on everything we do. I can't wear that at my size! I'm not hungry, I ate earlier, I swear! They would never be interested, just look at me. I'll do it once I've lost the weight. Our entire lives get tied up in the chains of the ideal body, only to be unlocked once we've earned it. Perfection is the key. And it's always just slightly out of our reach. There's always another pound to be lost, another problem area to fix (they seem to pop up out of nowhere, almost as if someone's invented them …). But we still believe that we can get there. We still believe after all this time that if we hate ourselves enough we'll end up loving ourselves. We don't realise that we've been tricked.

How did we get here? How did we reach a place where it's 100 per cent normal to hate your body? Every female I've ever known has disliked some part of her appearance, or all of it. We've been convinced that changing the way our bodies look should be our ultimate goal in life, and although women have been the primary target of these messages for the past century, these days no body is safe. Men are increasingly being told that their value lies in their muscles, and that looking like anything less than the cover of a fitness magazine isn't good enough. Thanks to toxic expectations of masculinity, they're also being told not to talk about the body-image issues they're struggling with. Hating your body is the new normal.

Most of us know someone who's had an eating disorder. Someone who's had cosmetic surgery. Someone who's lost and gained the same 20 pounds over and over again. People of all sizes, all ages, all genders, all colours, and all abilities are being affected by body-image issues. We're too fat, too wrinkled, too masculine, too feminine, too dark, too pale, too queer, too different. We're always 'too' something, compared to the ideal body. The pressure becomes too much for us to handle. Our societal self-hatred is spreading like wildfire, slowly but surely we're all being set aflame in the pursuit of perfection.

I'm sure I don't have to tell you this. You already know. You see it every day. It's in the adverts for the new! Easy! Fast! Lose 10 Pounds in 10 Days! Weight-loss plan. It's in the sky-high posters of model bodies selling everything from perfume to burgers. It's in the never-ending murmurs of how many pounds have been shed this week that you overhear on the train, at work, among friends. It's in the TV breaks telling you how breast enhancement could change your life. It's in the magazine pages you flick through to pass the time, raving about the latest juice cleanse or detox.

It's in the back-handed compliments about looking good 'for your age', and the concerned comments from family members about when you're going to do something about, well, you know … It's in the supermarket aisles you walk down filled with 'guilt-free!' reduced fat, sugar-free, zero carbs, made-of-nothing-but-water-and-air food products. It's when you try to unwind with your favourite film or TV show and parading before you is a cast filled with nothing but thin, white, beautiful, young, able bodies.

You might not even notice it, but you learn from it. You learn in millions of little ways every day that there is an ideal, and that you don't match up to it. So that when you get home, away from the murmurs, curtains drawn against the pictures, adverts silenced and screens turned off, only you, your body, your mind, and the quiet … You still know, because there it is in your mirror staring back at you. Everything that you're not. Everything that you need to change. All the ways that your body is wrong. You know.

If you're anything like I am then you've known for a long time. Ever since you were first old enough to take in the words, the images, and the lessons. The first time I remember thinking that I was too fat is when I was five years old. That's all the time it took in the world to believe that I was too much. I was too big, too soft, too brown, too ugly, my stomach was too round and my hair wasn't blond enough.

I remember spending hours in fantasies of what I would look like when I grew up, grasping for reassurance that one day I would be beautiful. Beautiful meaning thin. Thin was the only option, of course that's what I would become, that's what all the representations of beautiful women around me were: Barbie-doll thin, Disney-princess thin, Rachel, Monica and Phoebe thin. To my five-year-old mind, that's what women were supposed to look like. The fact that I was still a child didn't stop me from comparing myself to them.

Recent studies suggest that children as young as three years old have body-image issues and at four years old are aware of how to lose weight.[1] The biggest concern a child that age should have is whether they can do a cartwheel or memorise the alphabet, not whether they're too fat or how many calories it takes to change your body. The obsession is starting earlier and earlier. And this is what those thoughts grow into:

- 97 per cent of women in a survey conducted by *Glamour* magazine admitted to having at least one 'I hate my body' moment a day, with an average of 13 negative body thoughts every day.[2]

- In a survey of 5,000 women by *REAL* magazine, 91 per cent reported being unhappy with their bodies.[3]

- The Centre for Appearance Research found after surveying 384 British men, that 35 per cent would trade a year of their life to achieve their ideal body weight or shape.[4]

- 54 per cent of women would rather be hit by a truck than be fat, according to an *Esquire* magazine survey.[5]

There are thousands of statistics and surveys showing what the real story of our body image is. That we spend every day picking out our flaws and tearing our reflections to pieces. That we put our entire lives on hold because we don't think we're worthy of living in the bodies we have. That we would trade in years of life, risk illness, pain, and even death to turn our bodies into something worth loving. And that we're teaching our children to feel exactly the same way about themselves. Statistics are easy to glaze over, so here's the simple truth: we are destroying ourselves for an unobtainable and unrealistic body type.

The things that we're willing to do for the ideal body speak for themselves. We go hungry, we deny ourselves essential nutrients and ignore our most basic needs. We push ourselves past our physical limits until the room starts spinning and we can barely move the next day. We spend hours applying lotions and potions with promises of miraculous results on the label. We stuff ourselves into elastic casings to smooth out our silhouettes or train our waists into shapes nature never intended them to be. We drink teas and take pills that make our heartbeats race and make sure we don't leave the bathroom all night.

We attend groups every week where we sit in circles fantasising about goal weights and pretending we don't hear it when someone's stomach rumbles. We live off nothing but juice, convinced that our bodies are full of evil toxins that must be cleansed. We pay people thousands of pounds to cut into our healthy flesh, lift it, pin it, tuck it, suck it, staple it, reshape it and stitch us back together again. And it isn't a select few people who are going to any lengths necessary to get the body of their dreams, we're all doing it. The stay-at-home mum who lives down the street, the girl you went to school with, your old English teacher, the star athlete, the savvy businesswoman, the A-list celebrity, the millionaire entrepreneur. The pressure of perfection leaves none of us behind.

And besides the physical lengths we go to, the things we willingly inflict upon our bodies, there's an even darker side to our obsession with perfection, and that's what it does to our minds. The real cost of a diet isn't those irritating hunger pangs you have to ignore, it's the constant preoccupation with food, the never-ending counting and weighing and bargaining that takes up so much mental real estate. The hatred we have for our bodies doesn't stop at our thighs. It takes over our entire sense of self.

It affects our relationships, how we treat others and how we think we deserve to be treated. It seeps into our professional lives, determines what we have the energy to accomplish and the will to aim for. It saps our ambition beyond dropping dress sizes. You can't dream of becoming an artist, an explorer, or a leader when your dreams are occupied by visions of thin. It makes us believe that we don't even deserve to exist in the world, to be seen and heard and valued in the bodies we have. It takes away all of our power.

If we don't measure up to societal standards of beauty, we see ourselves as failures, burdens, and disgraces. We don't just hate our outer shells, we hate our whole selves. And it's exhausting. I know I'm not the only one who feels completely worn out by it all.

Those extra pounds we've learned to see as hideous flaws turn into the weight of the world on our shoulders. Do you feel it? That heaviness? That pressure? That's the weight of all the ways you've been told that you're not good enough. In our current cultural game of How To Be Beautiful, none of us are good enough. We keep playing by the rules because we've been promised that it'll all be worth it in the end. Even if we stumble, fall off the diet, or regain the weight, we get up and try again because we can still see it. The image of the body that will finally make us happy.

I want to let you in on a secret that nobody ever told me in all of my years chasing the ideal body: happiness is not a size. It isn't a number on a piece of fabric, it can't be found in a calorie count, and it sure as hell isn't hiding in your bathroom scales. I know that's hard to believe – after all, everything around us says otherwise.

We've been told for so long that if we just work hard enough the ideal body will be within our reach. Once we're there it'll all be worth it, we'll be beautiful, desired, successful, and, finally, good enough. Except by now you might be starting to realise that you've been playing by those rules for a long time, for as long as you can remember, in fact. You've tried everything you possibly could, you've sacrificed so much time, energy and life to get the ideal body and still you look in the mirror and see something so flawed. So imperfect. So human. How can that be possible?

I'll tell you how. Sit down, my love. Take that weight off your shoulders. If you're reading this book then that probably means you're tired of chasing the impossible. You're tired of waging war against your body and never ever feeling like you're good enough. The problem is that you just can't see another way. How do you let go of the rules and realise that you're good enough already? How do you make peace with your body?

First of all, we have to unlearn all of the lies we've been taught about the way we look. Then, slowly, we can learn the truth instead. If it doesn't happen straight away or if it feels like it's too difficult, I want you to remember that you are fighting against a lifetime of negative conditioning about your body. It's not easy to undo all of that and embrace a new way of thinking. So be patient with yourself, be kind to yourself, and most of all, keep reminding yourself that you deserve better. We all deserve better than spending our lives hating our bodies.

Lesson number one: the image of the ideal body you've been holding on to for all these years, is a lie.

The 5 per cent

We learn the ideal from what we see, and we see it everywhere we turn. The images that fill our minds when we think about what's beautiful aren't creations of our imagination, they're from the hundreds of media bodies we're exposed to every day. With every magazine page, every film, every advert, every TV show, every music video, every time we turn on our screens or walk down a billboard-lined street we see it. We see her.

The fashion model, the Hollywood star, the girl with the golden hair and honey smooth skin. Sometimes the hair is sleek and dark, the eye colour might vary and very occasionally the skin colour does too, but two things remain the same: she is beautiful, and she is thin. If Helen of Troy was the face that launched a thousand ships, we now have the faces that launched a thousand diets, a thousand beauty regimes and a thousand different kinds of self-loathing. From seeing their bodies plastered wherever we go, we learn what our culture's idea of perfection is, which bodies are celebrated and lusted after, what we should all be striving for. We're never allowed to forget.

If aliens ever did descend upon Earth, and confined themselves to a small room with only a television and a stack of magazines in order to learn about humankind before integrating themselves into the community, what would they think? Probably that our women are all five foot ten, weigh about 110 pounds, with gravity-defying globular breasts, faces without a blemish to be seen, are naturally hairless from the nose down and that we pretty much all die out after the age of 35 (except the few that become mothers, cougars, or sad-looking old women). They'd probably also think that a disproportionate number of our men have rock-hard abs and dazzling white smiles, although they'd notice that men are at least allowed to age visibly, and have identities beyond how attractive they are.

They'd probably assume that people of colour are a rare spectacle, and disabled people are far too rare to ever be seen in the outside world. And they wouldn't have any idea that people outside the gender binary exist at all. Imagine their surprise when they leave that room and encounter us, women especially, in all our glory. After the initial shock, they might be quite confused about why our media chooses to constantly represent a body type that 95 per cent of us don't have, and leaves the rest of us behind. They might even find it funny, seeing it as such an obvious distortion of reality. The problem is, we don't recognise the distortion.

Instead of seeing a single body type everywhere we turn as inaccurate, misleading or manipulative, we see our own bodies as the problem. Why aren't our legs that long and toned? Why is our hair so flat and lifeless? Why does our skin have lines on it? We compare ourselves with those images until we're left feeling worthless. Those images are nothing like us.

They're not supposed to be. They're supposed to be aspirational, superhuman enough for us to be in awe of, but with a beauty that we can still believe is achievable. That way, we can be sold the thing that promises to make us just as beautiful. We can buy the miracle diet pill that will give us the figure of our dreams. We can spend our money on the shampoo to get thick, flowing locks. We can splurge on that outfit that we've seen advertised on the most flattering (read: thin) bodies, because maybe it'll make us look like that too! Maybe we can be beautiful too! In all adverts we're being sold two things – the ideal image, and the product to get us there. Want one? Buy the other.

Female beauty ideals are the best marketing scheme in the world. What better way to make money than to make half the world feel ugly and then sell them the solution?

Outside of advertising, the media makes sure we all get the message that the ideal body is the only one worthy of being celebrated, admired, or loved. When was the last time you saw a leading female character get a happy ending without first fitting conventional standards of beauty? You only get a happy ending if you're beautiful, duh. When was the last time you saw a magazine cover with a red circle of shame drawn around a female celebrity's 'flawed' body parts? Inside, the article suggests that she's lost control of her entire life because her stomach folds when she bends over. She couldn't possibly be happy! The next issue shows how she's fighting to get her body, and her life back (cue eye-roll).

We quickly learn that the only way to be beautiful or happy is to spend our lives chasing the ideal body. And it will be a chase, since only 5 per cent of us naturally possess the body type that the media loves so much.[6] Even those of us who appear to be perfect on the outside carry the same nagging insecurities about not measuring up. When we look in the mirror we don't see ourselves clearly because we're looking through a lens of every perfect body we've ever seen. Against those images, we are always too fat, too ugly, too dark, too imperfect.

One study examining the effects of how seeing ideal female bodies on television impacts our own self-image found that 95 per cent of women overestimated their body sizes after seeing images of women with ideal body weights.[7] Meaning that when we constantly see images of the ideal thin body, we come away thinking that we're bigger than we are. What we see every day is shaping how we see ourselves.

We can't see the beauty in everything that we are because we've been taught to first see everything that we're not. All the rules of how we should look take the magic away from how we do look. Jes Baker sums it up perfectly in her book *Things No One Will Tell Fat Girls* when she writes:

> we do this terrible thing where we look in the mirror or at pictures and we expect to see a thin model. Unless you are a thin model, THIS WILL NEVER HAPPEN. So stop that shit. The second you start looking for you is the second you will start to appreciate what you are.

Things get even more complicated when we realise that the perfect body we're searching for in the mirror, the body we think we should have, the body we're killing ourselves for, doesn't even exist. The ideal isn't a real woman, one with history that comes to life on her skin, one with a moving, changing body. The ideal is a creation of a Photoshop wand. Nobody looks as perfect as the ideal, not even those 5 per cent.

Illusion

Fourteen years ago, Susan Bordo wrote the following in her preface to the tenth anniversary edition of *Unbearable Weight*:

> Now, in 2003, virtually every celebrity image you see – in the magazines, in the videos, and sometimes even in the movies – has been digitally modified. Virtually every image. Let that sink in. Don't just let your mind passively receive it. Confront its implications. This is not just a matter of deception ... This is perceptual pedagogy, How to Interpret Your Body 101. These images are teaching us how to see. Filtered, smoothed, polished, softened, sharpened, re-arranged ... Training our perception in what's a defect and what is normal.

Fourteen years later and things have only become worse. We compare ourselves to bodies that don't even exist and spend all our time, energy, and money trying to look like an illusion. When I was younger, I used to dream of spending my one magic wish on sculpting my perfect body. I would be able to mould myself like Play-Doh, pushing the fat from my stomach up to my breasts, making them perky and round, and perched above my ever-shrinking waist. I could carve out my collarbone and etch on my abs, make my eyes three sizes bigger and my chin three sizes smaller.

Which is exactly what editing software does to nearly every image of the female body we see in the media, except it goes so much further than I could have imagined. It erases all signs of ageing, tiredness, and character from female faces. It routinely makes dark-skinned women paler and light-skinned women tanned. It shrinks ears, noses, ankles, toes. It doesn't just shave pounds off the usual places like waists and thighs, it makes people thinner in places they never knew they had to be – necks, forearms, backs, knees, and everything in between. Not even our armpits are safe – they're consistently smoothed out, brightened up, and made to look like hair was never even intended to grow there. There is an ideal armpit. I'm not joking.

BELLY LOVE TIP #1

My belly was always my worst enemy. I've hated it at every age, every size, and in every way you can hate something. I never thought that I could be happy without washboard abs, but it turns out that I was wrong. These days, my soft, squishy stomach is one of my favourite physical features, and I'm going to teach you how to love your tummy too, no crunches required. Throughout this book you'll find these Belly Love Tips – read them, practise them, write them on sticky notes and put them around the house. It's time you made peace with your beautiful belly.

TOUCH

Change the way you touch your tummy. No more pulling, poking, punching or roughly squeezing, like if you just tugged hard enough it might come off in your hands. Stop. Stop treating your stomach like it isn't even a part of you. It is a wonderful part of you.

Try touching it gently. Try to feel its textures without a million thoughts about how it *should* feel clouding your mind. Imagine how inviting that softness is for a head to lie on or a hand to caress, how comforting, how uniquely **you**. Stop hurting yourself, and start exploring your body with kindness instead.

In a recent Refinery29 article, a former Victoria's Secret photoshopper described how the models all wore push-up bras underneath their bikinis during swimwear shoots, which were then erased in the editing process,[8] leaving cleavage far beyond what the actual swimwear could give anyone. A friend of mine working in the photography industry told me how women ask for another person's breasts to be cut from a photograph and pasted on top of their own. In 2013, over 3 million women worldwide had cosmetic surgery on their breasts.[9]

These aren't just harmless pieces of imagery that we all recognise as unrealistic and then go about our lives, these images teach us how to see ourselves, and everything that's wrong with us. It barely even matters whether we're aware of how the images are manipulated, we still compare ourselves to them. How could we not when they're everywhere we turn?

This is a game we cannot win. No matter how many sit-ups we do, lunches we skip, products we buy or hours we spend altering our appearance we will never look like the woman on the magazine cover. As the saying goes, 'even the girl in the magazine doesn't look like the girl in the magazine'. And it goes so far beyond those glossy pages.

The use of CGI (computer-generated imagery) means that moving bodies are being altered too – music videos, films, TV shows. In her videos, Britney Spears has the same chiselled stomach at 34 as she did when she was dancing with a snake wrapped around her shoulders aged 19. The only indication that we're being lied to is when the footage becomes slightly blurred, or when shots of the video pre-CGI get leaked online and we see her real body. A body that's already worthy of all the sweaty snake dances in the world! Apps that are free to download on our phones allow us to drop three dress sizes in just as many clicks before we post our pictures on social media. There is nowhere we can turn to any more for images of bodies that we know aren't edited.

This is a big deal. As Bordo wrote, this isn't a matter of seeing pretty (photoshopped) pictures that have no bearing on how we see ourselves, those pretty pictures are the standard we measure ourselves against, and we will always come up short. A picture really is worth a thousand words, and when the picture is a woman's digitally manipulated body seen by millions, all those words become variations of 'you're not good enough'.

Despite how obviously damaging constant exposure to these images is, the people often responsible for putting them into the world (namely magazine editors), still claim that they're harmless. When singer Kelly Clarkson appeared on the 2009 cover of *Self* magazine, it didn't take people long to realise that the editing fairy had done some serious weight-loss work on her body. A behind-the-scenes video of the shoot showed what she really looked like, and TV appearances at the same time as the magazine release proved it too. The editor-in-chief of *Self* came forward defending the cover, saying that those shots aren't supposed to be 'true to life' and that the editing was 'only to make her look her personal best'.[10] But hold on a minute … how can it be her personal best if it's not really her at all? What kind of message is that sending?

I went to an event a little while ago hosted by a popular women's magazine, the editor of which sat on a panel poised to answer our questions. When I asked what she thought about the toxic side of the media, particularly how it influences the body image of teenage girls, she told me that we don't give girls enough credit. She said that girls are smart enough these days to know when a picture is edited, and that they can control how much the media affects them.

Now, some of the most intelligent people I've ever known have been the ones to fall the furthest into eating disorders and self-hatred, so being smart has nothing to do with it. And as for credit, let's give it where it's really due: to every person who survives another day at war with their bodies because of the kind of poison that those magazines peddle, whether it's unrealistic airbrushing, lack of representation, or yet another 'How To Get Your Best Body Yet!' article.

I left the event really disheartened that someone who had the power to change things would rather evade responsibility and avoid the truth: that smart, creative, extraordinary people are being hurt every day by the image they're selling. And while those pages aren't the sole cause, they are a powerful part of the machine that works to reduce us to imperfect pieces, and sell us the solution. Denial isn't going to change that.

Do we know when an image has been photoshopped? I definitely didn't when I was flicking through my mum's magazines at eight years old. I still remember that feeling, the intoxicating glamour of womanhood beckoning me through those pictures, each one slowly seeping into my mind and forming my idea of what a woman should be. I couldn't wait until I looked just like them – polished, carefree and, most importantly, thin. Thinner than any of the women I knew in real life. I didn't stop to question how that was possible. Even once I knew about Photoshop, it didn't matter.

At 17, I filled an entire book with female bodies that I'd sliced out of those magazines. I made myself look at them every morning, channelling the strength to spend another day denying my hunger and chasing perfection. I knew about airbrushing by then. I knew how bodies were made thinner and so-called flaws were blurred out, but it didn't make a difference. Those bodies were still the goal, the dream, the ideal.

When we believe in the ideal body so ferociously, we're willing to ignore just about anything that flies in the face of it. It's why we still believe the right diet will work, even when the last 372 haven't. It's why we keep buying the lotions and potions that claim to make us younger and firmer, despite having a drawer full of them at home that did absolutely nothing. And it's why, when we see a picture of an impossibly beautiful body, we still compare ourselves to it, we still strive to look like it, even when we know it's been photoshopped. Even when we know that no real person could ever achieve a body that flawless. We still try. We just can't give up our belief in the ideal body.

Imagine if tomorrow all the images changed. No more Photoshop. No more exclusion. Real diversity and real bodies displayed for all the world to see. Imagine every person being able to open a magazine or turn on their screens and see themselves represented, see bodies just like theirs being celebrated as beautiful and worthy of cover pictures or leading roles. I think the effect on our self-esteem would be undeniable. Then all of the people who say that images are meaningless will have to deal with the millions of badass, confident women demanding an answer as to why we've been lied to for so long, and made to believe that we were anything other than perfect.

Thin is in

Have you ever thought to question where our image of the ideal body comes from in the first place? Who decides what beauty is, anyway? We treat the ideal body as if it's a sacred truth, passed down from Mount Sinai through generations – thou shalt be skinny. Our current beauty ideals are seen as undebatable, it's simply a fact that thin is beautiful and fat is not. To doubt the power of these truths would be blasphemous! But I'm going to anyway. Because if the ideal body is solid gold truth, then why has it changed so much over time?

It's hard to believe that there was ever a time when fat was in and thin was out. Actually, there have been plenty of moments throughout history when our body ideals today would be seen as bizarre. In Western culture 200 years ago, fat was viewed as healthy and beautiful, fat meant you had enough to eat, that you weren't poor, or in fragile health.

Once upon a time our hunter-gatherer ancestors relied on being able to store fat efficiently in order to survive, that extra jiggle was life-saving when food was scarce. Now we curse our slow metabolisms and see our bodies as less efficient the more fat they store. And sure, we're not hunters any more, for most of us food is readily available, so it's logical that plenty of body fat is no longer seen as essential. But why should it be seen as hideous? And why, over the last 100 years alone, have there been so many different ideas about fat, how much we're allowed and where we're allowed it?

Every so often an angry teenage boy who's mad about fat women loving themselves comes on to my Instagram page to tell me that we've evolved to see thin bodies as attractive, and I can't change people's instinctual preferences (I'm paraphrasing, usually there's at least one 'ur a fat whale!' thrown in there). Their argument is that the ideal body has been ingrained in our minds through evolution to ensure that we find the best possible mate. And sure, some of our personal preferences about what's attractive are hard-wired, but those preferences don't even begin to cover how extreme our current cultural idea of beauty has become.

When we think about female secondary sexual characteris-tics, the physical traits that we associate with feminine bodies like breasts and hips, and the parts that should play a key role in any evolutionary-driven ideal body, it's clear that sometimes, these are the parts that we've been taught are the most flawed. The parts that we should have evolved to admire the most are the parts we've been made to hate the most.

Wide hips and increased body fat in the thighs and buttocks are signs of oestrogen production in women, the sex hormone responsible for the development and regulation of the reproductive system. Surely, if the ideal body is so connected to instinctual survival, they would be physical features we would evolve to be always attracted to? But taking a glance back at any magazine, TV show or beauty icon of the nineties will show you how demonised those features have been in the past.

Back then 'does this make my butt look big?' was the question on women's lips everywhere, hoping for the answer to be no. Sir Mix A Lot didn't do much to stop the trend either; women kept trying to flatten their derrières way into the noughties. Why? Because that's what the image of beauty was at that time: tall, straight, and flat. Thick thighs are only just making a comeback (and only if they're cellulite-free). And what about stomach fat?

Women are genetically predisposed to storing more body fat than men,[11] and the fat around our stomach is there to act as protection for the reproductive organs.[12] In other words, it's supposed to be there. That pouch of squishiness at the bottom of your belly that you hate so much? You're meant to have it, it serves a purpose. Even the most slender, toned female bodies in the world usually have at least a small curve at that part of their stomach. If our body ideals were about what evolution has influenced us to see as positive qualities in a mate, then stomach fat would be all the rage. Instead we can barely go a single day without being bombarded with ways to Blitz Your Belly Fat! Battle The Bulge! Fight The Flab! Get Washboard Abs In Three Easy Steps!

Even while researching this chapter I searched Google for 'female stomach fat is good' and every single result, was an article about finally losing that stubborn belly fat, how to get flat abs and maintain them, fast and easy weight loss for your tummy.

The title of one *Bustle* article, which I did eventually manage to find, says it all: '"How Do I Get Flab Abs" Is A Biologically-Rigged Question For Women To Be Asking Themselves'. It is rigged, making something as natural and normal as stomach fat into the ultimate female sin is rigging the game so that we always lose. So as for evolutionary body ideals, I think we left that reasoning behind a long time ago. We're playing by a whole new set of rules now. Besides, I'm not sure what kind of evolutionary instinct would make defined eyebrows and thigh gaps a priority.

The only possible reason that the ideal body keeps changing, and exists in the form it does today, is because groups of very powerful people make it so. Just like the ones who make pleather fashionable one year and tell us that it's hideous the next, these people, instead of playing with fabric textures, play with our self-image. The rules spread fast, and soon all the people in charge of what we see on a daily basis are clued in. They enforce the new ideal body by saturating our surroundings with images of it, selling us new miracle products to help us reach it, and writing headlines that reinforce the ideal into fact, even if the proof was built on shaky ground.

There is no higher reason why the bodies we idolise today are different from the bodies we idolised 50 years ago, just like there's no higher reason why bootleg jeans were gradually replaced with skinny jeans (and probably a new type of jeans by the time you're reading this). It's fashion. It's a cultural preference built on nothing more than what we're told. We hate our bodies for not fitting well enough into a standard that is literally made up. And if we weren't living in this time and place in history, things would very different.

One of my favourite body positive artworks called *Wrong Century* by Tomas Kucerovsky shows a beautiful fat woman in a striking red top standing in an art museum. A man passes by, raising his glasses to glare at her body with a deep frown on his face. Behind her two younger men whisper to each other and laugh, gesturing at her size. We then see her face, staring sadly up at a piece of art. The piece she's staring at is Peter Paul Ruben's *The Rape of the Daughters of Leucippus*, where the two women's bodies he painted are soft and dimpled, with thick thighs and rolling stomachs. She stares, knowing that things were once so different. You see it and you can't help but think if only those people judging her size understood that they're just blindly following the trends, then they might see her very differently. Open your eyes: bodies like hers were once worthy of great art and admiration.

Botticelli's *The Birth of Venus* shows the Roman goddess of sex, love, and beauty emerging from the water in her shell. Her stomach has a fleshy pouch at the bottom and her thighs definitely touch. She is mesmerising. There's a sculpture called *The Crouching Aphrodite*, showing the ancient Greek interpretation of the same goddess bent forwards with three distinct soft rolls flowing down her belly. The figure considered to be the very epitome of beauty at those times had belly rolls. Yet we're supposed to feel disgusted with them now.

The Venus of Willendorf is a small statuette carved in the Palaeolithic period (around 25,000 years ago) showing a female body with enormous rounded breasts resting on an even bigger stomach. She could walk into any modern-day diet centre and instantly be dubbed a morbidly obese apple shape who needs to cut the calories immediately. She's thought to have represented fertility and sexuality all that time ago. My oh my, how times have changed.

Even since the beginning of the twentieth century an array of different bodies have been idolised at different times. We need to remember that our idea of beauty today isn't immutable truth. It isn't unshakeable fact. It's fashion. Why do we take something so seriously that changes by the decade? Can't we see how meaningless ideal bodies really are, constantly changing and being dictated to us by the celebrated shapes of each generation?

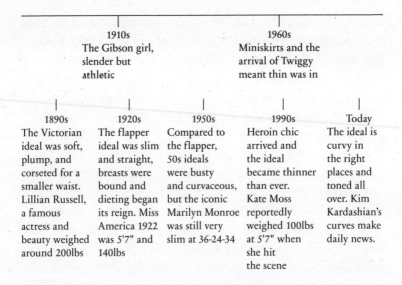

	1910s The Gibson girl, slender but athletic		1960s Miniskirts and the arrival of Twiggy meant thin was in	
1890s The Victorian ideal was soft, plump, and corseted for a smaller waist. Lillian Russell, a famous actress and beauty weighed around 200lbs	1920s The flapper ideal was slim and straight, breasts were bound and dieting began its reign. Miss America 1922 was 5'7" and 140lbs	1950s Compared to the flapper, 50s ideals were busty and curvaceous, but the iconic Marilyn Monroe was still very slim at 36-24-34	1990s Heroin chic arrived and the ideal became thinner than ever. Kate Moss reportedly weighed 100lbs at 5'7" when she hit the scene	Today The ideal is curvy in the right places and toned all over. Kim Kardashian's curves make daily news.

Body positivity is often misunderstood as wanting to make a new body type the ideal, one that's bigger and curvier and represents those of us who've spent years on the ideal body sidelines. The truth is that we don't want to change the ideal, we want to abolish it. We want absolutely all bodies to be celebrated and idolised, represented and glorified. The women on the magazine covers can stay, but they're going to have to make some room for the rest of us too. We're tired of being told that there's only one kind of beauty when we see that all of us exist on the spectrum of beauty, no matter how well we fit into the standards of today.

Today's ideal body is deceptive. It tells women that they're allowed body fat, embrace your curves! It insists that fitness is just as important as beauty, strong is the new skinny! It claims to be a relief from the years that Kate Moss measurements dominated the beauty conversation. But it really isn't. Sure, curves are allowed, but only in exactly the right places and only in exactly the right proportions. The Internet is overrun with people declaring who gets to call themselves 'curvy' and who doesn't ('this isn't curvy, this is just fat').

We're allowed our hips and our breasts back, but our stomachs, legs, arms and faces have to stay in line, and our arses are a whole different story. As for fitness, the only thing that really counts is if you can see physical results, chiselled torsos and high, firm glutes. Today's ideal is the hourglass shape of the past taken to its extreme. Is it really any easier to maintain a body that's thin, toned and hard in the specified places and overflowingly voluptuous everywhere else, than it was to be thin all over? Or is it just as unattainable for the majority of us?

Now every girl is expected to have Caucasian blue eyes, full Spanish lips, a classic button nose, hairless Asian skin with a California tan, a Jamaican dance hall ass, long Swedish legs, small Japanese feet, the abs of a lesbian gym owner, the hips of a nine-year-old boy, the arms of Michelle Obama, and doll tits.

– Tina Fey, *Bossy Pants*

Unless you hit the jackpot in the cultural beauty standards' genetic lottery, achieving today's ideal body is going to take more time and energy than any past ideal body. Working for a body type that so few of us could ever naturally possess becomes a full-time job. Every waking hour is dedicated to fighting your flesh into submission. The obsession takes over. And maybe that's the point?

The myth

Female beauty standards are never simply about being beautiful. How a woman is supposed to look also dictates how she must act, and ultimately how she fits into the world. Because the road to the ideal body is made up of superficial things – which low fat yoghurt to choose, which size to pick up, which shade of eyeshadow to wear or brightly coloured magazine to take from the shelf – we forget that it's about so much more than that.

If we think about our own experience, it's easy to see how striving for the ideal body changes us far beyond the physical. It prescribes to us how we should spend our time, our money, and our energy. It becomes the thing we focus on the most, the thing we talk about the most, the thing we want most in the world. It becomes a core part of our identity, which is why the thought of giving it up is so terrifying – what will we be without it? The answer, of course, is whatever the hell we want to be. Female beauty ideals have been used to limit us, who we can become, and how much space we're allowed to take up in the world. They are about so much more than what we look like. Here's a mini history lesson to show how fucked up beauty ideals really are:

In China, female foot-binding was once the ultimate symbol of feminine beauty and status. Women who had 'lotus feet' (feet altered in shape by binding, making them around three or four inches long), were seen as the most attractive, and were the most likely to earn prestigious marriages. The process of achieving this beauty standard involved breaking all but the big toes, tying them flat against the soles, breaking the arches of the foot in two, and binding them together until they were crushed into place.

The women also became symbols of the husband's wealth – having lotus feet meant that even walking was painful. The women couldn't work, so their feet showed the world that they came from wealthy homes, where men didn't need the women's labour to earn enough money. It was an ideal that caused immobility, pain and sometimes death.[13,14] By keeping women's feet tiny and broken, their roles in the world remained that way too. But at least they were considered beautiful, right?

The Victorian woman's corset had the same effect. A cinched waist was a sign of beauty and class. It was 'considered essential for real femininity', despite the fact that 'corsets put so much force on women's bodies that they often constricted the lungs, squeezed the liver and small intestines, dislocated the stomach, and compressed the bladder. Some women's corsets were laced so tightly that, over time, their ribs grew into their livers and other organs'.[15] Do we seriously believe that's just about looking beautiful? Why does female beauty have to come at the price of so much pain? That painful ideal wasn't a simple aesthetic preference for small waists – it served to keep women confined, laced into their roles in the home and too short of oxygen to question it.

In her 1991 work *The Beauty Myth*, Naomi Wolf charts the rise in women's social, economic and political power with the increasing pressure of the rules of beauty, showing how connected the two are. In other words, the extreme thinness that became the ideal body type at that time isn't accidental, it's an effective method of keeping women hungry, preoccupied, and without enough energy to fight for real equality. On the surface it's about looks, but underneath it's about controlling what a woman can be. As Wolf famously writes 'a cultural fixation on female thinness is not an obsession about female beauty but an obsession about female obedience'.

The ideal body serves a social purpose beyond just telling us how we should look. So what's the social purpose of today's ideal? We're still hungry, and preoccupied, and so obsessed with our bodies that we don't realise how much extraordinary potential we have. When I think back over the dieting years and the rare moments I managed to force my body into looking more like the ideal, I don't wish for that body back. I wish for that time back. All that time that was supposed to be about discovering the world and who I was became wasted on making myself smaller and smaller. Imagine if we all stopped expending so much energy on trying to change our bodies. We could do anything we dreamed of. We could get shit done.

Another purpose of upholding an unattainable ideal body is making cold hard cash. Some of the biggest industries in the world make billions from our belief that we're not good enough. Just think about how much we spend on diet plans, beauty supplies, exercise equipment, anti-ageing products and all the other things we hope will finally fix our physical imperfections.

The thin body ideal has stuck around for so long because it's such a profitable one – it's one that so few of us can ever successfully obtain, and one we're willing to spend whatever it takes to achieve. We'll talk more about that in a bit. For now, it's clear that the beauty myth still has a firm grip on us, and it will do as long as we continue to believe that beautiful is the most important thing a woman can be, whatever form beautiful takes at certain times in history.

Real talk

Let's get real about the ideal. It sucks. It doesn't represent us, and it doesn't even try to. It refuses to acknowledge that people of all sizes, shapes, ages, skin colours, genders and abilities exist and are worthy of being seen, heard, and valued. It isn't even real, it's built on digital manipulation and deception. And yet we're still told to do everything we can to look like something only a Photoshop pro could create.

It changes over time so that even if we do come close to fitting the standard it slips from our grip and transforms into something else. Which shows us that it's only really about fashion, not truth, not necessity, not evolutionary purpose, just a made-up rule. A rule that keeps us trapped, small, and believing that we don't deserve better. Why are we still buying into this?

Mostly because it promises us so much; it doesn't just sell us the image, it sells us the dream. Everything that we've always wanted wrapped up in a pretty thin bow. But just like the image itself, those promises are all lies. For everything it claims to give, it takes more away.

- **Aspiration:** The ideal body gives us something to aspire to, something to achieve. It promises that we'll be rewarded when we work hard enough. It gives us ambition. But what kind of life aspiration is losing 20 pounds? Our ambition is really being wasted on things that don't matter. We could aspire to true greatness, to career success, to travelling the world, to helping others, to spreading love, to spiritual enlightenment, whatever floats your boat and makes you feel genuinely fulfilled. Instead we're stuck aspiring to empty numbers and convincing ourselves that it's enough.

- **Identity:** The ideal gives us a sense of who we are. We get to be the one who goes to the gym, the one who wears the best clothes, the one with the rocking body and the will-power of a saint. Except all those superficial things do is distract you from everything you could be. Who wants an identity that's built on a calorie count? And what happens to your identity when your body changes, when you fall off the diet, miss the gym, grow or age? Wouldn't you rather be known as the one who's kind, the one who's talented, the one who's caring, compassionate, intelligent, funny, thoughtful, brave, adventurous, serene, confident, or reliable? Whatever it is that makes you uniquely you? You really are so much more than a body.

- **Love:** We all know how this one goes. Get the perfect body, find the perfect man/woman/person. Contrary to popular belief, all kinds of people find love. There are people out there who haven't been completely brainwashed by exclusionary cultural standards of what's attractive, and besides, why would you want to be with anyone who values what you look like over who you are? You deserve someone who adores your true identity, not the outer shell you've crafted to try and survive in an image-obsessed world.

- **Happiness:** This is the one we're fooled into believing the most. We learn it with every success story of the person who lost the weight and turned their whole life around. The thousands of adverts showing women gleefully smiling down at their plates of salad or prancing around fields with a bowl of cardboard-tasting cereal in hand. They show us that as soon as we reach the ideal all of our problems will disappear and we'll get the life we want, finally.

Even Oprah Winfrey, self-made media mogul, beloved around the world and dubbed as one of the most influential figures of the twentieth century, has repeatedly said that it doesn't mean anything if she hasn't lost the weight. So much success, and yet the ideal body is the one thing that she thinks will bring her happiness. The only problem is that she keeps regaining the weight, we all do. We never reach the ideal because, as we know, it changes, it's impossible, and most of us just aren't genetically cut out for it. If we keep playing by the rules of the ideal we'll be waiting for happiness for ever. So what if we just took happiness now, as we are? Weight loss doesn't solve our problems. Dress sizes don't bring us fulfilment. And spending your life believing you're not good enough will never make you happy. I hope Oprah realises that too.

The ideal works incredibly hard at convincing us that it's all our fault. That the reason why we're not beautiful enough, successful enough, happy, or in love is because we're not working hard enough for it. We're not following the rules well enough. We're undisciplined. We're lazy. We're failures. We're the problem. And we believe it, we soak up all that guilt and all that self-loathing and we don't stop to question that maybe the problem isn't us and our bodies.

Here is something that I want you to try your hardest to believe right now. I want you to say it to yourself, read it over and over until it sinks in:

> You are not the problem. Your body is not the problem. The problem is the culture. The problem is the rules. The problem is the ideal. Not you. How you feel about your body is not your fault. All those insecurities aren't something that you've just made up and decided to torture yourself over. This is something that has been done to you, to all of us. There is absolutely a problem, but it's not you.

You might still have a hard time believing that, after all you've been blaming yourself for so long. But you did not ask to be born into a culture that values how we look above who we are as people, and prizes thinness so highly. You didn't ask for the ideal, and if you're still in any doubt about how damaging it truly is, just take a look at one of the most well-known eating disorder studies in the world, conducted by Anne Becker, to test what effect exposure to Western body ideals had on the body image of adolescent girls in Fiji.[16]

Before 1995, the Nadroga province of Fiji didn't have access to television. Traditional Fijian values showed a preference for robust, strong bodies, and encouraged hearty appetites with feasts. People would be wary if someone showed a lack of appetite or lost weight. The Miss Fiji beauty queen of the time described how people saw slim women as weak, saying 'people are always telling me to put on weight'.[17] Most notably, before TV arrived in Fiji, eating disorders were practically unheard of, with only one reported case of anorexia by the mid-1990s – and dieting for weight loss before the nineties was non-existent. Until TV came along.

Within three years of television shows from the UK, USA and New Zealand being broadcast on the island, 74 per cent of the teenage girls surveyed said that they felt 'too big or fat'. And 15 per cent of girls reported using self-induced vomiting in order to control their weight.

Some of the quotes from these girls say it all: 'When I look at the characters on TV, the way they act on TV and I just look at the body, the figure of that body, so I say "look at them, they are thin and they all have this figure", so I myself want to become like that, to become thin' … 'I just want to be slim because [the television characters] are slim. Like it's influencing me so much that I have to be slim'.

The study is a perfect snapshot of how damaging images of the ideal body can really be. These images had the power to cause so much pain in just three years, in just one format. Take a minute now to reflect on how many years you've been exposed to the ideal body, all the hundreds of images in all different formats you see every day, and ask yourself, is it really any wonder that we feel the way we do about our bodies?

We weren't born hating our bodies. The Fijian girls didn't even hate their bodies until the image of the ideal body came along. Even if it seems too distant to remember, there was a time when your body was not your worst enemy. A time before the flaws became visible, a time before the diets became mandatory, a time before you got swept up in the way the world told you that you should be. I know that at some point I was carefree, safe from comparison and perfectly content in my soft, fascinating body. I know that slowly I learned the self-loathing that took over my life. Hating our bodies is something that we learn, and it sure as hell is something that we can unlearn.

A new ideal

The new ideal would be no ideal at all. It would be all of our bodies celebrated and represented. It would teach us to see the beauty all around us, and to see ourselves through kinder eyes. It wouldn't use yet another exclusionary image to divide us, making fat 'in' and thin 'out'. It isn't the body-shaming slogans that some people think of as body positivity: 'real women have curves'. It would recognise, as Hanne Blank wrote, that 'real women are fat. And thin. And both, and neither, and otherwise'. It wouldn't leave us feeling less than, unworthy, not good enough. It wouldn't place us in competition with one another. It would raise us all up instead of tearing 95 per cent of us down. We are the ones with the power to make it happen.

I want you to fall in love with your body. Truly, madly, deeply in love, as the song goes. I want you to be wonderstruck by all the ways it works to keep you alive. I want you to be in awe of how the signs of your life trace themselves on your skin. I want you to feel like a goddess. Or god. Or gender-neutral deity. I want you to see the beauty that comes from your body and beyond.

I also know that for some of us, that kind of body love seems impossible and way too daunting to even contemplate. If body love feels unachievable right now, that's okay. Nobody can jump from a lifetime of body-image issues straight into self-love. Instead, we can take some stepping stones along the way. One option is to aim for body acceptance.

Body acceptance is about accepting that this is the body you have, and feeling neutral about that fact. It means not thinking that you're flawless and bootylicious 24/7, but also not thinking that you're hideous and need to change. Actually, it's not thinking about your body very much at all, just accepting that how it looks is how it looks, and getting on with your days.

A stepping stone down from body acceptance could be body respect. You might feel like you can never make peace with how your body looks. You might feel like you can never accept your stretch marks, or your loose skin, or your softness. So for now, let's forget about accepting the outside. Instead let's work on being thankful for all the incredible things our bodies allow us to do.

If your arms allow you to hug the people you love, let your body know that you're grateful for that, instead of focusing on whatever shape those arms might be. When your body tries its best to heal you when you're sick or injured, recognise how hard it's fighting for you, not how it looks while it's fighting. If your body takes you places and lets you experience the world, you can still be thankful for that, even if the gratitude disappears as soon as you look in the mirror. You can respect your body, even if you can't make peace with your reflection. Hopefully the stepping stones of body respect and body acceptance will lead you to body positivity, but if not, that's okay too.

No matter where you land on your journey to making peace with your body, remember that it's not about being beautiful to others. It's not about being beautiful according to the rules. It's about knowing that you're good enough and knowing that your outer shell is one of the least important things about you. What every step on this journey has to start with, is realising that you deserve better. And you deserve to have your body represented in our culture's idea of beauty, always.

So show me it all. Show me the fat bodies and the thin ones. Show me the belly rolls, the cellulite, the jiggling upper arms. Show me the muscular and the soft. Show me the wide hips and the narrow ones too. Show me the breasts of all shapes and sizes, perky and droopy, uneven or absent. Show me the scars, the marks, the freckles, the blemishes. Show me the darkest skin and the palest, and every shade in between. Show me the able bodies and the differently abled bodies, the bodies in wheelchairs, the amputees, the bodies with disabilities visible and not. Show me the wrinkles and the lines, the hair in all tones of silver and grey. Show me the tall bodies and the short bodies. Show me them all. Let the world see them all, and let us call them all the new ideal.

The F-word

Let's talk about the word FAT. If you've read this far then you've already seen it plenty of times. You might have wrinkled your nose at it, squirmed in your seat a little bit, felt your face flush with heat or wondered why a body positive book would drop so many F-bombs. After all, fat has become one of the most powerful insults in the world. We've all felt the white-hot shame that slices through your insides when someone says those two words: you're fat.

Not too long ago those words had the ability to catapult me into a spiral of self-hatred faster than you can say 'bikini body'. I've spent my life running from fat, living in fear that it would catch up with me. I ran when I was five years old on the playground. I ran when I was 10 years old on my first diet. I ran when I was 14 years old and in a hospital bed, still convinced that I could feel it creeping up on me.

I nearly ran right into an early grave, desperately looking over my shoulder for its shadow. And then after recovery, when all that extra softness suddenly appeared and I didn't know what to do with any of it, I start running again. I kept running from fat for so many years, through crash diets, exercise addiction, and hundreds of pounds gained and lost. Fat was always there, the enemy, the threat, the fear.

When we see the word 'fat' we don't just think of a body size or a food group or a type of cell that covers our bodies. We see all the meanings that our culture has given those three little letters. Fat is ugly. Fat is unhealthy. Fat is disgusting. Fat is lazy. Fat is unintelligent. Fat is failure. Fat is disgrace. The list goes on and on, there are no three letters in our culture quite as loaded with negativity as F A T.

So what's it doing here amid words on self-love and body acceptance? Surely I should be telling people to stop calling themselves fat, and saying things like 'you're not fat, you're beautiful!'. But really, who said you couldn't be both? Who said you can't be fat and beautiful, fat and successful, fat and sexual, fat and intelligent, fat and healthy, fat and happy? Fat is not a bad word. I know that's a pretty unbelievable statement, but bear with me.

Reclaiming the words that have been used to tear us down in the past is part of this journey. When I first found the body positive community, the word fat was still unspeakable to me, unthinkable even, and yet here were hundreds of people declaring themselves as fat. Why weren't they running from it like I was? Why weren't they hiding from it? Why would they insult themselves like that so openly?

It turns out that they weren't insulting themselves, they were celebrating themselves. They were taking back the words that have been used to make them feel worthless and stripping them of their power. They were fat babes rocking fatkinis and all other kinds of flabulous fatshion. They were embracing their fatness in every way and they were powerful as hell.

Marilyn Wann wrote in *Fat! So? Because You Don't Have to Apologize For Your Size*, that 'reclaiming the word fat is the miracle cure you've been looking for, the magic trick that makes all your worries about weight disappear'. You can't be hurt by a word that you no longer see as a threat. People can jump up and down all day long raging about what a fat whale you are and when your only response is 'so?', you've pretty much burst their bubble. Marginalised groups have historically reclaimed the words of their oppressors to strip them of their power, for example, the word queer was used as a derogatory slur towards LGBTQIA+ community long before it was reclaimed and

Is 'fat' really the worst thing a human being can be? Is 'fat' worse than 'vindictive', 'jealous', 'shallow', 'vain', 'boring' or 'cruel'? Not to me.

- J.K. Rowling

became a celebratory term. Why shouldn't the word fat be taken back too?

All the negative things that society has taught us fat is synonymous with just aren't true. Fat doesn't mean anything other than just that, fat. Some people have fat bodies, some people have thin bodies, some people have chubby bodies, some people have muscular bodies, and every other variation of size and shape in between. The amount of fat cells your body carries does not define who you are as a person, it doesn't dictate your beauty or your value. You don't need to keep running from it.

So start! Say the F-word out loud, say it until that nervous feeling in your stomach goes away and it becomes just another three-letter word (it's a pretty cute one actually). Find some unapologetically fat babes and notice how they're living their lives in full fat force. Call out people who say that someone's fat like it's a bad thing. Stun the next person who tries to tear you down with an F-bomb by taking their words as a compliment. I wouldn't suggest going around calling other people fat unless you know they're comfortable with it – most people haven't realised how fabulous fat can be yet. But get comfortable with it yourself, take back a little bit of your power with just one word.

I'll say it again: fat is not a bad word, it's just a way of describing bodies. It should hold no more negativity than 'brunette' or 'blue-eyed', and it definitely shouldn't be something that has the power to destroy our entire sense of self and leave us living in fear of our own bodies.

LOSE WEIGHT FOR GOOD!

(ONLY £29.99 A MONTH)

The Industry at the Root of Our Bad Body Image

'If tomorrow, women woke up and decided they really liked their bodies, just think how many industries would go out of business'

– Dr Gail Dines

'Dieting is the cure that doesn't work for the disease that doesn't exist'

– The Fat Underground

The first

I remember that first diet well. It was around the time that the girls in class started changing for PE in a separate room (before that we all just changed together). A few of us had started wearing bras that held nothing but a swelling sense of pride mixed with fear – womanhood was coming. I'd noticed that my body was different to the others' a long time ago, but the rest of them didn't seem to notice that they had bodies at all. They ran and jumped and played and talked to boys at breaktime like their bodies were things they didn't even give a second thought to. Mine was already the thing I thought about the most.

I spent every cross-legged assembly staring down at my thighs and keeping them hovering in mid-air so that they wouldn't splay out and overflow like batter swelling over the sides of the cake tin. I had the posture of a saint in class, making sure that my stomach was properly sucked in and not bulging against my blue-and-white school dress like it did when I let myself relax. I've forgotten now how that feels, spending every moment from when you leave the house to when you get home determinedly sucking it in. Tighter if you feel someone's eyes on you, tighter still if you hear the click of a camera, forcing a hollow-necked smile and waiting until you can breathe again. If anyone reading that felt the need to tense their body and check that they weren't all hanging out – please breathe. Let it go, be comfortable, there is nothing wrong with your unsucked-in stomach!

I was already an active child, moving my body for fun before the dreaded thoughts of calories burned and pounds dropped crept in and ruined it. I was on the netball team, the football team, dance class, I spent summers in clubs filled with sports (I fell in love with softball one year and fell out of love with it just as fast when the boy I liked told me that I was 'good for a big girl'). After school, I rode my bike up and down our slanting road with the girl who lived across the street for hours every day. Indoors I had an older brother who always needed to practise his wrestling moves, occasionally ending in tears and once with him breaking his thumb – you can imagine the shame I felt thinking that I was fat enough to break a thumb just by sitting on it.

Truthfully, I wasn't fat. No sensible adult would have looked at me and cried out 'childhood obesity!' before calling for a ban on turkey twizzlers at lunchtime. I wore an age 10–11 when most of my friends were wearing age 8–9. I might have been 10 pounds heavier than them. I had a round face and solid limbs and the kind of puppy fat that adults insisted was cute and that I spent hours pulling and squeezing and wishing away. But in that child-hood bubble I was huge.

It's disturbing just how distorted childhood body image can be, even when looking at other people's bodies. One of my favourite parts of the day used to be getting to watch *Sabrina the Teenage Witch* at teatime and imagining when my magic would kick in (no prizes for guessing what my first spell would be). The two aunts in the show, Hilda and Zelda, are perfect examples of how messed up my ideas about bodies were. I always saw Zelda as normal-sized and beautiful, and Hilda as the fat one. Having bought the complete boxset a few years back and rewatched every episode with my best friend, I see now that Zelda is in fact extremely thin, probably weighing in at around 100 pounds, and Hilda is just a curvaceous woman, not even what most people would consider plus size. Yet to me she was huge.

Recently Mattel made headlines for rebranding Barbie after decades of accusations that her unrealistic body proportions sent a dangerous message to the young girls who adore her. They proudly presented the new dolls with a range of skin colours, available in tall, petite, and curvy. Even though the idea of Curvy Barbie was seriously exciting to all of the women who'd grown up staring at Barbie's plastic perfection and feeling inferior, Mattel made sure they didn't push the beauty boundaries too far. Curvy Barbie has fuller calves, no thigh gap, a very slightly rounded lower belly, wider hips, and arms with a hint more flesh on them. Blown-up to life size proportions she would still only wear a UK 6/8[18] (that's a 2/4 US), where original Barbie would wear a UK size 2 (US size 00). But hey, it's progress.

So what did young girls think of having a more realistic fashion icon to play with? 'Hello, I'm a fat person, fat, fat, fat,' says one six-year-old playing with the doll. Another spells out 'F-A-T' so she doesn't hurt Barbie's feelings saying it out loud. When the adults leave the room, the girls undress Curvy Barbie and laugh at her.[19] Which shows how believable it is that my few extra pounds made me see myself as the class whale – an hourglass size 8 is big enough to be ridiculed and labelled as an outcast by six-year-old girls. If that's not fucked up I don't know what is.

So there I was, 10 years old and chubby. I had a crush that year, too. He wore mismatched green socks and hopped down the school corridors like a frog – the height of charm when you're 10. I already knew that I would never tell him how I felt, there was no way he would choose me over my long, slender friends with perfect pigtails and bright blue eyes.

I decided that if I was going to become the beautiful, thin version of myself I imagined when I closed my eyes that I better start doing something about it. I knew all about diets by then, I'd read enough 'Lose 10 Pounds a Week!' articles in my mum's magazines, seen enough TV adverts for meal replacements and overheard enough conversations between the mums at the school gates. When we got home one day I announced to my mum that I was 'getting healthy'. I knew it was a diet, but I didn't want her to know, that would have meant having to talk about my body and why I hated it so much. These were the rules of 'getting healthy':

- NO chocolate

- NO crisps

- NO biscuits or cakes

- Only snack on fruit or low-calorie cereal bars

- Smaller portions

- Run more at school

- Weigh self every day

And when I decided that there would be NONE of the foods I liked the most, I meant it. I wasn't just cutting them down, I wasn't rationing myself, I was banishing them from my life for good. If it was 'fattening' (i.e., high calorie, high fat, delicious) it had to go. Parents – that is what I would call a serious warning sign. It was the same all-or-nothing attitude that meant that within a year I was skipping lunch, within two years I was having a small bowl of cereal for dinner, within three years I was forcing myself to do hundreds of sit-ups every night before I let myself eat anything, and within four years that was it – I had anorexia.

My first dieting attempt was successful. I lost some of my puppy fat and my mum managed to convince me that enough was enough, time to go back to normal. I relinquished my fierce control over calories for a while, but I never thought about food the same way again. I knew how it worked now – I knew which foods made you fat and which didn't, I knew that I could say no to food I really wanted, and I knew what that hunger felt like.

That dieting hunger is intoxicating. The lightness of living on hope more than actual sustenance gets addictive fast. The will-power of denial makes you feel invincible. Refusing to listen to your basic instincts gives you a sense of control unlike any other. For every night I went to bed with a half-empty stomach I fed myself on dreams of how perfect everything would be once I was thin. I ignored the fact that PE suddenly got harder without those extra calories to turn into energy. I ignored the confused looks from my friends when I turned down a piece of birthday cake. I ignored the sense that everything I did seemed so much more serious now that it was tinged with the beginnings of obsession. Goodbye, childhood. I was doing what I had to do. I was becoming a woman. That's what women did: deny their hunger, make their appearance their top priority and do anything they could to shrink smaller every day. I already recognised what a crucial part of growing up it was.

It wouldn't be long until I was back on the wagon, asking Mum to make my sandwiches without butter and swearing off more and more foods with each diet. By the time I started developing anorexia I was already a UK size 8. I remember my Nan sending me clothes two sizes too big and saying she wished that I would get a bit more meat on my bones, but I wasn't gaining weight for anyone. All I could see when I looked in the mirror was how much I needed to lose. Then everything spiralled. You'd think that brushing so close to death would make me see my body differently. You'd think that nearly starving myself out of this world would put me off ever dieting again. But you'd be wrong. Dieting was my religion. And not even coming back from the brink was going to take it away from me.

In the years after I'd supposedly 'recovered', I tried everything to lose weight again. I tried to starve again and ended up binging, I tried to live on nothing but fruit and ended up binging, I tried to cut out carbs and ended up binging. I tried fat free. I tried high protein. I tried not eating before 6 p.m. and not eating after 6 p.m. I tried intermittent fasting. I tried eating clean and exercising for three hours a day. I tried weight-loss groups and protein shakes. I tried juice cleanses and laxatives. I tried diet pills and even hypnosis. I always ended up binging, and I always ended up hating myself even more when the weight came back like clockwork.

There are still people who tell me that I just didn't find the right diet. That even I, a recovered anorexic, should still keep trying, keep dieting, keep chasing that thin dream that kept me up at night when I was 10 years old and led me to a hospital bed. But you know what? I'll never diet again. Because diets suck. We all know it, no matter how hard we try to convince ourselves otherwise. Diets leave us miserable, hungry, and feeling like failures when we can't keep them up (spoiler alert: it's not your fault when you can't keep them up). I hope by the end of this chapter you'll be ready to say goodbye to starvation too, but first we have to make the trek through Dietland. Hold on tight, and feel free to snack along the way.

Diet culture

If I were a body positive superhero saving people from self-loathing, then diet culture would be my evil nemesis (their outfit would be made of measuring tapes and tears and mine would be gold spandex, naturally). I would travel the world destroying all the weight-loss companies that make billions convincing women that they're not good enough as they are. I would outlaw diet pills. I would ban juice cleanses. I would make the term 'bikini body' illegal and declare summer to be self-love season instead. And I would look super cute doing it.

In 2013, 29 million of us in Britain went on a diet.[20] That's 55 per cent of the entire adult population. The percentage of Americans on a diet at any given time is the same – 55 per cent, or close to 116 million people.[21] That means that over half of us are consciously restricting our food intake in order to shrink our bodies. We've found plenty of ways over the years to try to do it, from cutting out entire food groups like fats or carbohydrates, to cutting out food altogether and trying to fast ourselves to thin.

We are a society obsessed with dieting, and it has a seriously detrimental effect on our health, well-being, and happiness (and ironically, not the effect we want it to have on our weight). Even those of us who've realised this, and have waved goodbye to diet-land forever, have a hard time escaping the ever-present messages that our bodies are wrong and must be fixed by an almighty weight-loss solution. That's because diet culture is everywhere. And when you're in it, you don't even notice that it's a problem.

So what is diet culture? Diet culture is the sum of all the things that make us so obsessed with weight, and how to lose it. Every advert, article, TV show and testimonial selling weight loss as a means to happiness, add up to make diet culture. Diet culture is why we believe that weight loss is the most important thing in the world, and why 33,000 women told *Glamour* magazine that they would rather lose 10 to 15 pounds than achieve any other goal.[22] Diet culture is why you can't leave the house without hearing whispered conversations about pounds lost and food regretted, or seeing mile-high billboards beckoning you into weight-loss groups, and selling products that promise to finally give you the body you've always wanted.

Diet culture is why every time you log into your social media, women with 'perfect' bodies pop up on the side of the screen urging you to just click once for their secret. A little while ago, when I was researching the mortality rates for different eating disorders, almost immediately a message popped up promising to tell me how to lose weight fast and get perfect abs. Diet culture strikes again. Diet culture is the catalyst of so many eating disorders – it's how we first learn to starve ('beat cravings!'), binge ('cheat day!'), or purge ('work it off!').

Diet culture is dangerous detoxes, liquid fasts, poisonous pills, and 'magic' potions. It's fitness as an obsession and self-hatred as a motivator. Diet culture is what teaches us to base our worth on things that we can weigh, measure, and burn off. Diet culture is being able to find 50 different ways to starve yourself at your local magazine stand. Diet culture is why girls start dieting, on average, at age eight.[23] EIGHT.

It is so deeply ingrained that we barely even notice it's there, it's just the way things are, nothing to be questioned. Diet culture is why we hate our bodies. Not because we're hideously flawed, and not because of some unchanging truth about what it means to be beautiful, but because we have been taught to. We have been taught to hate our bodies by the culture we live in. A culture that has convinced over half of us that shrinking ourselves is a worthwhile and necessary pursuit.

How diet culture has been created is simple: people realised that a lot of money can be made from teaching us that our bodies are a problem, and selling us the solution.

The weight-loss industry is one of the biggest and baddest in the world, ensuring a constant stream of cash by supplying us with new ways to hate ourselves every season. What started as a quaint little advert in a local newspaper for 'reducing cream' over 100 years ago has boomed (along with our insecurities), into a more profitable business than any entrepreneur could ever dream of. In 1990 Naomi Wolf wrote that 'dieting is the essence of contemporary femininity', that was back when the US diet industry was worth $33 billion. In 2013, Americans spent $60 billion on weight-loss products,[24] and market researchers predict that the weight-loss and weight-management industry will be worth over $200 billion worldwide by 2019.[25] I believe the correct response to those numbers is 'daayuummn'.

REDUCE, REDUCE, REDUCE!

Before the boom of the diet industry in the early twentieth century, restricting your food intake was largely religious territory. One famous diet guru of the 1830s was Sylvester Graham a.k.a., the cracker dude. Graham was a Presbyterian minister who sought to cure his flock of their gluttony and sexual urges by making food as boring as he possibly could. Everything had to be bland – no meat, sauces, alcohol, tea, coffee, pepper or mustard.

People would swarm to watch Graham preach about the importance of dietary reform and how what they ate made them morally better or worse as people (sound familiar?). Graham converted countless devoted followers into his Grahamites, and invented his extra-bland wholewheat cracker. But after a while, people started to realise that following his diet made them weak, not strong like he promised it would. Graham was nicknamed 'Dr Sawdust' and his popularity waned. I like to think that people went back to having as much mustard and sexual activity as they pleased after that.

Another popular diet of the early 1800s belonged to Lord Byron, renowned Romantic poet and ladies' man. Because many of the prominent poets and celebrities of the Romantic era contracted tuberculosis, looking sickly thin became fashionable. Byron decided that the secret to weight loss was vinegar (seriously). He drank it straight and soaked meals of flattened potatoes in it.

He was probably responsible for more than a few body-image issues in his young female fans after writing that 'A woman should never be seen eating or drinking, unless it be lobster salad and champagne', as nothing else was delicate or feminine enough to consume publicly. Ladies – the next time you're feeling insecure about eating in public, just consider it as an eff you to old Byron and every other sexist moron who doesn't think women should be seen eating. Towards the end of his life Byron had managed to slim down, but his diet took on a level of obsession that most of us are all too familiar with today. Plus his breath must have smelt like vinegar all the time.

But one of the most bizarre early diet fads has to go to Horace Fletcher, otherwise known as 'The Great Masticator'. I've tried plenty of diets over the years that emphasise chewing your food slowly and thoroughly before swallowing, but this guy took it to the extreme. Every bite was to be chewed at least 100 times until it was pulverised into a liquid, anything left over could then be spat out. People started having Fletcherism dinner parties where the main activity was timing the chews of each guest. Not only was mastication the key to dropping pounds, Fletcher also credited it for his physical strength and intellect. Nobody seemed to mind that he was obsessed with his own faeces and even carried a sample of it around to show people as proof of his amazing diet plan. They bought into the craze anyway, making Fletcher a diet-industry millionaire.

Then came the Roaring Twenties, and the birth of the diet industry as we know it today. The flapper redefined the image of womanhood and fashion: hemlines got shorter, body ideals got thinner, and the diet industry boomed. Women had money to spend and they quickly bought into the message that it should be spent on their appearance. As Laura Fraser wrote in *Losing It: America's Obsession with Weight and the Industry that Feeds On It*, 'It was during the 1920s that advertisers hit on a problem that was visible enough for women to be embarrassed about, difficult enough to require buying lots of products, and best of all, would never go away: fat'.[26]

In came the advertisements for all manner of reducing products and obesity cures: vibration devices to buzz away fat cells, bath salts, creams and soaps to melt the pounds away. Brushes and stimulating belts (didn't work then, doesn't work now, I'm looking at you, Slendertone). Dangerous diet pills, cigarettes and chewing gum laced with laxatives that you could purchase on the street. Musical reducing records and diet books that sparked the obsession with weight loss in paperback form, which still thrives today.

Along came calorie-counting. Dr Lulu Hunt Peters is credited with starting the calorie craze with her book *Diet and Health, with Key to the Calories*, which sold two million copies after being published in 1918. Dieters were to start with a fast, and then use her 'key', which listed 100 calorie portions of different foods to add up to a daily intake of 1,200 calories (that's medically known as semi-starvation, by the way). She encouraged her readers to always think about food in terms of calories – 'you are going to eat calories of food. Instead of saying one slice of bread, or a piece of pie, you are going to say 100 calories of bread, 350 calories of pie'. I wonder if she had any idea of the level of obsession she was creating.

The Hollywood 18-Day Diet prescribed less than 600 calories a day and become so popular that even restaurants knew how to accommodate it. The lamb chop and pineapple diet was also popular, and is exactly what it sounds like. Delicious. The citrus fruit industry also thrived as the Grapefruit Diet took the US by storm. And if dieting wasn't enough, you could always 'reach for a Lucky instead of a sweet', as Lucky Strike cigarettes encouraged in their adverts (cigarettes are probably still one of the most widely used appetite suppressants today).

One pearl of wisdom from a 1918 issue of *Vogue* magazine firmly planted itself in the minds of image-conscious women everywhere – 'there is one crime against the modern ethics of beauty which is unpardonable; far better it is to commit any number of petty crimes than to be guilty of growing fat'.[27]

As white women won the right to vote and new contraceptives became more widely available, women were more politically and sexually liberated than ever before. The Flappers thought that they were free, drinking cocktails and dancing all night. It turns out that sense of freedom was an illusion, as the bodies that they danced in became bound by rules as oppressive as the ones they'd just left behind. They could do what they wanted, as long as they devoted enough of their time, energy and money to maintaining the perfect figure. The Flappers are also acknowledged as the first generation of women to widely use bulimia as a means to staying slim.[28]

The diet industry took a dip in the 1930s and 1940s since people had more important things to worry about than their waistlines. The Great Depression and wartime rations shifted the focus from not eating too much to making sure there was enough to eat. But it came back with a vengeance in the 1950s, with help from mass-marketed women's magazines that transformed into weight-loss manuals.

That's when the template was created for the 'inspiring' transformation stories that still fill our magazines today, featuring before and after pictures and the promise of happiness that only comes once the weight has been lost. *Ladies Home Journal* ran articles titled 'I Was a Hopeless Fatty, Now I'm a Model', 'Don't Let Your Child Be a Fatty!', 'I Lost Weight and Am Just Beginning to Live', and the seriously awful 'From Hippo to Slimmo'[29] (I hope whoever came up with that one was immediately sacrificed to a herd of hungry hippos). Countless advertisements for diet plans and weight-loss products ran opposite the stories, and the lines between editorial (what the writers truly think) and advertorial (what the writers are paid to think by advertisers), became blurred.

Advertisers knew that after the war they couldn't keep selling women the same old picture of housewife domesticity to aspire to, they needed a new money maker, one that all women would feel the pressure to buy into. Thinness was the perfect plan. It's genius, when you really think about it: saturate the media with ideal bodies, convince women that they can only be happy if they look like those bodies, sell women products promising to give them those bodies, and when those products don't work, tell the women that it's their fault for not having enough willpower, and sell them more.

If women begin to achieve the current ideal body, change the ideal so that they'll need to keep buying products (that don't work) to attain the impossible. Rinse and repeat. They go home rolling in their billions and we're left with shattered self-esteem, empty bank accounts, wasted years and useless products, and we still blame ourselves instead of seeing it for the manipulation that it is. And all along the whole thing rests on that one big lie, that your body needs to look a certain way in order for you to be happy. We bought it. We still buy it.

After the 1950s, the diet industry was a runaway train. The snake-oil products kept coming – lotions and potions, gadgets and gizmos, pills and plans advertised in ever-growing numbers of magazines. Thanks to the newly popular televisions appearing in family homes, weight-loss companies could deliver their sales pitches without women even having to leave the sofa. Grainy black-and-white pictures of men with slicked-back hair promised to help 'lose ugly fat, fast', and all there was to do was mail away for the miracle product that would finally make you beautiful. Kerching.

FACT: CELLULITE HAS ONLY BEEN A 'FLAW' FOR THE PAST 40 YEARS!

Not long ago our harmless thigh dimples were thought of as a normal variation of female flesh. Then in 1973 Nicole Ronsard, a New York beauty salon owner, was featured in an issue of *Vogue,* describing cellulite as a 'disfiguring' attribute.

She released a bestselling book called *Cellulite: Those Lumps, Bumps and Bulges You Couldn't Lose Before*, and we were convinced once and for all, that another part of our bodies were flawed, while she went home with the profits.

In the 1950s the first ever weight-loss groups appeared, TOPS (Taking Off Pounds Sensibly) began after Esther Manz recruited three of her friends to meet weekly and cheer each other on in their dieting efforts. Manz was inspired by Alcoholics Anonymous, creating a group atmosphere of 'organised will-power, sugar-coated with fun and relaxation'.[30] It was so fun and relaxing that any members who gained weight were booed, had cardboard pigs pinned on them, and were made to sing songs about being fat pigs who ate too much.

Soon chapters of TOPS were springing up across the US with names like Shrinking Violets, Tops Not Tubs, Button Busters, Thick N Tired and Do or Dieters. Surprisingly, Manz kept the organisation as a non-profit, as did Overeaters Anonymous, who popped up in 1960. Then came the diet industry giant: Weight Watchers.

Jean Nidetch began the group in 1963, using a diet sheet that she was given at an obesity clinic, and charging local housewives for weekly meetings in her living room. In 1970, Weight Watchers made $8 million,[31] and that was only the beginning. In 1978, the company was bought by H.J. Heinz for $71 million, and in 1999 it was taken over by Invus. By 2013, Weight Watchers had approximately one million members with 40,000 weekly meetings held worldwide. In both 2013 and 2014 consumers spent $5 billion on Weight Watchers-branded products and services[32] – meetings, online subscriptions, food products and magazines. Convincing people that their bodies aren't good enough has become one of the most profitable businesses in history.

Today the number of plans that promise to help take off the pounds are endless. You can head to a meeting at groups like Weight Watchers, Slimming World, Lighter Life or Jenny Craig. You can buy into the latest diet craze sweeping the nation – the Atkins diet made a comeback in 2016 after Kim Kardashian credited the low carb method for her post-pregnancy weight loss. The 5:2 diet was the most popular weight-loss trend in 2013 in the UK: 39 per cent of dieters tried it. You could check your local book store for the next paperback fad, try Dukan, Paleo, Cambridge, South Beach, Beverly Hills, Alkaline, Lean in 15, Genotype, Zone, Raw Food, Mediterranean, or Macrobiotic.

You can get meals delivered to your door or cut out meals altogether with a juice fast or liquid cleanse. You can get pills claiming to suppress your appetite, boost your metabolism or block fat being absorbed from food, via prescription, over the counter, or from any number of unregulated online sites. You can still mail away for as much snake oil as you like, waist-trainers, detox teas, body wraps, cellulite creams, ab-toners, they're all still in business.

A hundred years and billions of pounds later, we still can't seem to grasp one basic piece of logic: if any one method of losing weight actually worked, none of the others would exist, and we'd all be thin by now. Instead we internalise diet culture's lesson that we're to blame. We tell ourselves that we failed the diet, rather than realising that the diet failed us. The diet industry has failed us since the first moment it started proliferating and profiting from our insecurities.

It's time we realised, as Terry Poulton puts it in *No Fat Chicks*, that we are the victims of a 'billion-dollar brainwash'. That 'the whole diet phenomenon is not about beauty or how much women weigh at all. It's about how much we can be persuaded to spend trying to be thin'. We are being manipulated every single day by an industry that rakes in billions while we stand crying over our bathroom scales. And I don't know about you, but I'm sick of the lies.

HOW MUCH DID YOU LOSE THIS WEEK?

The time had come. I'd tried to do it by myself. I'd tried over and over again. I'd tried every way I could think of. But I couldn't do it. I was a failure. My appetite just couldn't be tamed. It was time to reach out to a greater power. It was time to join the flock of my fellow sinners at their place of worship. It was time to follow the diet bible. It was time for a weight-loss group.

I walked up the creaking stairs of my local YMCA with dread building in my empty stomach. I'd been starving myself for a couple of days already, just to make sure that I didn't die of shame when I stepped on those scales in front of everyone. I'd done a full face of make-up and styled my hair, I desperately wanted the people there to think that I was beautiful, at least then I'd be the chubby girl with the pretty face. By the time I reached the top of the stairs I was sweating in nervous patches, I waited until my face dried up and my breathing steadied – God forbid they thought that I was unfit enough to be left panting from the journey up. Then I went in.

About 30 women and one man were in the room, some fat, a few slim, most somewhere in between. Some talked animatedly in small groups while the others formed a line against the back wall, I spotted the scale at the end of it. There was a sign to the right welcoming newcomers, I made my way over and saw the tell-tale lump of fake fat sat in the centre of the table, ready to scare us into signing up.

There were two other people joining that week, and we waited for our indoctrination while staring at the lump of fat, wondering how much of its gelatinous horror we had attached to us in that moment. Soon someone came over to tell us all about the plan (I already knew, I'd tried it alone, I gained the weight back but told myself it would be different if I actually joined the group). They handed out our forms to fill in and presented us with shiny new books and weekly food diaries. We all started hastily scribbling out our details, and then my stomach hit the floor.

'Please tick here if you've ever been diagnosed with an eating disorder such as anorexia nervosa/bulimia, or have had any experience with eating disorders in the past or currently'. What did I do? If I told the truth they'd surely kick me out. I'd have to listen to someone telling me that I wasn't allowed to lose weight again, that I'd have to be fat for ever. But if I didn't tick it and they found out I'd be in even more trouble. I thought I saw the woman beside me tick hers. I decided to be honest.

It turns out that it didn't matter. Nobody ever asked me about it, it wasn't mentioned when I turned in my increasingly sparse food diary, or when I told the group that I rack up 18 hours of workouts a week, which got nothing but praise and envy. Nobody batted an eyelid when I wasn't willing to relent on my low goal weight or have anywhere near the amount of treats I was allowed. I silently slipped back into all kinds of eating disorder behaviours, but since I had about 50 pounds to lose nobody saw it as that – I was just really dedicated.

Someone said to me years later that it's not the fault of a weight-loss group if someone develops an eating disorder while on their programme. I replied that if a recovered anorexic walks in, ticks the box, and gradually falls back into dangerous levels of restriction and exercise addiction without anyone questioning it week in, week out, then it's pretty disgusting of the group to deny any responsibility whatsoever.

After a couple of months I'd cut the recommended plan in half, and I stopped attending meetings altogether. Plates got smaller, workouts got longer, the numbers dropped and dropped. That summer I finally hit my goal weight of 130 pounds, I was drinking weight-loss shakes for lunch and eating no more than 1,000 calories every day. I decided that 110 pounds would be my new goal weight, I wanted to be so thin that people wouldn't even recognise me as they passed by. Thankfully, I didn't fall into a total relapse. I found body positivity instead. But that's skipping ahead.

After ticking the box and giving back the form with shaking hands, it was time to line up and receive the almighty starting weight. We all knew that this was the weight that would one day be emblazoned on our before and after pictures. People would look on and gasp – 'I can't believe she weighed so much, look at her now!' It would be the weight that we were in a past life, never to be returned to again. Those images propelled us forwards, palms growing clammy and nervous smiles flitting back and forth.

The woman in charge of the scales had wire-rimmed glasses and pale grey hair, she seemed soft and kind. She was the least threatening of the members, chosen to govern the most terrifying part of the meeting. I'd seen women in line before me taking off their jackets, their shoes, stripping down to skimpy summer dresses even though there was an early spring chill outside. Clothes can add countless extra pounds, we all knew that. Before I'd left for the meeting I'd stood in my room holding up each pair of leggings to see which was the lightest.

The moment arrived. I stepped on the scales. My mind flashed back to weekly meetings in a blue room where a man in a suit told me over and over again that the number had to be higher. Back then I'd worn three layers of clothing, studded belts hidden underneath two jumpers and old ceramic kitchen weights anchoring my pockets. I shook the memories away and reminded myself that this was different, I was different. Everything would be okay this time once I'd lost the weight. The number popped up on the screen and I immediately fell into the deepest shame I'd ever felt. I was fatter than even I thought I was, and now other people knew it as well. The owl-eyed woman behind the table must have seen the disgust on my face and tried to comfort me by saying that she wished she weighed that much. It didn't help.

I eagerly took my seat, ready to dive head first into my new lifestyle. That's what it was. A lifestyle. That phrase was echoed over and over again – it's a lifestyle, not a diet. Weight-loss groups do everything they can to distance themselves from the D word these days. Jenny Craig calls its plan 'a pattern of healthy eating'. Nutrisystem sell 'safe effective weight loss; no fads, no gimmicks!'. Weight Watchers Australia lure former yo-yo dieters with the comforting line: 'the best bit? It's not a diet. Everything's still on the menu'. And Slimming World have dedicated an entire page on their website to denouncing the D word, titled 'It's not a diet', where they promise that the counting, deprivation and rules of normal dieting are nowhere to be seen in their plan ('at Slimming World, DIET is a four-letter word!').

It's a clever tactic, and we fall for it. Most people know by now that crash diets don't work. We've been on the weight-loss merry-go-round enough times to learn that extreme fasts, semi-starvation rations, liquid detoxes, and magic gizmos and contraptions that promise miraculous body transformations are bullshit. We still buy them, because as we know, hope is stronger than rationality when it comes to attaining the ideal body, but more and more people are catching on to the fact that those diets just don't deliver. As early as 1990 there was even a US congressional hearing about the failures and deception of the diet industry.[33]

So what do the biggest players in the diet industry do once people start to suss them out? 'Who us? Oh no, we're not a diet. Diets don't work. We know that. No dieting here! We're all about lifestyle changes and errr … health! No diets, boo diets!' And people believe them. I definitely believed it, even when all the warning bells were ringing in my mind that what I was doing certainly felt a lot like dieting. Even as I was weighing out my small cube of cheese every night for my dairy allowance and counting up the points in olive oil. Some lifestyle that is.

So how do you know if you're on a diet? It's quite simple, actually. If you are consciously restricting your daily food intake in any way for the purpose of losing weight, you are on a diet. Even if 'no food is off limits' (Weight Watchers US). Even if there's 'no complex counting' (Slimfast UK). And even if the company goes out of its way to insist that it isn't a diet. If they are selling a food plan that promises weight loss, they are a diet company. And if you are following a food plan with hopes of losing weight, you are on a diet.

Marilyn Wann wrote a chapter in *Fat! So?* called 'How to Tell When You're on a Diet'. The checklist includes statements such as 'if you're comforted by the thought that you can eat all the mushrooms you want, you're on a diet', 'if you plan your social life around what you can or cannot eat, you're on a diet', and of course 'if you've ever said, "This isn't a diet, it's a lifestyle change!" you're on a diet'. There is such a thing as a lifestyle change with the aim of eating more nutritiously and moving your body more often, but if it comes with a goal weight, it's a diet.

The key is that if you believe that it's a lifestyle, you believe that it'll work for life. And it will, as long as your definition of 'working' is that you keep coming back to it time and time again for the rest of your life having regained the weight you lost in the first place. Nearly every member of the weight-loss group I went to had been there before. This wasn't their first rodeo. The one man in the group probably weighed around 300 pounds and had previously lost 100 pounds on the plan, only to gain it back and wind up right where he started, promising himself that it would be different this time.

Even the leader of the group was fat – she openly discussed how she fell off the wagon and regained 40 pounds, but she had no doubt that she would lose it again, with us. I'm sure she did, but she's probably found it again by now. Because that's how it works! That's how diet companies are in business. If everyone went on the plan once, lost all the weight they wanted and kept it off for life, that wouldn't be a very lucrative business, would it? Slimming World isn't going to make much money handing out free lifetime memberships left, right, and centre to all the people who hit their target and stay there – the only reason they can offer free lifetime memberships is because so few people do hit their target and stay there.

Weight-loss groups rely on repeat customers. They want you to believe that you'll reach your goal weight and sustain it, but they don't actually want you to. Weight Watchers has recognised that its members have 'demonstrated a consistent pattern of repeat enrolment over a number of years', and the former chief financial officer of the company has even said in an interview that 'that's where your business comes from'.[34] And yet we still blame ourselves when the weight comes back – it's our willpower, it's our weakness. It couldn't possibly be because our lifestyle change is in fact a diet, and just like diets that call themselves diets, it doesn't work.

There was one woman who had kept the weight off. She'd been a lifetime member for nine years, 30 pounds down and successfully kept at bay. Every week we grilled her for the secret, which was, in her own words 'just don't eat the things you want to eat'. That's how she sustained the die— ahem, lifestyle. We all laughed as if it was a joke. She was a walking example of what it takes to be a success story, strictly monitoring yourself every day for the rest of your life. Dieting isn't a casual undertaking that anyone can master, it's a full-time job. It's a battle against your body's natural instincts. It's an obsession.

Still, I believed that I would be one of the 5 per cent. I spent hours trawling the brand's magazine, imagining myself one day gracing the cover, beaming down at all the peasants still striving to shift the pounds. Superior, poised, the object of so many people's envy. Weight-loss queen. Clearly being hungry made me a bit of a bitch, too.

While I was at the group I was a devoted member. I learned my scripture. I repented for my sins. I prayed for my thin salvation and I followed our leader unquestioningly. Each week I showed up and took my place front row in the circle, ready to receive my judgement. And I know weight-loss groups place a lot of emphasis on weigh-ins being confidential and never revealed to the group, but there is still judgement. Whether it comes from the leader or from within.

Everyone in the circle got their turn, their name called out with either an enthusiastic reading of how much they'd lost followed by applause, or a condescending questioning – 'what happened then?', 'not such a good week was it?'. I writhed with envy as my fellow members described how far off plan they'd fallen and celebrated their miraculous 6lb loss. I was the perfect disciple, I trusted the plan, I hung on the words being preached and I vowed to do better next week. Always better next week.

You've probably picked up on how religious I'm making this all sound, and truly, it is religious. We worship our body idols, we pray for our salvation, we sacrifice our needs and we believe with unrelenting faith in the power of the diet, the power of thin. We believe in our weight-loss dreams so fiercely that they've become our new religion. And nowhere is this more obvious than in weight-loss groups.

The circled plastic chairs are our pews. The group leader is our minister. The magazines and food charts are our scripture. The scale is our confessional. We say our prayers as we walk towards our judgement, we go to the bathroom one last time to try and disguise our sins. We vow to remain chaste: where women once took oaths to be sexually pure, we now take oaths to be nutritionally pure. We keep our mouths shut around temptation rather than our legs. We dream of redemption in our next life, our thin life, where we've been saved from the shame of existing in fat, gluttonous bodies.

Weight-loss groups know this. They know that our devotion is biblical and that they can play on our holy sense of guilt. Slimming World calls its off-plan foods 'syns', for crying out loud.

With religion comes community, and a sense of community is one of the biggest selling points of weight-loss groups. It's why

I was so convinced that I would finally succeed this time around, I would have support, encouragement, and be surrounded by people who understood. 'Slimming World truly is the club that cares', and with LighterLife: 'You never need to feel alone. -#WeGetIt'.

DIETING RELIGION

Sometimes the link between dieting and religion isn't so subtle. Check out these popular weight-loss books from years gone by:

Pray Your Weight Away, Charlie W. Shedd
More of Jesus and Less of Me, Joan Cavanaugh
Help Lord, the Devil Wants Me Fat!, C. S. Lovett

Considering there are so few (if any) body positive spaces offline where people can come together, share their body-image issues, and feel connected and inspired to overcome them, it's no wonder weight-loss groups become the only sense of community so many of us have. At least there you can share your pain, at least there people will get it. Those meetings are the only public space we get to talk about our body struggles. It's sad that the support given then focuses on how to heal those struggles by changing our bodies, rather than changing the culture that taught us we weren't good enough in the first place. It's sad that in order to feel a sense of community, we have to go somewhere that profits from our self-hatred.

For women especially, our female community is so rooted in the topic of our bodies and everything that we think is wrong with them. When Wolf wrote that 'dieting is the essence of contemporary femininity', she didn't just mean that women diet a lot. She meant that dieting, body dissatisfaction, and disordered relationships with food are central to our shared experience as females. They lie at the core of womanhood. They are what we get to bond over and feel connected by. It's ironic that weight-loss groups offer us a space to do that, while simultaneously lying at the heart of why we have all these issues in the first place. And although we may go there and feel less alone, feel understood and have others empathise with all the ways we hate our bodies, we deserve better.

Our sense of community should not be rooted in body shame. We should feel connected to one another by more than our desires to lose weight. We instantly bond with another woman in a cafe over how 'naughty' those cakes look, or how we need to be 'good' this week, but why can't we bond over a shared sense of food freedom instead? We compliment a friend and they reply with the expected 'oh no I took terrible today and I've already gained two pounds this week', but why shouldn't we feel connected by self-love instead? Why must we file into town halls and pay our oppressors in order to feel valid, to feel seen and heard and understood? Why can't we have meetings of empowerment instead?

When I attended those weekly meetings, I did feel like part of a community. And there were all the things weight-loss groups promise there will be: praise, encouragement, everyone cheering you on each pound of the way. There was one woman whose weight loss plateaued. She must have been about 70 years old, and she followed the plan religiously. When her body decided that it was happy to settle at the weight it was she was put on a fast-track diet plan, designed to shock your body into shrinking again.

We're talking low calorie, even fruit and vegetables rationed, everything weighed and measured to fit the correct number of 'units' for the day. The plan is so restrictive that it's been affectionately termed 'The Straight Jacket' by members who've undergone it. It worked. A 70-year-old woman put herself in a mental straight jacket in the pursuit of thinness, and we all cheered her on. The best part? She was already slim. And if that's the community that weight-loss groups give us, I'm out.

TEATOX

Word on the street is that there's a new magic potion in town, sure to make all of our weight-loss dreams come true. If you're on social media you've probably already seen it. Everywhere you click there's another colourful packet, held up to the camera by your favourite celebrity. 'Time for another cup!'; 'Ready to start working on the bikini body!'. If some of the most famously beautiful bodies in the world are using it, then it has to work, right? You rush to the website where the miracle product is sold, only £29.99 for a 28-day supply! Any doubts you might have about what the product contains slip away as you're reassured that everything is 'all natural'. Nobody tells you that 'all natural' isn't the same thing as 'safe'.

I'm talking about detox teas. And while these teas aren't anything new (dieter's teas have been around for decades), this time they're back with a vengeance. Millions of people worldwide are going to bed with their nightly 'cleansing' drink, hoping to slim down, tone up, and finally get that flat stomach. What the companies don't want you to know is that all they're really selling are laxatives in pretty packaging.

Bootea is the UK's leading teatox brand, with over a million customers in the last three years. Their '100 per cent natural' detox teas are endorsed by the likes of Vanessa Hudgens, Lindsay Lohan, Ashley Benzo and Michelle Keegan a.k.a., a whole bunch of beautiful, young, thin female celebrities with a hell of a lot of influence. Like many other teatoxes, the key ingredient in their popular bedtime cleanse tea is senna, along with Chinese rhubarb root – both completely natural, and both laxatives. Although it would be easy to miss these ingredients, since the online disclaimer uses their lesser known (and more ambiguous) names *Cassia angustifolia* and *Rheum officinale*.

So what's so bad about senna? According to WebMD, 'Senna is an FDA-approved non-prescription laxative. It is used to treat constipation and also to clear the bowel before diagnostic tests such as colonoscopy'. Laxatives have absolutely no lasting effect on weight loss, but a bout of self-induced diarrhoea will certainly leave you feeling lighter. After a night glued to the toilet you'll be left severely dehydrated, having lost a whole lot of fluids from your body. Any weight loss you see on the scale the morning after will disappear faster than you can drink a glass of water. Not only do these teas have zero effect on weight loss, they can be seriously dangerous.

The side-effects of laxative abuse range from painful cramps, dehydration and fatigue, to stroke, heart failure, and even death. When all that water gets flushed from your body, essential minerals and electrolytes get flushed with it. The sodium, potassium, magnesium and phosphorus in our bodies ensures that our nerves and muscles function properly (including the heart), and if they become imbalanced, you're in trouble. Of course, you won't see any warnings about that on the teatox box, in fact, many don't carry a full list of ingredients at all. When I asked an employee at Bootea why there were no ingredient lists on their website, I was told that they're renovating. When I asked if there was any way that I could get hold of a full list including the amounts of each ingredient, I was told no, but not to worry as their products are all completely safe.

Most medical professionals advise a maximum of one to two weeks of unsupervised dosages of senna, and yet popular tea-toxes containing senna come in 28-day packs. Bootea's cleansing tea contains 18mg of active senna, while the NHS recommends 2.5–20mg a day 'adjusted according to response' for the treatment of constipation. Except detox teas aren't being used for the treatment of constipation, they're being used, and no doubt abused, by people who are desperate to lose weight. And if they believe that one cup will help them do that, they'll believe that two, three, or four will work even better. In an E! News interview Kendall Jenner is quoted saying 'I usually start my day off with a cup of detox tea. I have like 12 cups a day'. Considering she's still alive, I'm sure she doesn't, but plenty of her adoring fans will be more than willing to if they believe it might help them achieve a body like hers.

Laxative abuse is widely recognised as a serious symptom of an eating disorder. According to the Alliance for Eating Disorders Awareness, 'Laxative abuse is defined as a use (or overuse) of laxatives over a long period of time, and used as a means of weight control'.[35] Isn't that just what detox tea drinkers are doing – using laxatives over a long period of time as a means of weight control? And why is nobody saying what these teatoxes are really selling: eating disorders?

Currently the purchase of these teas is completely unregulated, anyone can walk into their local health food store and pick up as many boxes as they please. When I asked Bootea if any regulations were being put in place to prevent the abuse of their product by people with eating disorders, such as limiting the number that one person can buy, I was told that there is no limit, just like there's no limit to how much alcohol one person can buy. A strange comparison to make about a product that only a few minutes beforehand I was being assured was completely safe.

When I was at the height of my eating disorder I started taking laxative pills to force the number on the scale down even further. The problem was that it didn't take long until the effects wore off, and I needed more and more each time. Another side effect of laxative abuse is dependency. Take them for long enough and soon the colon won't work properly without them, it can also become stretched or infected. But, of course, detox teas are all about health, they're not simply the latest spawn of the diet industry out to profit from our body insecurities at all. Bootea boasts on its website that 'We will never encourage our customers to go on a "diet" as we believe (in fact we know) that healthy eating is a lifestyle and not a short-term fix', which roughly translates to 'we know diets don't work but here! Take these laxatives instead!'. Really healthy.

Perhaps the most dangerous aspect of the teatox craze is the glamour being sold along with the product. Thanks to social media, we have more insight into celebrities lives than ever before: what they wear, where they go, how they eat and work out to maintain the bodies we covet so fiercely. Brands know perfectly well that using celebrity endorsements online will tap into a major market of impressionable young people looking for the route to get the ideal body. Teenagers trust their favourite stars, and they're willing to fork out all of their cash to be just like them. Most of them have no idea how much these celebrities are paid for one picture of them in a bikini, smiling slyly down at an unopened packet of laxatives with a cute name. Kylie Jenner, the face of SkinnyMint detox tea, currently has 78 million Instagram followers where she posts paid ads for teatoxes, teeth whiteners and even gummy vitamins.

SkinnyMint is another teatox brand reassuring its online customers that with them there's 'No dieting. No pill popping'. We all know that diet pills can be dangerous, but who would suspect a simple, all-natural tea? Certainly not the many people who've reviewed the product on Diet Pills Watchdog and reported experiencing bloating, fatigue, dizziness, nausea, vomiting, headaches, severe diarrhoea, mouth rashes, extreme abdominal pain, lower back pain, impaired kidney function, heart palpitations and hospitalisation.[36]

Of course, on SkinnyMint's website all you'll see are glowing reviews and countless before-and-after weight-loss pictures. Their Night Cleanse tea also contains senna, which customers are advised to drink every other night, but 'if you're an experienced Teatoxer, you can try drinking Night Cleanse every night'. SkinnyMint's slogan is '#DareToBeGorgeous', playing right into the low self-esteem of millions of girls who already believe that they're not.

Instagram is an ideal advertising space for teatox companies, and even though there are plenty of celebrities and lifestyle bloggers willing to help peddle their poison, these brands still reach out to the body positive community in an effort to boost their sales. Flat Tummy Tea is one company who don't seem to understand that laxative abuse and body positivity do not go together. Despite their name, they insist that 'we're not about weight loss and never promote that' in emails that have been sent to nearly every body positive blogger I know.

One look at their website tells a different story. While not explicitly promising to help shed pounds, their detox tea is aimed at people who feel 'bloated, fat and sluggish'. They promise that 'We get it, babe, some days you look (and feel) like you're five months pregnant'. Luckily, their senna-filled Cleanse tea is there to help 'get you back to flat'. The underlying message is clear: this tea will help you get your ideal body, focusing on the body part women hate the most, their stomach.

After your four-week Flat Tummy Tea detox there's a subscription programme to 'maintain that kick-ass tummy you've been working on'. The Maintain sachets (containing senna, obviously) are to be taken once weekly 'to combat those whoops moments'. Anybody fluent in diet speak knows that a 'whoops moment' means overeating, falling off plan, binging. Luckily a nice cup of laxative tea will supposedly make up for our overindulgences. There's another word for when people try to purge themselves of the food they've eaten with the use of overexercising, laxatives or self-induced vomiting. What's it called again … oh yeah, bulimia. Taking laxatives after a 'whoops moment' in an attempt to undo the calorific damage is bulimia. Even when it comes in a pretty pink package.

In fact, forget the weight-loss side of this business. Forget the promises of flatter tummies and sly suggestions that sipping tea will transform your body. Because even focusing on the core message of the teatox industry – that our bodies require a detox – we can see the web of lies we're being sold.

The idea that our bodies are full of toxic, fat-inducing substances that we need to clear out of our systems to be healthy, is 100 per cent made up. The only valid form of detoxing is in the treatment of people with serious drug and alcohol addictions. Otherwise, our bodies do a damn good job of detoxifying themselves. Our kidneys, liver, skin and lungs all work constantly to eliminate any toxins in our system, and drinking pints of expensive herb water won't help.

We've been duped, yet again, by the diet industry. And if you don't believe me, maybe you'll believe the British Dietetic

Association: 'Detoxing is nonsense, it's a complete fallacy that the body needs to detox. Removal of waste products and toxins is a continuous process and we don't need to periodically flush them out. The body does a perfectly good job of eliminating any substances on its own'.[37] The entire concept of needing to detoxify, purify, or cleanse your body with these regimes is literally made up by the diet industry to sell us more shit (that doesn't work) to fix our bodies (that don't need fixing).

DIET PILLS

In the autumn of 2013, I remember hearing another news headline about a young woman who'd died from taking diet pills. I heard people talking about how awful it was, what a tragic loss. What dangerous lengths people go to, to escape the cultural condemnation of living in the wrong type of body. She wasn't even that fat. Why would she do such a thing? I shook my head and agreed, such a shame, such a loss. The next morning I took my two metabolism-boosting pills and began my daily workout, the fifth that week.

I thought that I was being smart about it – I'd researched every ingredient listed on the label (ignoring the fact that no amounts of each ingredient were there). I read the reviews, I weighed up the pros and cons. Pro: it could help me lose weight. Con: there were no cons big enough to outweigh that one glaring pro, the thing that I wanted more than anything in the world. They were easy to get hold of, not even a box to tick online confirming my age before they were shipped and on their way.

I ordered another batch labelled as 'carb blockers', not that I was eating enough carbs to block anyway. Still, if I took them after a binge day, maybe they'd undo the damage. This time round the usual starvation diet wasn't working as well (I realise now that years of anorexia followed by extreme yo-yo dieting and weight-cycling had probably wreaked havoc on my metabolism and cranked my set-point weight up more than a few notches), but I was willing to do whatever it took to make it work. At least until I'd saved up enough money for liposuction. That was the plan. I wish I could go back and hug that girl who hated herself that much.

I had a retail job at the time and it seemed like no matter where I stood there were mirrors pointing accusingly at me from all angles. But that would be all right once there was less of me reflected. I took my pills each day, shaking that little bottle of hope and sending a prayer to the diet gods. At first the pills just gave me an energy boost. I was dashing up and down the shop floor without stopping for so much as a yawn.

I lost five pounds in the first week, and I didn't even feel hungry! I'd discovered a miracle pill! I ordered another batch straight away. In the second week, I started to notice the not-so-ideal side effects. By the end of the working day my top felt damp with sweat, and there had been more than one moment when my heart seemed to skip and it felt like I'd forgotten to breathe. Not to worry, small nuisances compared to the payoff of my dream body inching closer into sight by the day.

About three weeks in I was out one morning walking the dogs with my mum. My limbs felt heavier and the energy from the pills was taking longer to kick in; it was probably time to double the dosage like it said on the bottle. Halfway round our usual route I suddenly had to stop. I bent over the nearest bush and started uncontrollably retching, dark spots creeping into my vision. I told my mum that it was probably the iron supplements I'd taken that morning. (I was taking those too, I'd seen on the Internet that my fatigue may have been due to a lack of iron. Obviously, it was actually due to overexercising and barely eating all day, but I wasn't going to face that fact.) But I knew.

I knew it was the pills, with their mysteriously sparse information label and too-good-to-be-true results. When I started waking up in the middle of the night in a terror-induced sweat, heart racing and mind spinning, I stopped taking them. I didn't throw them away, just pushed them to the back of the cupboard, I might have needed them again in the future if I got desperate.

When I tell people that body positivity saved my life, I don't think they realise how literal I'm being. Sure, it saved me in the sense that it gave me a life back that I never thought I deserved to live in this body, it saved my mental health and freed me from years of self-torture. But I also genuinely believe that I may not have lived many more years without it. Because taking mystery pills and ignoring dubious side effects was only a scratch on the surface of what I was willing to do for thin.

I tried more diet pills after that. I'm incredibly lucky not to have been around at any number of points over the last 100 years when medical professionals dished out potentially fatal drugs to anyone who wanted to lose a few pounds, while taking the profits straight to the bank. Time and time again the latest miracle weight-loss chemical has been discovered, patented into a formula and peddled to thousands (or even millions) of unsuspecting customers, only to be recalled when pesky side effects start coming to light, like heart palpitations, blindness, and sudden death. Here are some horrific examples of how much damage those magic pills can do:

- In the 1890s people were starting to believe that being fat was bad for your health, so medical professionals turned to drugs for a solution. They started prescribing Frank J. Kellogg's Safe Fat Reducer to patients looking to lose weight. With a trustworthy name like that, what could go wrong, right? The pills contained thyroid extract, which, it turns out, isn't great for humans to consume. They burned through lean tissue in the body, causing osteoporosis, heart palpitations, chest pain, and if enough internal organs burned up, sudden death.

- In the 1920s the papers started advertising 'a new and safe way to lose weight'. The drug was called Dinotrophenol, it was derived from benzene and had many uses – herbicide, insecticide, component in First World War explosives, why not try it for weight loss too? Genius. By 1935, over 100,000 Americans had taken the drug, before people realised that high doses sped up the metabolism enough to cause a fever that burned the body alive, otherwise known as hyperpyremia. Other side effects included a rash, loss of sense of taste, and blindness.

- Amphetamines were quick to pick up where Dinotrophenol left off, marketed as Dexedrine or Appetrol. They became known as 'mother's little helpers', since so many housewives in the 1950s and 1960s were on them. By 1952, 3 billion dosages of amphetamines were being produced annually in the US, they were even prescribed to children until the 1970s. The pills helped people lose a couple of pounds before the weight-loss effect wore off, and users were left with addiction, increased heart rate and blood pressure, anxiety, insomnia, hallucinations, heart damage, stroke, kidney failure, and sudden death.

- Next up we have phenylpropanolamine (PPA), an amphetamine-like chemical branded as Dexatrim, Accutrim, Thinz and Appedrine. In 1989 alone, 47,000 people reported side effects of the drug to poison control centres that were serious enough to require medical attention. In 2000, the FDA issued a public health warning about the drug, after conducting a five-year study that showed it increased the risk of stroke in women. FDA scientists estimated that 200–500 strokes per year were caused by PPA. Several hearings took place where the parents of young people who'd abused the diet pills and died from cardiac arrest spoke out against the drug. Other users also experienced seizures, hallucinations, insomnia, anxiety, cardiac irregularities, hypertension and psychosis. It wasn't until 2005 that the FDA proposed a rule to reclassify PPA as 'not generally recognised as safe and effective'. Bit of an understatement, if you ask me.

- Probably the most well-known diet pill disaster is Fen-Phen. The combination of fenfluramine and phentermine worked as an appetite suppressant and amphetamine, dexfenfluramine

(Redux) followed shortly after. Fen-Phen was the magic weight-loss cure of the moment, it was advertised everywhere and was so in demand that many doctors devoted their entire practices to dispensing it, even to people who weren't overweight by medical standards (one member of California Medical Weight Loss Associates justified this by saying 'a lady who weighs 120 and should weigh 100 is obese'[38]).

In 1996 alone, 18 million prescriptions were given out, Jenny Craig and Nutrisystem even started offering the pills to their members. In 1997 they were withdrawn from the market following over 100 reports of heart valve damage, and further studies showing that 30 per cent of its users tested with echo-cardiograms showed abnormal valve findings. While researching Fen-Phen, I found it being sold on online weight-loss forums, with people who were aware of the risks saying 'it's worth it if you can lose 30 pounds in one month' – the original study showed that people could lose 30 pounds in a year, either way, definitely not worth betting your heart on.

Today hundreds of diet pills are available with and without prescription, many unregulated and available for anyone to find online or in their local health food store. Currently the most popular brand of non-prescription diet pills in the UK is XLS Medical, whose fat binder pills are 'clinically proven' and stamped with the 'lose 3x more weight than dieting alone' slogan.

The key ingredient in the pills is Litramine, and according to its website over 2.6 billion doses of Litramine have been sold. While checking the 'clinically proven' results, the only study I found showing Litramine to be effective on weight loss was entirely funded by the 'exclusive' manufacturer and distributor of Litramine. Some people may call that a conflict of interest, just saying ... Elsewhere online, hundreds of independent reviews list side-effects ranging from constipation, bowel pain, diarrhoea, and headaches, to faecal impaction leading to hospitalisation – and even weight gain.[39]

Other popular diet pills in recent years have been fruit-based: raspberry ketones, African mango, acai berry. Raspberry ketones blew up a few years ago as a 'miracle' fat-burning supplement after being endorsed by Dr Oz, an American TV presenter whose show focuses on health and wellness. At the time, there were absolutely no human studies to back up the claims, only rat studies showing that one group of rats gained less weight while consuming high-fat diets and taking raspberry ketones than other rats on the same diet taking nothing.

But the rats were taking 100 times the recommended dose for raspberry ketone supplements.[40] And one other thing – rats aren't humans. In 2014, Dr Oz stood before a Senate subcommittee to be investigated for his on-air claims about the 'miracle' effects of dietary supplements, which no doubt thousands of people take as certain truth and rush out to buy the cure that will finally make them thin. Why would a medical professional knowingly endorse a product that doesn't work? I'll give you three guesses; £5 per guess.

So what can we learn from the history of diet pills? Firstly, that there is no miracle pill. If there were, then everyone in the world would know about it, and again, we'd all be thin (and alive). Secondly, that we should always remain sceptical of products that claim to be the magical solution, even when they're endorsed by medical professionals. And lastly, that those professionals, the ones we entrust with our health and well-being, are often willing to pull the wool over our eyes for the sake of their bank balance. The market for weight-loss drugs is worth billions, and it's time that we sent a clear message to the diet industry that our lives are worth more.

I WANT MY MONEY BACK

To anybody who's ever been on a diet and gained the weight back, I want you to pay close attention to what you're about to read: Diets. Don't. Work. And I don't just mean the kind of bizarre crash diets that tell you to eat nothing but individually skinned grapes and peppercorns while rubbing yourself all over with palm leaves to stimulate fat loss. Those definitely don't work, but all the others? The ones that are 'scientifically proven', 'GUARANTEED TO HELP SHED POUNDS FAST', endorsed by celebrities the world over, or masquerading as 'a lifestyle'? They don't work either.

It's not that you won't lose weight, you probably will. But it'll come back like a boomerang every time. There are plenty of studies that diet companies use to prove that their plan will make you thin for life. The problem with those studies is that they usually only follow 'successful' dieters for a year or two before shouting hallelujah and taking the results to the bank.

If they followed those dieters for five years, the numbers would tell a different story (which is probably why they don't). Time and time again, the actual number of people who lose weight on a diet and keep it off for five years comes in at between 3 per cent and 5 per cent. Dieting might help you lose weight in the short term, but in the long term you'll wind up right back where you were.

When Traci Mann, a UCLA professor and psychology researcher, decided to gather a team to review the scientific literature on dieting in 2007, the results were clear: 'We found that the majority of people regained all the weight, plus more'.[41] In fact, at least one-third to two-thirds of people were shown to regain more weight than they'd lost. After analysing 31 long-term diet studies, Mann concluded that dieting was ineffective, i.e., diets don't work.

If someone had shown me those numbers back when I was still living in Dietland I would have scoffed and said something about people having no willpower. After all, that's what we're taught: the diet doesn't fail, we do. We believe that if we just try hard enough, we'll be able to reach that goal weight, and if we don't, we're terrible people with zero determination and deserve to hate ourselves for ever. In reality, the reasons why 95 per cent of diets don't work are far more complicated, and no amount of iron will is ever going to change them.

We are biologically programmed not to stick to diets. Way back when we were hunter-gatherers, food could get scarce at times. The only way to survive famines was to have plenty of juicy fat stores that the body could use for energy when it got desperate. Thanks to natural selection, we still have that same survival technique, meaning that when we experience starvation (and many diets prescribe exactly that), our bodies hold on to their fat stores extra tightly by slowing down our metabolisms.

If you do manage to lose body fat, you'll disturb the balance of hormones, produced by adipose cells, that regulate hunger and fullness signals in the brain. In other words, lose weight, and you'll start feeling even hungrier than usual, your metabolism will slow, and your body will start fighting back against the diet. Why? Because your body already knows the weight it wants to be.

Set point theory suggests that all of our bodies have a natural weight range that they are most comfortable in (I know from experience that after every dieting attempt my body always settled back into its safe, soft size 12/14, no matter how quickly or slowly it gets there). Usually we have about 10–20 pounds either side of our set points that our weight can fluctuate to, but when we try to force our bodies beyond those limits, our bodies work against us. And every time we attempt to mess with our internal weight regulation system, our set point can change, getting incrementally higher with every failed diet.

Which means that most of us would be thinner than we are now if we'd never dieted in the first place, and yet the only way we believe that we'll get thinner is by dieting. Catch-22 anyone? Maybe it's time we started trusting that our bodies know better than the ridiculous outside demands of how we're supposed to look. As Linda Bacon writes in *Health at Every Size: The Surprising Truth About Your Weight*, 'more than 50 years of research proves that your body tries to maintain your fat at the level at which you are designed to function best (not necessarily a size 4 or even 24, however)'.

Our set points are all different, and yet here we are fighting against our bodies to all fit one, impossible mould. Here's a wild idea: what if actually, we're all supposed to look different. I know that goes against every message that the mainstream media tells us about beauty, health and body size, but bear with me.

A little while ago ASDAH (the Association for Size Diversity and Health) released a short video called *The Problem with Poodle Science*. In it, adorable illustrations show how unjust it is to make one breed of dog (the poodle) the ideal image of health and beauty, and try to make all other breeds conform to an image that nature never intended for them to be. All dog breeds are supposed to come in different sizes and weights, but because the poodles are running things and refuse to recognise this, the mastiffs end up starving and convinced that it's what's best for them. Now I'm not saying that dogs and humans are exactly the same (although that would be my ideal world), but why shouldn't humans exist with as much deliberate diversity and difference in size as other species of animals do? And if that is the case, then of course no amount of dieting is going to change it.

So what about the people who are dieting for their health, rather than their looks? Well, unfortunately for them, not only does dieting not work, it's actually bad for our health – mental and physical. Since 95 per cent of diets don't work, most of us have made more than a few attempts at weight loss in our lives, meaning we've lost and regained weight several times. This is called yo-yo dieting, or weight-cycling, and has been linked with an increased risk of diabetes, high blood pressure, hypertension, stroke, coronary heart disease, and increased all-cause mortality.[42]

If you've ever felt the euphoria of breaking a diet and diving headfirst into all the forbidden foods you've been craving but denying yourself, you'll also know that dieting leads to binging. Most of the time we go for the high-fat, sugar-laden foods we weren't allowed on the diet, the ones that aren't exactly great for our health. Again, this isn't a failure on our part, it's exactly how the diet–binge cycle is designed to work, using guilt, shame, and gained weight to lead us right back to the start of the merry-go-round again.

For some of us the damage that diet–binge cycle does leads us down the eating disorder rabbit hole – dieting is a serious risk factor in the development of eating disorders, with evidence suggesting that 35 per cent of normal dieters will progress to pathological dieting, and of those, 20–25 per cent will develop partial or full syndrome eating disorders.[43]

When we diet we lose touch with our natural hunger and fullness signals, we rely on outside cues to tell us when we're supposed to eat and how much, rather than listening to our bodies. Which means that when the diet inevitably fails, we often lose control around food. We lose something else as well: time. I can't begin to imagine how many hours I've wasted over the years obsessing over calories and weigh-ins instead of living my life, but that's for another chapter.

When the National Institutes of Health held a summit in 1992 to evaluate the safety and efficacy of dieting, they found the same failure rates as Mann did years later, and added that dieters are at risk of 'poor nutrition, possible development of eating disorders, effects of weight-cycling, and the sometimes serious psychological consequences of repeated failed attempts to lose weight'.[44] That was over 20 years ago. Why the hell are we still taking part in this culturally accepted form of self-harm?!

If we need any more evidence of how badly diets hurt us, all we have to do is look at Ancel Key's Minnesota Starvation Experiment,[45] the most famous study of the effects of hunger on mental and physical health there is.

In 1944, Ancel Keys recruited 36 conscientious objectors to help the war effort by taking part in an experiment. He wanted to understand more about the effects of starvation on the body, and how best to rehabilitate those who had been starving, with hopes that the results would help rebuild communities living in near famine conditions towards the end of the Second World War.

The men chosen were all physically strong and psychologically stable. For the first three months of the study the men were given 3,200 calories daily, which was then followed by six months of 1,800-calorie rations with a 22-mile per week walking requirement (to burn around 3,000 calories a day). The men were each expected to lose 2.5 pounds per week to meet their target weights, and their calorie allowances were adjusted accordingly if they weren't keeping up.

It didn't take long on the semi-starvation rations for the men to start changing. They become increasingly impatient and irritable around each other, snapping and getting jealous if one was assigned higher rations than the rest. Almost immediately after the diet began, several of the men lost all interest in dating and their sex drives disappeared. They began developing strange rituals at mealtimes, doing whatever they could to make the meals seem bigger and last longer.

They became distracted, some had to withdraw from their studies, and many became completely obsessed with food – collecting dozens of cookbooks and planning on starting a career as a chef, when previously they hadn't taken much interest in food at all. They deteriorated physically as well, experiencing dizziness, extreme tiredness, muscle soreness, hair loss, reduced coordination, ringing in their ears, anaemia, swelling in their ankles and legs, and emaciation. But it's the mental side-effects that are the most shocking.

One man started having dreams about cannibalism towards the beginning of the experiment, and when he couldn't stop himself cheating on the diet, he threatened to kill himself or Keys. Another started eating scraps of food from rubbish bins. Both men were admitted to the psychiatric ward and recovered upon resuming normal eating.

Others had violent urges and told fellow members that they felt like they were going crazy. One man literally chopped off one of his own fingers with an axe. These are men who were previously mentally and physically healthy, living on around 1,800 calories a day (remember the Hollywood 18-Day diet prescribed less than 600 calories a day!). Someone tell me again how dieting is good for your health?

Diet culture promises us that if we work hard enough, buy the right products and spend enough time, we can whittle our bodies down to the ideal. We'll have health, happiness, and our real lives will finally begin! When we believe that promise what we're left with is obsession, destroyed self-esteem, empty bank accounts, eating disorders, wasted years, and hunger. We give everything we have to a system that strips us bare and leaves us forever reaching for the mirage of beauty that they planted in our minds. They get away with our money and we get nothing, we don't even get thinner. We've been tricked. And it would be laughable if it didn't hurt so much.

The good news is that once you see through the lies, you can stop believing them. You have the power to break out of the diet cycle, to stop giving money to companies that profit from our self-hatred, to refuse to believe the manipulation any longer, and to take your happiness right now, instead of 10 pounds from now.

You can start living your diet-free life, and be rid of the guilt that you learned so long ago. It won't be easy, unfortunately, the rest of the world hasn't realised what utter bullshit diet culture really is yet. But it will be worth it. So to end this section of the book I'd like to reiterate one highly scientific piece of information that I mentioned earlier that is of utmost importance, and with which I hope that you'll all agree: diets suck.

The pledge

Here is the diet-free pledge, ready for you to sign and start living your delicious, diet-free life. I know that if you're currently on a diet then the concept of giving it up is pretty scary. Terrifying, in fact. Leaving behind everything you've ever believed about your body, your worth, and how food should be treated is terrifying. I get that. It's okay if you're not ready to sign the pledge just yet, you can always come back to it at the end of the book, or at any time in the future.

But for now, if you're looking for something to help you decide whether it's time to say goodbye to constant counting and bathroom scale meltdowns, consider this: are you willing to follow this diet for the rest of your life? Are you willing to restrict and punish yourself for decades to come? Are you willing to hate your body until you're old and grey and still clinging on to those numbers? Do you really think that on your deathbed you'll look back and say 'hey, I wish that I'd counted calories more'? And if the answer to those questions is no, it's time to take the pledge. I promise that you're not signing your soul away, in fact you might be getting a long-lost part of it back. You'll find this pledge at the back of the book too – cut it out, sign it and stick it up somewhere you'll see every day.

I _____, hereby pledge to stop dieting.

I promise to stop counting every bite and obsessing over the numbers.
I promise to stop letting my scales tell me how beautiful, valuable, or loved I am.
I promise to stop buying miracle weight-loss cures that don't work.
I promise to stop giving my money to companies that rely on me feeling like my body is wrong.
I promise to respect my body's hunger.
I promise that I will no longer use exercise as punishment for what I've eaten.
I promise to stop taking part in self-deprecating diet talk.
I promise to try my best to unlearn all the toxic lessons about my body that diet culture has taught me.
I promise to stop dieting, and start living instead.

Signed: _____

Can I be body positive and still diet?

If you've read the rest of this chapter, you'll probably know how I feel about diets by now. Just in case you missed it: I am anti-diet, and I know that doesn't sit well with a lot of people. Some of you have probably been reading and wondering why you can't have both. Why can't you believe in body positivity but still want to lose those last 20 pounds? Why can't you love your body and still want to shrink it? Why can't body positivity and dieting go together? I hear you, and I hope what you're about to read gives you some answers.

Since body positivity has gone mainstream, there are plenty of people promoting the idea of body positive weight loss, even diet industry giants like Weight Watchers and Special K have jumped aboard the BOPO train in an attempt to boost their profits. Body positivity has become so watered down that some people actually believe that changing your body to better fit societal ideals is the most body positive thing to do.

But body positivity has never been about that. Body positivity is about accepting our bodies as they are, at any size, and challenging the oppressive systems that teach us we aren't allowed to do that. What is the number-one most oppressive system teaching us that we aren't worthy of happiness and self-love until we look a certain way? Bingo. The diet industry.

The monster that is the diet industry, and the overwhelming diet culture that it's created are at the very root of our body-image issues. If those clever advertisers had never realised that women's weight was something they could capitalise on way back in the early 1900s, the obsession with female thinness that holds so many of us captive today probably wouldn't exist.

Body positivity is the counter-culture to fatphobia and thin obsession, it was created as an alternative to buying into the messages that keep us small and at war with our bodies. Body positivity is an escape route from diet culture. Which means that dieting is not body positive, and never will be.

Now, it's important to clear up a couple of things here:

There is a huge difference between pursuing physical health in the form of lifestyle changes and buying into diet culture. One can go hand in hand with body positivity, the other is its arch-nemesis. Wanting to improve your physical health by eating more nutritiously and being more active can fit perfectly with body positivity (in fact, there's an entire movement within body positivity called Health at Every Size (see page 210) dedicated to encouraging healthful behaviours at, you guessed it, any size). The key difference between that and diet culture is that pursuing physical health is based on improving how your body feels, whereas dieting is entirely based on changing how your body looks to fit a one-dimensional idea of beauty, health, and happiness.

Actual healthy lifestyles (not the kind that have been co-opted by the diet industry), don't come with a weight-loss requirement. They aren't fuelled by the belief that you'll be more valuable in a smaller body. There's no painful restriction, no pressure to drop dress sizes, and no guilt over weekly weigh-ins and calorie tallies. Can you prioritise your physical health and be body positive? Hell yes. But you are equally never required to do so to be worthy of self-love, you're worthy of self-love no matter what your current health status might be.

Diet culture, on the other hand, is poison. Diet culture is the 'Lose 10 Pounds in 10 Days!' articles that little girls stumble upon and learn that they aren't good enough as they are. Diet culture is pills and potions and wraps that offer magical transformations for extortionate prices and even more extortionate health risks printed in teeny-tiny writing on the bottle (if printed at all). Diet culture is the product of one of the biggest and meanest multi-billion dollar industries in the world, it teaches us to hate ourselves so it can sell us 'cures' that don't work. Diet culture is why so many of us believe that thinner is always better, and thin can never be thin enough. Diet culture is why we're at war with our bodies, and it has no place in body positivity.

Weight loss in and of itself can still be body positive. Some people lose weight as a by-product of adopting more healthful behaviours. Some people lose weight in recovery from a binge-eating disorder. All of us have natural weight fluctuations with age, activity levels, hormone changes, and personal circumstances that have absolutely nothing to do with dieting. And since body size does not affect how worthy we are of self-love, you can be body positive whether your body is smaller or larger than it once was. Weight loss itself isn't the problem, forced weight loss through dieting is the problem.

At this point I reckon there are probably some people thinking 'But shouldn't we let people do whatever they want to their own bodies? Isn't that body positive?' And hey, I'm not here to tell anyone what they can and can't do with their glorious bodies. Your body, your rules. If you feel like it you can cover every inch of that fabulous skin in tattoos, you can get jiggy with as many people as you please (consensually, of course), you can take up extreme sports while wearing a T-rex costume, and, if you really want to, you can diet.

But reserving the right to do whatever you want to your own body isn't body positivity, it's body autonomy, and they are two different things. Body autonomy means that what you do with your own body isn't anyone else's business, which means that anything goes, even diet culture. Body positivity is a much more specific concept based on accepting our bodies as they are and fighting against the forces that tell us we're not supposed to. It has barriers that keep things like diet culture out, because they go against its very meaning.

Those barriers are what allow body positivity to be a safe space for so many people. The body positive community was the first and only space I'd ever found free from diet and weight-loss talk. It's the only space that I've ever felt able to heal from a lifetime of diet-culture-induced body hatred and eating-disorder demons. It's a refuge away from the ideal body obsessions that have hurt us so much. And since we can barely leave the house without hearing about pounds lost and desserts regretted, we need it. We need a diet-culture-free zone. So, as you can tell, I feel pretty strongly about keeping the body positive community safe for us diet survivors, because I really needed a safe space when I was younger. A lot of us did. And many people still do.

There are already millions of places to go if you want to celebrate weight loss. There are countless online spaces dedicated to dieting where you'll be cheered on every pound of the way. You can still talk about food diaries and dropped dress sizes with 99 per cent of the population. Is it really too much to ask that we preserve one space away from it? One part of our lives that diet culture can't get its hands on? Body positivity is that space.

So sure, you can pursue your physical health and be body positive. You can lose weight for any number of reasons and be body positive. You can do whatever you please with your own body outside of the necessary barriers of body positivity. But you cannot buy into a system that teaches us that we'll only be good enough when there's less of us, and still be body positive. I mean, that's just common sense.

DESSERT EVERY DAMN DAY

Hunger, Food Guilt, and Intuitive Eating

'Guilt may be an appropriate emotion when you have hurt another person or committed a crime, but guilt has no place in your eating world'
— Evelyn Tribole & Elyse Resch, *Intuitive Eating*

'Life is too short for self-hatred and celery sticks'
— Marilyn Wann, *Fat! So?*

One more bite

Once upon a time when I was a little girl, food was just food. It was something that stopped me being hungry, that tasted good, that my mum lovingly prepared and that I ate without any of the inner turmoil that was soon to arrive. It's probably hard for most of us to imagine it now, but there was once a time when none of us even knew what calories were. When we didn't even realise that the stuff we put in our mouths had any connection to the size of our bodies. When we ate because we were hungry, stopped when we were full, and didn't spend our time obsessing over each bite. That was before the guilt about what, when, where and how much we should be eating crept up and swallowed us whole.

Some of my favourite childhood memories are rooted in my taste buds. Going out to the arcades in the evening with my grandparents and coming home to a plate of cheese and crackers. Family holidays bundled in the back of my dad's car playing 'who can eat a sugared doughnut without licking their lips'. Walking to my mum's allotment and eating all the strawberries I was supposed to be picking as the sun set in the background. Settling down with my brother and sister on the sofa on a Friday night after we each picked the packet of crisps we got to eat while we watched *Friends*. Food was comfort. Food was fun. Food was pleasure.

And then the guilt seeped in. Slowly I learned that my appetite was shameful. That food was something to fear, not enjoy. That I had to earn my calories, burn off the fat, be careful of the sugar, weigh, measure and write down every bite. Food stopped being the simple pleasure I knew it as, and instead it became the thing that could make me fat. And I learned young that fat was the worst thing I could be.

It's hard to see how any of us could live in this diet-culture-drenched world and still have a healthy relationship with food. Most of us don't see food as sustenance, we see it as the thing that can either make us fatter or make us thinner. It's either good or bad, allowed or banned. In *Never Too Thin: Why Women are at War with Their Bodies*, Roberta Pollack Seid sums up just how twisted our ideas about food and eating have become:

> All societies set up complex food rules, but in most of them, food is considered a necessity. In contemporary America, we have come to the odd conclusion that it is not a necessity. Eating has become a moral issue. We must ask ourselves if we are 'entitled' to nourishment. We have to be 'good' enough – work out enough, diet enough, and above all, be slim enough – to deserve it.

Our relationship with food has been royally fucked up. Every meal comes with a side order of shame. Every bite has to be calculated and considered. We believe that we have to earn every snack and burn off every indulgence while clocking in every calorie, fat gram, carbohydrate and protein percentage in the never ending food calculator in our minds. Forever counting.

We've reached a place of complete disassociation from our bodies and what they tell us they need. Instead of seeing hunger as a necessary and important signal that our bodies send us for survival, we see it as suspect. We've spent so many years buying into the lie that listening to our hunger makes us weak, that those pangs in our stomach just need to be ignored so we can follow the latest diet plan promising to finally bring us happiness.

We've become so used to relying on external cues (like diet rules) telling us what we should be eating that we've forgotten how to listen to our bodies, and trust that our bodies actually know better than another ridiculous diet guru urging us to eat 17 bananas a day and go for a walk when we crave anything else.

Kate Moss famously said that 'nothing tastes as good as skinny feels'. So I thought I'd put together a little list of things she's obviously never tried before that taste *so* much better than buying into an oppressive body ideal could ever feel:

Pasta, pizza, mango, avocado, doughnuts, peanut butter, sushi, bacon, chocolate cake, lemon cake, any cake really, blueberries, garlic bread, smoked salmon, poached eggs, apples, roast dinners, cookie dough, sweet potato, whipped cream, freshly squeezed orange juice, watermelon, gelato, paella, oh and CHEESE.

You're welcome, Kate!

What we now think of as 'normal' eating patterns have fallen into the category of disordered eating. Things like cutting out entire food groups in fear that they'll make us gain weight. Obsessively counting and recording everything we eat. Purging our calories with daily intensive exercise. Abusing laxatives in the form of detox teas in an attempt to 'undo' indulgences. Having 'cheat days' where we binge on every forbidden food possible. And developing secret, shame-filled rituals around our food. All of these behaviours fall within eating-disorder territory. And yet my friends and I all spent years not only doing them, but being encouraged to do them by the mainstream media in the name of 'health'. Screw mental health, right?

We have learned these disordered eating habits from diet culture, and most of us don't realise how dangerous they truly are. The latest trend of clean-eating has spawned a whole new eating disorder called orthorexia, characterised by an all-consuming need to only eat nutritionally 'pure' foods, to the point where fixating on healthy eating ends up destroying mental health. Orthorexia isn't yet recognised as an eating disorder in the Diagnostic and Statistical Manual of Mental Disorders, but more and more people are seeking help as their preoccupation with clean-eating starts to rule their lives and eventually hurt their health, mental and physical.

Others fall into binge-eating disorder, compulsively gorging on huge quantities of food, often followed by starvation periods or purging. Bulimia disturbingly parallels the all-or-nothing, make-up-for-it mentality that our culture has taught us about eating. And some experts have even commented that 'anorexia nervosa could be called the paradigm or our age, for our creed encourages us all to adopt the behaviour and attitude of the anorexic. The difference is one of degree, not of kind'.[46]

Food has become the enemy. And the battle is exhausting. It's exhausting having so much mental real estate taken up by thoughts of food every minute of every day. It's exhausting lying awake at night, recalculating the day's calories and feeling the weight of guilt and regret over not being 'good' enough.

Even more exhausting is the punishment we inflict on ourselves to make up for what we see as the crime of eating. How dare we enjoy food or refuse to be ashamed of our appetite? How dare we give into the sin of being a human being with hunger and functioning taste buds?! Why can't we just be good and live on lettuce and chickpeas like we're supposed to?

We've all been made to forget one simple truth: we are allowed to eat. No matter what we ate yesterday. Regardless of whether we've worked out or not. At any size. Without any need to justify or repent. We are allowed to eat. And it's about time we took that truth back.

So how do we fix our relationship with food? How do we banish the guilt, learn to listen to our bodies and leave disordered eating patterns behind? We can start by taking a look at the lessons diet culture has taught us about food and throwing them out. Then we can learn a new way of eating, one that doesn't compromise our mental or physical health. One that doesn't make us feel like crap for eating a bit of cake or convince us that shame is a healthy part of our diet. Food freedom is possible, and it tastes damn good, so let's go and get it.

The good, the bad, the guilt

As anyone who's ever been to Dietland will know, there are good foods and bad foods. They're not always referred to in that way, sometimes it's junk food vs healthy food, syns vs free food, on-plan vs off-plan, zero-points food vs way-too-many points food. But the bottom line is still the same: these foods are okay, these foods aren't, and it's pretty much universal knowledge which foods belong to which category.

We all know what 'good' and 'bad' foods are. The good foods are usually green, fat-free, and low calorie. The kind that you see in brightly coloured arrangements on Instagram sprinkled with the must have health food of the moment (I still don't understand what a chia seed is). When we eat them we feel virtuous. We go to groups and sit in circles boasting about how 'good' we've been. We make promises about how 'good' we're going to be this week. We know that we're doing the right thing and praise awaits us. Even if we can't stop thinking about cake.

Then come the bad foods. The ones we worry about people judging when we put them in our trolleys. The ones we secretly stash and binge on when the 'good' foods just aren't good enough. The ones that, three days into our latest diet, we start spending every waking moment fantasising about. The ones we hate ourselves for eating. The rules are clear and must be followed if we ever want a chance to win the weight-loss jackpot.

I've known which foods are good and which are bad since I was around six years old and people started telling me to be careful with that sweet tooth of mine. When the diets started, all sweets, chocolate and desserts were placed firmly in the 'bad' category. Slowly the savoury snacks made their way there too, the crisps, the pastries. Then came the carbs, bread, pasta, and chips were all banished.

Eventually all snacks were bad foods and any meal larger than a small plate slipped over into that category too. Then when anorexia hit there was no such thing as a good food. Every food was bad, dangerous, fattening, filled with fear and off limits, except the ones with the very lowest numbers, the ones that could just barely keep me ticking over without making any more of me.

In my dieting years, there was never any room for compromise – every food was given its category and it stayed there without exception. I remember my final diet, the longest and strictest of them all. It spanned entire seasons and became my sole purpose in life. Of course, at the time I called it a lifestyle change, but now I just call it my Almighty Diet Summer From Hell© (ADSFH for short).

My friend Terri and I were both committed to the ADSFH. In fact, it formed the entire basis of our friendship that year. It was all we talked about, every single day, for about five months. We checked in with each other daily to see how good the other had been, i.e., how many calories we'd manage to cut that day. We adopted a constant dietspeak where 'how are you?' was actually code for 'what have you eaten today?' We'd give each other praise or consolation and spend hours rehashing every single detail of our plans, our goal weights, our projected progress, and how other people just didn't understand how important it was for us to finally lose the weight. Our entire friendship was distilled into calorie counts and weekly weigh-ins.

During the ADSFH I held on to those good food/bad food categories so tightly that food wasn't food any more. Food was either my salvation or my damnation. It was either my ticket out of Chubsville or my doom. Those categories were my key to health, happiness, and the holy grail of thin. So there was a whole lot weighing on how closely I followed the rules. My entire sense of self hung in the good food/bad food balance (except, of course, there was no balance about it). And that's the real problem with putting food into those two categories: it's not about the food at all, it's about how we see ourselves when we eat it.

When we moralise food, we moralise ourselves every time we eat. It isn't just the food that's good or bad, it's us. When we talk about food in those two terms what we're really saying is that *we* are good or bad. We're believing that the amount of calories, fat, sugar, macros, carbs or anything else we consume is what makes us a better or worse person. We are judging ourselves morally by what we put in our mouths. And that's not okay.

Sure, all foods are not nutritionally equal, and we can distinguish between more or less nutritious foods without falling into the good food/bad food trap. We can even choose to prioritise our physical health by being nutrient-conscious and body positive and still banish food guilt (more on that in a bit). But let's not pretend that most of our food categories are created with just our health in mind. For most of us, bad foods mean fattening, and when we hear someone say they've been bad on their diet, the rest of us know exactly what that person means.

The dichotomy of splitting food into these two categories means that we're always trapped. We're either being good and craving the bad (because intensified cravings are our brain's way of getting us out of diet-starvation mode), or we're being bad and feeling guilty for not being good. Our overwhelming sense of food guilt starts with believing in good food/bad food labels. It's why we spend entire days regretting the dessert we let ourselves have at the weekend. It's why the constant food calculator runs in our minds bargaining our next fridge visit. It's why everything we choose to eat becomes a reflection of our self-worth.

Along with those two unbreakable categories comes our all-or-nothing diet attitudes. We're either all good or all bad, anything in between is pointless. You know how it goes, one bite of chocolatey pleasure sneaks its way into your mouth and in your mind that means the whole operation is blown, might as well eat the entire cake and chug it down with a milkshake and just a small pizza to finish it off, maybe some fries and some ice cream too. Might as well, after all, you'll have go back to being good tomorrow.

During the ADSFH, Terri and I always set aside our designated 'cheat' a.k.a. binge days in advance. We'd collect every bad food we'd been denying ourselves and eat until we could barely move, then it was back to good foods only until we earned another binge day.

The good food/bad food dichotomy is the perfect set up for the diet–binge cycle that most of us know all too well. Labelling something as bad and off-limits is a sure-fire way to make sure it's the thing we want the most. It's the most alluring, the most tempting. Diet-food companies are forever playing on that sense of temptation with their chemical-infused dessert substitutes – give in to temptation, this one's guilt-free! Guess what? All food is guilt-free once you realise how harmful those two categories are and stop judging your value by the numbers you consume.

Here's a radical idea: what if food is just food? What if we took away the moral implications and stopped judging ourselves for every damn thing we eat? Cake is not sinful. Kale is not saintly. As Jes Baker puts it 'you're not a better person if you eat carrots, and you're not a fuck-up if you eat pie'. Other than actual moral/religion-based food choices (like vegan, vegetarian, kosher or halal), food should have no moral value. Which is why we need to stop referring to it as good or bad and believing that it has the power to define who we are as people.

So the next time you start to tell a friend how good you've been this week or how bad you are for giving in and eating the thing you've been craving for the last month (sacrilege!), stop and remind yourself that you are more than what you choose to eat. You are not a good or bad person based on your calorie count, and you deserve to eat without guilt.

Eat clean, train dirty

Clean-eating is the latest dietary trend that's taken social media by storm, and it isn't just about making sure you wash your lettuce before you eat it. At its core, clean-eating began as a way of consuming less processed, factory-made goods and more whole, nutritious food. Sounds reasonable, doesn't it? But like any dietary trend, it took on a life of its own and is now thought of as anything from raw fruitarianism to sugar-free paleo-veganism.

Ultimately, clean-eaters aim to limit or eliminate foods from their diet that aren't nutritionally pure enough, in the name of health. It isn't a new idea; Roberta Pollack Seid traced the health food craze back to the 1970s, and wrote in 1989 that cultural attitudes of food felt 'as if every time we put something in our mouths, we must re-evaluate our life-expectancy hopes'.

But in the last five years especially, the idea of eating clean has become an online lifestyle. Instagram is a haven for photos of rainbow-coloured clean eats, hashtagged with #eatcleantraindirty and #instahealth. Social-media personalities have built entire empires from boasting of the benefits of clean-eating, making the usual promises about how their plan is the easiest route to the perfect body, the perfect life, and even the cure to illness and disease. Happiness awaits at the bottom of a bowl of organic kale – haven't we heard another version of that one before?

With rising numbers of clean-eating devotees has come rising numbers of people struggling with orthorexia, an eating disorder characterised by an obsession with food purity and healthy eating. Orthorexia hasn't been officially recognised as a psychiatric diagnosis, but countless people have come forward sharing their experience of how clean-eating took over their lives. Wanting the health benefits of organic kale isn't a problem, the problems arise when the need for food purity becomes an overwhelming preoccupation. People with orthorexia are often admired for their willpower and dedication to health – it's difficult to recognise something as a disorder that our culture only sees as praiseworthy.

Here's a typical response in discussions about orthorexia: wait a minute, you're saying that eating healthy is a DISORDER? Sounds like an EXCUSE to eat CRAP all day! Point = missed. Here's how orthorexia is defined by Steven Bratman, the person who first coined the term in 1996: 'for people with orthorexia, eating healthily has become an extreme, obsessive, psychologically limiting and sometimes physically dangerous disorder'.

People cross the line from eating clean to having orthorexia when the pursuit of physical health comes at the cost of mental health. When thoughts about how to make meals more 'green' pop up every other minute. When you start sacrificing your entire social life because it endangers your dedication to food purity. When you start drowning in guilt and shame for eating something that isn't 100 per cent clean.

Recognising orthorexia isn't the same thing as damning nutrition or encouraging fast-food diets, it's simply shedding light on a very real problem that's spreading through social media fast. It's also important to call out a culture of healthism that tells us the better our physical health, the more worthy we are. The moral implications of this trend are clear: if you're not eating clean, you're eating dirty. And dirty implies all kinds of failure and shame, teaching us that what we put in our mouths places us higher or lower in the hierarchy of human value. Which just isn't true.

The clean-eating trend has gone far beyond promoting healthful food choices and instead has spawned thousands of new anxieties around what we're supposed to eat to be 'good', and to take absolute control of our health destiny. Ironically, the extreme lengths that some clean-eaters go to – like cutting out entire food groups – could actually harm their physical health by causing nutrient deficiencies. And the potential effect on mental health is clear.

By all means, teach people the value of a nutritious diet, but why must that turn into teaching them to live in fear of the things they choose to eat? An important reminder about so-called 'unclean' foods from Kate Harding and Marianne Kirby in *Lessons from the Fat-o-Sphere* reads: 'eating ice cream is not actually equivalent, health-wise, to pouring battery acid down your throat, no matter how much people who dispense dieting advice might like you to believe it is'.

So what should we be eating, according to body positivity? The honest answer is that true body positivity doesn't give a flying frittata about how 'clean' your diet is, because your food choices will never be part of a criteria for how worthy you are of body peace and self-love. You're worthy regardless of what you choose to eat. And you certainly don't need to justify yourself in conversations about food and health by saying things like 'I eat well so why shouldn't I love my body?!'. Those kind of comments only perpetuate the idea that food has moral value and that only some types of people (and only Good Fattys) deserve to feel good about themselves.

You won't find any specific food rules in this book. There are already far too many books capitalising on false nutritional claims and food shame. Most of the time they completely gloss over one very important thing: our relationship with food is complicated. It isn't as simple as Eat This, Be Happy, Live For Ever. Not only is our mental health and emotional well-being often ignored by the latest health craze, inherent classism is ignored as well.

Clean-eating can be just plain elitist: it expects everyone to have the access, funding, and education to adhere to a lifestyle that's often expensive, white-washed, and dripping in superiority. Green smoothies and yoga classes are great, but they're simply not an option for everyone, and that should be acknowledged.

Mostly, I just want us all to be able to eat in a way that doesn't sacrifice our emotional well-being. When we have conversations about food and health, I want us to include mental health, always I want us all to feel food freedom, however that looks for each one of us. If you can do that while eating nutritiously, sustainably, ethically, even cleanly, that's cool. If not, you are still 100 per cent, unrelentingly worthy of self-love. Kale or no kale.

Hunger

How many of us have spent our lives being ashamed of our appetites? How many times have we felt those familiar pangs in our stomachs and fought to convince ourselves that we don't actually need to eat, those twinges of hunger are just trying to trip us up, throw us off plan, lead us to temptation and make us fat. We have to stay in control and rise above the hunger. It's not as if those pangs are a crucial message our bodies send us necessary for our very survival or anything like that. They're just weakness, right?

I'm willing to bet that most of us are highly experienced in denying our hunger. We know all the techniques to distract ourselves when it hits. We're well practised at taking portions smaller than we really want and telling ourselves that we've had enough even when we still feel half empty. We've learned that eating freely in public is a no-no, except if we stick to the list of socially approved foods. Unless, of course, you're fat, in which case you learn that no matter what you eat in public there will be scrutiny, criticism and commentary – eating a salad? Yeah right, who are you trying to kid? Eating anything other than a salad? Looks about right, no wonder you ended up like that.

Every time we dare to listen to our cravings in public we have to weigh up whether it's worth the fear of being food-shamed, since our culture has yet to start teaching people that other people's food choices are our business roughly 0 per cent of the time.

Don't even get me started on the terror of first-date dinner choices. Growing up it was irrefutable knowledge that you could never eat what you actually wanted to on a date. I have no idea where this knowledge first came from, whether it was a magazine, a TV show, friends or family but it was a fact. If you're a female on a date then you eat as little as possible, as daintily as possible, and for the love of god, make sure you don't order anything that's going to get stuck in your teeth. Because how could anyone be attracted to a woman who's uncouth enough to actually eat what she wants, what a monster!

BELLY LOVE TIP #2

SIT AND WATCH
Save some time before you get dressed in the morning and find a space in front of your mirror.
Sit, relax, breathe, let your body fold.
Instead of zooming in on the parts that you've been taught to see as flaws, take a minute to look at the shapes that your body makes. Look at your stomach.
Does it flow like soft folds of velvet?
Does it roll like a breathtaking mountain landscape?
Does it ripple like waves calmly brushing the sand?
Keep reminding yourself of how beautiful those shapes are when they're found elsewhere in the world.
Why should they be any less beautiful when they're found on your body?
After all, you are a force of nature as well.
Sit for a while and appreciate the landscape of your body.

Body image and food issues are definitely not gender specific, especially with rising numbers of male eating disorders and the growing pressure for anyone who identifies as male to be leaner, fitter, and stronger every day to fit an idealised image of manhood. But there is something very specific about female hunger, and why it's still being demonised even today.

Young boys are still being praised at the dinner table for wolfing down 'man-sized' portions and young girls are still being encouraged to eat delicate portions and restrain themselves. It's not uncommon to see men bragging about their mammoth appetites while female celebrities swear in those awful magazine food diaries that a few nuts and seeds keep them going for hours! Of course, people of all genders struggle with their relationship to food, but the demonisation of female hunger specifically is rooted in history and has greater implications than we realise.

In *Unbearable Weight: Feminism, Western Culture, and the Body*, Susan Bordo traces modern women's shame around their hunger back to Victorian conduct manuals – pieces of literature that taught upwardly mobile women how to act appropriately to reach their desired social status, from dressing to eating to speaking. The advice on eating contained gems such as these from Florence Hartley's *The Ladies' Book of Etiquette, and Manual of Politeness* published in 1860:

Eat your soup quietly. To make any noise in eating it, is simply disgusting.

To eat fast, or appear to be so much engrossed as to be unable to converse, is ill-bred; and it makes those around you suspect that you are so little accustomed to dining well, that you fear to stop eating an instant, lest you should not get enough.

It is equally ill-bred to accept every thing that is offered to you. Never take more than two vegetables; do not take a second plate of soup, pastry, or pudding. Indeed, it is best to accept but one plate of any article.

Never eat every morsel that is upon your plate; and surely no lady will ever scrape her plate, or pass the bread round it, as if to save the servants the trouble of washing it.

Never make a noise in eating. To munch or smack the lips are vulgar faults ... Do not eat so fast as to be done long before others, nor so slowly as to keep them waiting.

Laid out like that, these little pieces of sexist wisdom seem blatantly excessive – but aren't they also quite familiar? I know I'm not the only one who learned that eating quietly, declining seconds, and leaving food on the plate were part of the rules of public eating.

Back in the Victorian era, femininity and food restriction went hand in hand. And just like today, it wasn't really about the food at all, but the behaviours that the food rules prescribed. Victorian women's denial of appetite had three main functions. First: it was a sign of wealth and social status. Second: it was a sign of higher spirituality. And third: it was a sign of chastity.

The well-provided-for woman who had plenty didn't need to give into her hunger whenever food was presented, in fact, she didn't need to be interested in food at all, since she could separate herself from the labour of food preparation by hiring help. Towards the end of the nineteenth century, thinness was fast becoming a sign of upper-class distinction. Thanks to industrialisation, food was more and more readily available to all social classes, and plumpness was no longer a sign that one was wealthy enough to eat well. As most people's bodies grew stockier, well-to-do women started prizing thinness as a sign of superiority instead. Upper-class Victorian women were among the first to popularise dieting even before the diet-industry boom of the early twentieth century.

Men suddenly wanted trophy wives who were frail and slender as a sign of their riches ('I'm so rich my wife doesn't even need to eat!' #manpoints). Beyond money, a lack of appetite also stood for a developed sense of spirituality. Self-restraint around food indicated a woman who could rise above her animal instincts to focus on a higher moral purpose.

Picture a luminously pale young woman, hollow-cheeked and floating around ethereally while reading Romantic poetry, and swearing off cake because she's too at one with her spiritual self to be a basic bitch who cares about food. Young women even idolised fasting saints from the past for their religious abstinence from the pleasures of the flesh. So you can guess what other pleasures of the flesh also came into play in ideas about women and hunger.

Let's talk about sex, baby. A woman who dared to have an unrestrained appetite for food was clearly also showing an unrestrained appetite for sex. This was in an era when women had to be chaste and pure above all else. At the same time as 'Victorian women were told that it was vulgar to load their plates',[47] they were also being told that masturbation was self-abuse and there was a widespread practice of female circumcision to cure women of supposed hysteria. As Joan Jacobs Brumberg puts it in *Fasting Girls*, 'appetite ... was a barometer of a woman's moral state'.

Before the fashion for thinness truly set in, one of the most iconic beauties of the late nineteenth century was Lillian Russell, a famous actress whose 200-pound figure was held up as the epitome of feminine beauty. Russell was known for her unrestrained appetite for food, which is part of what made her so popular – stories about her indulgences titillated her male audience – meanwhile upper-class women were being taught to be restrained in every respect.[48] Given that slut-shaming and food-shaming are still rife in today's society and aimed at every woman, I'd say that we've never truly detached ourselves from the archaic idea that femininity has to come with self-denial and unsatisfied hunger.

In *The Beauty Myth*, Naomi Wolf explores food and modern-day female hunger in terms of power and social status. She suggests that creating a body ideal that requires 95 per cent of women to go hungry to achieve it is no mistake, but in fact is a tool to keep us small and distracted. 'The beauty of thinness lies not in what it does to the body but to the mind, since it is not female thinness that is prized, but female hunger'. Remember the Minnesota Starvation Experiment and the effects of hunger on men who were previously completely healthy – obsession, preoccupation, lack of motivation, and for some, a complete deterioration of mental health. Now think back on all the time that you've spent on extreme diet regimes – how did that hunger make you feel?

Every so often I think back on my dieting years and wonder what else I could have been doing with that time. Because it's not just the time you spend preparing food, going to the gym or tracking weight-loss progress, it's all the hours you spend thinking about food, weight, and nothing else. Dieting makes us obsessed with things that, in the grand scheme of life, don't really matter.

I spent all my teenage years consumed by the need to shrink my body, when I could have been learning and growing and exploring and living. We've been fed a lie that being thin is the most important thing we can be, but just think what we'd all be capable of achieving if we stopped believing it. And if we stopped forcing ourselves to go hungry all the damn time.

The physiological effects of hunger alone stop us from fully engaging in the world and reaching our full potential. Our bodies and brains just don't function properly when they're deprived of nourishment. And since diet culture has been primarily aimed at women for the last 100 years, hunger could be seen as one of the most effective tools for suppressing female advancement. It keeps us thinking about things like waistlines and sugar substitutes rather than the need for social, political, and economic equality. Which is what led Wolf to famously write – 'dieting is the most potent political sedative in women's history'. Or, in other words: we cannot take on the world while we're hungry.

So you see, female hunger is not simply about food. It's not even simply about body size. It's about power, and liberation, and wholeness. When we refuse to be ashamed of our appetites we send the message that we are whole beings with needs that deserve to be fulfilled. We let the world know loud and clear that we will not spend our lives starving and shrinking instead of flourishing and living.

In this way, listening to our hunger and respecting the needs of our bodies is radical. Eating what we want when we want is a delicious way of kicking diet culture's arse and giving a giant 'fuck off!' to a system that's determined to reduce us all to flesh and bones, when we are so much more than that. So yeah, Florence Hartley, I'll have seconds when I want them and I'll lick the whole damn plate clean, and I sure as hell won't subscribe to any idea of femininity that tells me I'm less valuable for doing so.

The next time you feel that familiar pang in your stomach, don't try to convince yourself it isn't there. When you're on a date, be a badass and order what you want. And if you're following a diet plan that leaves you hungry and obsessed, well, stop following it. Respect your body enough to listen to it when it tells you that it needs nourishment. Honour your appetite. And go take on the fucking world.

The diet-binge cycle

Once everyone had gone to bed, that was the best time. I could creep down the stairs without making a noise, check all the lights were out and make my way to the kitchen. The only thing in my mind was a command on repeat: eat, eat, eat. My hands felt like they were buzzing as I reached into the cupboard to start what was fast becoming a familiar routine. One more glance round to make sure nobody was coming downstairs to catch me in the act. I was alone. Just me and a cupboard filled with all the foods I swore I'd never eat again.

I'd been thinking about this moment all day: what time I'd go downstairs, how it would taste, what I'd eat first, next, and last. The urge to binge had been building since I woke up that morning, filling every corner of my mind with those three neon letters until I couldn't stand the brightness any longer: EAT. The wrapper was off and the first bite of sweetness set my taste buds alight. That sudden sense of relief swept over everything, and I knew I wouldn't be going back upstairs for a long while.

Some nights I told myself I would start slow, really savour those forbidden foods and enjoy them. Other nights I had no intention of doing anything except devouring whatever I could get my hands on in the largest quantity possible. I didn't care if it was hot, cold, sweet, savoury, fresh, or old. Once the binge started, there was no telling where or when it would end. Once I gave in, that was it. The binge would engulf everything, leaving behind all thoughts of the day passed, all rules around food, all awareness of bodily sensations, fullness or discomfort. Just uncontainable animalistic hunger. One thing was guaranteed: the hunger wouldn't stop until I literally couldn't eat another bite.

I'd spend the whole week being 'good', sticking to my latest restrictive diet plan and spending every moment obsessing over the numbers. I'd tell myself that this time would be different. This time I'd beat the binge cravings and finally lose the weight. I'd learn how to control my hunger, tame my unruly body fat and reach my dream body. I wanted it more than anything in the world, and yet I somehow still found myself crouched in front of the cupboard after just six days of my 1,200-calorie plan, drowning in guilt but seemingly unable to control the urge to binge.

As we've already seen from the I Want My Money Back section of the last chapter, diets set us up to binge. Starvation, even if it isn't extreme, causes real physiological changes in the brain. When we go hungry our brain gets the message that we're living in a time of famine. Our evolutionary survival instincts kick in and our brain does everything it can to get us to fall off the wagon.

This includes lowering our metabolism, kicking our hunger signals into hyper drive, and even making us more sensitive to cravings so that food is more appealing.[49,50] Which is why falling off a diet isn't about a lack of willpower; our brains are biologically programmed not to stick to diets (hence the whole 95 per cent of diets not working thing). As Susan Bordo puts it in *Unbearable Weight* – 'restriction and denial of hunger ... set up the contemporary binge as a virtual inevitably'.

I spent years in the diet–binge cycle. Every time I dieted, I unwittingly sent the message to my brain that a famine was occurring. Existing in a state of semi-starvation caused my survival instincts to kick in and produce physiological changes in my brain so that food was all I could think about, until I couldn't fight the urges any longer and binged. But every time I binged, I convinced myself that I was an out-of-control glutton and I needed to restrict more and more to make up for the binge. Cue the start of the cycle. I had no idea that my restriction was a direct causal factor of my binges. Instead I bought into the diet-culture message that I was a failure with no willpower and the cycle continued.

Anyone who's experienced it knows how the cycle goes.

Stage 1: you think that you're too fat, so you go on a diet. You lose weight short-term which you take as proof that the diet plan works.

Stage 2: your weight loss slows as your body fights back to stay in its set-point range, so you restrict your intake further. You might be able to keep this stage up for weeks, even months, but you are literally fighting against your own body and will inevitably get the urge to binge.

Stage 3: you've blown it. You've eaten all the things you're not allowed to eat. According to the plan you're a failure, and if you're going to fail, you might as well fail hard – bring on the binge. Before you know it you've gained back the weight you lost, and maybe more.

Stage 4: you think that you're too fat, so you go on a diet ...

The stages will last different amounts of time depending on how many diets you've been on, and how long you can fight against your body's internal weight regulation system. Some people can keep the weight off for weeks, others months, some even years. One thing is the same for all of us: we blame ourselves when we fall off the wagon.

We don't see that the cycle has been created to guarantee that we keep going round in an endless loop. It isn't about willpower or hard work; yo-yo dieters have willpower in abundance, how else would they keep forcing themselves to do something so exhausting despite overwhelming evidence that it won't work? How else would they keep trying, over and over, even with years of experience telling them how it's going to end? Dieters have willpower, but the cycle isn't about willpower. The cycle is about biology, and you can only fight your own biological instinct for so long. The diet industry has made billions convincing us that that's not the case.

For six years, I alternated eating huge quantities of food with purging through over-exercising and restricting, and I was stuck. Shortly before I found body positivity I broke down in front of my dad and started crying uncontrollably. I told him that it felt like I was always either dieting or binging, and I couldn't see a way out. I imagined spending the rest of my life constantly either hungry or overtaken by compulsive eating. I was ashamed and confused but, most of all, I was tired. I just couldn't do it any more. I wanted to know how to eat normally and I wanted to live without every minute of every day being consumed by guilt and obsession.

It turns out I wouldn't need to worry about it for much longer, because once I started learning about body positivity, the diet–binge cycle stopped. My relationship with my body and food started to heal, and I began to relearn how to eat in a normal, non-disordered way. And these are the first steps I took.

I made a promise to myself to never diet again. The cycle had to stop somewhere, right? I'd told myself time and time again that it would stop after I'd lost the weight. That once I'd starved myself down to my perfect body then all of the food cravings would disappear, along with every other problem in my life (classic magical When-I-Lose-The-Weight thinking). After six years, I had to consider the possibility of letting the illusion go, and facing the truth: this wasn't working. It wasn't making me love my body. It wasn't making me happy. And it wasn't doing anything to heal all of the pain left over from my eating disorder.

I started learning about diet culture and how we've all been made to see our bodies as problems for profit. I learned the truth about dieting – the 95 per cent failure rate, the mental and physical harm it causes, the money that's made from teaching us to hate our bodies. I thought back to five-year-old me, learning that weight loss was the key to beauty, happiness, and womanhood and already terrified of being fat. And do you know what I did then? I got really fucking mad.

Because none of us, especially not five year old children, asked to live in a world that values what size our bodies are over who we are as people. None of us should have been taught that our bodies are battlegrounds and that fighting against our flesh should be our ultimate purpose in life. None of us. We all deserve better than that. So with my newfound diet-culture rage I waved goodbye to dieting. And without fully realising it, waved goodbye to the cause of my binge-eating urges, and hopped off the diet–binge cycle.

I removed all 'good' and 'bad' food labels. You've already read about why this is important, so this is just a reminder of the effect removing those labels has on binge-eating. It means that all the typical binge foods are no longer forbidden temptations luring you over the 'bad' side. They're just foods. Which means that they won't hold the same emotional significance any more.

Don't get me wrong, I still love a lot of my old classic binge foods, give me a slightly undercooked, gooey chocolate brownie any day of the week. But when I get pleasure from eating them, it's not a pleasure that's tainted with shame and guilt. Enjoying one brownie no longer makes me feel like I'm a terrible person and have to eat four more because I've already been 'bad', so I might as well bury my shame in batter. The old 'bad' foods don't have that power over me any more, because I've detached all the old negative emotions I used to feel when eating them.

I stopped telling myself I had One Last Binge. Without another impending diet, I no longer had that last-supper mentality that takes hold of us before a new diet starts. When you're always waiting for the next round of starvation to begin, it's easy to tell yourself that you might as well eat everything that's soon to be off-limits. Especially since this diet is going to be different and you'll definitely never eat those foods ever again.

Except when you're starting a new diet every week, all you're really doing is setting yourself up for a weekly binge. When you stop dieting, you don't need a last supper, you don't need to binge until you can't move because all those foods will still be there tomorrow. And if you want them, you're allowed them.

I stopped beating myself up for binging. Remember that dieting sets us up to binge? And that hunger produces real, physiological changes in the brain that create the urge to binge? You're not a failure with no willpower – you're a human being with a brain that's functioning in its necessary biological role. It isn't your fault that you got caught in the cycle; our culture sells dieting as the route to success and our bodies react how they've evolved to react to ensure our survival. So basically, as soon as diet culture got hold of you, you were screwed.

It's time to let go of all the guilt that comes from you believing that you're the problem. Diet culture is the problem. And all that built-up shame only becomes the force that pushes you into the next binge. Be kind to yourself, realise that all your body has ever wanted to do is take care of you, and let the guilt go.

I let the hunger unfold. When you quit dieting, you'll probably experience an oh-my-god-I-can-eat-anything-I-want-GIVE-IT-TO-ME phase. You might even binge, especially if you've been dieting frequently and strictly for a long time. What's important is that you let yourself experience that hunger non-judgementally and without forcing yourself to restrict to make up for it. You need to send a message to your body that it can trust you again, and that you're going to start feeding it when it sends a signal that it's hungry.

You'll also probably want to dive right into the foods that you've spent a lifetime believing are 'bad'. Which is bound to provoke internal accusations of 'you're an insatiable slob who's out of control and needs to diet'. When I first jumped off the diet wagon, I ate a lot of half-baked cookie dough. But I kept reminding myself that choosing cookie dough over more nutritious options didn't make me a worse person, that my hunger signals and cravings should be respected, and that if my body changed as a result, that was okay. Gaining weight and letting my body get back to its set-point weight wouldn't make me any less worthy of self-love.

But after a few weeks of cookie dough-topia I found that I just didn't need as much of it to satisfy my cravings. The forbidden allure had worn off, I knew I could have it if I wanted it, but also that it would still be there tomorrow and I never needed to deny myself again.

I'd always thought that as soon as I stopped dieting I'd just want to live on a buffet of baked goods for ever, but as I started allowing myself total food freedom, something strange happened instead. My body told me that it didn't want dough-nuts all day every day, it wanted more nutritious food as well, even (and this was previously unheard of), green things! Here's the biggest way I healed my relationship with food: I started listening to my body.

I learned to eat intuitively. And this is how ...

Intuitive eating

By now you're probably thinking something along the lines of 'Okay, Megan, you keep dropping hints about intuitive eating without handing over the information, so what is it?'

Here's the most basic answer I can give you: intuitive eating means eating what you want, when you want it, and stopping when you're full. I realise that sounds way too simple to be the answer to all your food worries, but hold on. If intuitive eating was powerful enough to banish my food demons after years of anorexia, binge-eating, and yo-yo dieting, then it might just work for you too.

Besides being too simplistic, a lot of you will have immedi-ately thought that intuitive eating sounds just plain dangerous. If you've spent years in Dietland, then experience will have taught you that allowing yourself to eat whatever you want usually ends with a stomach that feels like it's about to burst, an overwhelm-ing sense of shame, and countless empty jars and packets strewn around like a snack-food crime scene at 11p.m. on a Sunday night before the diet starts tomorrow. I get it.

The thought of letting go of all the food rules that years of dieting has ingrained in your mind as 'right' is a scary prospect. In fact, a very loud warning message is probably playing in your mind right now about what it might do to your body. How the hell could you ever let yourself eat whatever you want whenever you want it? There wouldn't be enough ice cream in the world!

What if I told you that you already know how to eat intuitively? Sure, it's probably buried under years, even decades of diet-culture damage, but it's there. You were born with it. We're all born knowing how to respond appropriately to our hunger, eat when we need to eat, and stop when we're satisfied – just think of a newborn who cries when feeding is needed and turns away when enough is enough. Without these innate internal signals of hunger and satiety, we wouldn't survive as a species. We only learn to distrust our own internal signals when all the external rules about what, when, and how much we should eat interfere with our ability to trust our own bodies.

The good news is that we can get that trust back. The people who literally wrote the book on intuitive eating – Evelyn Tribole and Elyse Resch – refer to this process as a 'journey back to intuitive eating', you won't be learning anything new, just getting back in touch with the power that you've always had to listen to your body. This is the key to healing your relationship with food, to mental freedom, to banishing food guilt, and to reconnecting with your body.

Take a minute to imagine the worst diet food you've ever forced yourself to eat. Mine is probably those zero calorie water noodles that you buy from health food stores, although I'm not too sure what's so healthy about pretending that water and chemicals tastes the same as noodles. You never have to eat that food again. You never have to feel guilty about not eating that food again. You never have to feel guilty for eating what you really want again. You never have to compromise your mental health with food restriction ever again. From this point on you are the only person with the authority to decide what you get to eat, and you'll learn to see that your body is a trustworthy source of authority. Sound good? Keep reading!

NO MORE DIETS

Just in case you're still holding on to dieting as the route to happiness, this is where it has to go. You cannot keep dieting and expect to heal your relationship with food. Why? Dieting teaches us to ignore our bodies' signals and instead follow outside rules about eating: e.g., drink water when you're hungry! Go for a run when you have a craving! If you want pasta, fill up on courgette instead!

Dieting teaches us that our own bodies can't be trusted when it comes to decisions about food. Intuitive eating on the other hand, teaches us to listen to our bodies and forget those rules. As Janet Polivy puts it in her foreword to *Overcoming Overeating*, 'the crucial problem with all restrictive dieting is that it drives a wedge between a person and his or her body'. It's time to take the wedge out, and rebuild the bridge between food and our bodies.

Every intuitive-eating programme worth its salt puts breaking up with diets as step number one. More specifically, these parts of the diet mentality have to go:

- The constant internal food calculator – turn that shit off.

- The idea of forbidden foods (a.k.a. 'bad' foods) and safe foods (a.k.a. 'good' foods).

- The guilt and shame for 'failing' when you eat so-called forbidden foods: remember that you've never failed for ending a diet, the diet has always failed you.

- The magical 'when I'm thin' fantasy. The one where having a smaller body has instantly led to more romance, a more satisfying career, a more exciting social life, no more worry, stress or sadness and, most importantly, no more cravings for baked goods. Because that's all so believable, right?

- Every Do, Don't, Should and Shouldn't that diet plans have made you believe about eating. Shouldn't eat after 9 p.m.? Forget it. Don't touch anything with refined sugar? Nope, not listening to that one any more. You should just tap into your willpower to resist all edible temptation! Seriously, get out of here with that twisted food morality nonsense. We're starting from scratch here, no more rules.

And this bit is really important: for you to genuinely start healing your relationship with food and become an intuitive eater: you can't treat this like an experimental new diet plan, hoping for fast results and a new body. This is not a weight-loss gimmick or a quick fix, but it is a way to make peace with food for life.

Any lingering diet hopes will only alienate you from your body and undermine your new way of eating. I realise this probably feels like a giant leap of faith, but you've already tried everything else, haven't you? Haven't diets already wrecked your relationship with food, wreaked havoc on your metabolism, and made you see your body as a problem that needs fixing one too many times? Don't you think it's time to call a truce with food and your body? Me too.

LEARN TO LISTEN TO YOUR BODY

Step 1: Get back in touch with your hunger signals. Chances are that you've spent a long time seeing your appetite as the enemy. You're probably an expert at ignoring when your stomach rumbles and telling yourself that it's not time to eat yet. The problem with ignoring your appetite is that your body learns that you can't be trusted to pick up on its hunger signals. Some of you might have distanced yourself from them so much that you only become aware that you're hungry once you're ready to devour everything in sight.

Now you've ditched the diet rules, you no longer have to see your hunger as a problem. Instead, you can see it as the amazing way your body communicates its needs to you so that you can survive. Which means that you can start listening to it in a completely non-judgemental way – whatever level of hunger you feel at any given time isn't good or bad, it just is, and it deserves to be responded to.

Some intuitive-eating programmes recommend using a 1–10 hunger chart to get back in touch with what you're feeling, ranging from completely empty to overstuffed, with 5 being neutral. Everyone feels hunger and satiety in different ways, so you can make your own chart based on your experience, this is what mine looks like:

1. So hungry I can't feel it any more and just feel nauseous instead (tired, grumpy, generally zombiefied).
2. I WILL EAT YOU IF YOU COME NEAR ME (shaky, irritable, difficulty concentrating on anything except FOOOOD. This is the stage where my boyfriend starts telling me that I'm not the same when I'm hungry).
3. Give me something with cheese on it soon please (ready to eat but still functional, fair amount of stomach-rumbling and what's-for-dinner thoughts).
4. I could use a little something to keep me ticking over! Maybe a snack or light meal (small stomach twinges and some thought about food choices).
5. Neither hungry or full, not really thinking about food.
6. That was tasty! (Feeling energised and quite satisfied, though not weighed down.)
7. Hunger = satisfied, but there might still room for dessert if I fancy it, did somebody say brownies? (Comfortably full, might have a craving for something sweet, but no longer hungry.)
8. Yep, I'm full (heaviness in my stomach, feeling a bit tired, ready to sit down for a while).

9. WHY DID I WEAR JEANS?! (Sneakily unbuttoning jeans, second trimester food baby, feeling very tired and maybe a tiny bit nauseous.)
10. Christmas-dinner-level stuffed, never want to think about food again (stomach-ache, sick feeling, need to sleep off this food coma).

When it comes to hunger signals, the aim of intuitive eating is to respond when you're at a 4 or a 3 on the hunger scale, giving you a better chance of choosing the food you really want, and being able to tell when you're really satisfied.

If you frequently find yourself at a 2 or even a 1, it's likely that you end up eating everything you possibly can and catapulting yourself to the other end of the scale, finishing way past comfortable satiety on a 9 or even a 10. Which is not a failure on your part, it's simply how we're wired to react to deprivation, by engulfing everything in sight once it's available. And since we're taught to ignore our hunger, it's no wonder we end up on the extremes.

Read this next part carefully: you are allowed to respond to your hunger. It doesn't matter what time it is, it doesn't matter what you've already eaten that day, you don't have to tell yourself that you shouldn't be hungry if you are.

Listen to your body non-judgementally. If you're feeling any symptoms of physical hunger (from stomach twinges to full-on rumbles, feeling empty, light-headed, shaky, tired, faint), then it's time to eat. You have permission to eat when you're hungry. And you don't need to turn to any external cues for what to eat, no more charts, points systems, safe food lists or diet substitutes for what you're actually craving. Pay attention to your hunger signals, and then ...

Step 2: Eat whatever the fuck your body is telling you it wants. Before the thoughts about spiralling out of control and eating all of the 'bad' foods pop up, remember that nothing is off limits any more. What you choose has no effect on how you get to feel about yourself. Just try to focus on what your body is telling you it wants, and match that with your food options.

If nothing calls out to you immediately then take a minute to ask yourself: do I want something hot or cold? Sweet or savoury? Mild or flavourful? Dense or light? Smooth or crunchy? If your mind sets on something then imagine yourself eating it, if it's available maybe go and try a small amount, you'll know if it matches up with what your body's craving. You have permission to eat whatever you truly want.

HOLD ON, BUT WHAT IF I REALLY CAN'T STOP EATING ICE CREAM? SURELY THAT'S NOT GOOD FOR MY HEALTH? Like I said, there was a time when I was convinced I would never want to stop eating cookie dough from morning until night. It's normal to gravitate towards your previously forbidden foods, but once you truly convince yourself that they're no longer banned, that they'll always be allowed, and there isn't another diet lurking around the corner as a punishment, those foods will lose the allure of the forbidden.

Once you really believe that cookie dough has the same moral value as chickpeas, and it's there for you to eat whenever you really want it, you won't feel that desperate craving to devour a whole batch whenever you get a whiff of vanilla from the oven.

Allow yourself all the previously forbidden foods. Whatever your cravings lead you to, make sure you enjoy it. Be present when you eat, appreciate the food, and savour it. As Linda Bacon writes in *Health at Every Size*, 'the best attitude toward eating is not one of denial and restriction. The best approach is one that cultivates pleasures and honors food and the act of nourishing yourself'. Allow your body to feel nourished, your taste buds happy and your cravings listened to, and keep checking in with your body to see when you're satisfied.

Step 3: Stop eating when you're full. That is, when your body has really had enough, not when you think you should stop eating according to some outside rule. If you're an experienced dieter then you've probably learned to eat the portion assigned to you by the plan, no more, no less, regardless of how it left you feeling. Sometimes you'd end up unsatisfied and not allow yourself to go for more; other times overstuffed from thinking that you might as well get as much as you can while you're allowed it. Now that you're eating intuitively, you will always be allowed more whenever you want it, so there's no need to eat past the point of comfort like the last supper pre-diet days.

If you tend to eat without paying much attention and wind up full to the brim, slow down, take your time, and maybe pause throughout the meal to ask yourself if you're still hungry and if the food is still satisfying. You're the only person who gets to decide how much is enough, and if you listen to your body, it will tell you. Susie Orbach wrote in *On Eating* that 'No diet, no doctor, no trainer, no scheme can know better than you what suits your body'. You're already equipped with everything you need to decide what, when, and how much to eat, so start trusting yourself.

When it comes to being full, different levels on the hunger scale suit different people, and you get to choose what feels best for you. I like breakfast and lunch to take me to a 6 or sometimes a 7, not so full that I start feeling sluggish, but satisfied enough to feel energised and content. If I'm having dinner at home and some sofa time in the evening, an 8 feels good to me. I like going to bed with my stomach feeling full, others are more comfortable hitting a 5 or a 6 and going to bed feeling lighter.

If you eat past the point of comfort, you haven't failed, you're not a bad intuitive eater. If you eat sometimes when you're not hungry, you still haven't failed. This is not a diet! You don't have to measure how good or bad you've been depending on how you've followed the rules. There are no rules, just guidelines for eating in a way that suits you, mentally and physically. Nobody eats intuitively 100 per cent of the time, because food isn't just fuel, it's tradition, it's pleasure, it's ritual, it's comfort. There's no way that we can reduce it to a filler, nor should we.

In *Overcoming Overeating*, Jane Hirshmann and Carol Munter explain the difference between stomach hunger and mouth hunger. You feel stomach hunger when there is a physiological need to eat, when your body needs nourishment and sends you a signal to say so. You feel mouth hunger when there's a psychological need to eat. Maybe you just want the taste of something, maybe you're eating for comfort, out of habit or just for pleasure, but it's not to satisfy physical hunger.

The aim of intuitive eating is to be more attuned to your stomach hunger and satisfy it. That doesn't mean you'll never feel mouth hunger, but that it won't be the prompt for most of your eating experiences. Rest assured, you can still choose to eat something just because it looks really fucking good.

What about nutrition?

Most intuitive-eating programmes advise against focusing on nutrition straight away. If you're just starting to break away from the diet mentality it's still all too easy to turn 'healthy eating' into a moral obligation fuelled by guilt and secret body-shrinking motives. You have to be free to explore your appetite without any 'this is what I should be eating' thoughts looming over your food choices. Once you've neutralised the old 'good' and 'bad' foods and really started to trust your own body, you might want to make a conscious choice to eat more nutritiously.

What's important is that the decision comes from a place of wanting your body to feel good, wanting to fuel it with things that help it function well, and make you feel energised and ready to kick some ass. Not from wanting to force your body into a different shape to better fit societal standards of beauty, that's where the guilt and body shame will start to seep in again.

If you feel secure in your intuitive-eating experience and want to start eating more healthfully, listening to your body is the best place to begin. At some point, it's probably going to say, 'hey, all this cookie dough has been really great, but maybe it's time to get some other nutrients and broaden our horizons a little bit'. When you're making your food choices you can start to think beyond what taste/texture/temperature you're craving and also consider how you want your body to feel after eating.

For example, if you're thinking of having a full English fry-up for breakfast but you've got a busy morning ahead and fry-ups tend to make you feel sluggish, is there another option that'll still satisfy you and leave you more energised? Maybe some poached eggs on toast with a side of fresh fruit? If your body still says 'nah, I need the whole shebang', then dig in and enjoy every bite! Wanting to eat more healthfully shouldn't mean forcing yourself to eat things you don't want.

Fun fact: studies have shown that the more we enjoy our food, the more nutrients we absorb from it. In one study that Linda Bacon describes in *Health at Every Size*, two groups of women were served a traditional Thai meal, one group was from Thailand, the other Sweden.[51] The Thai women liked the meal more, and absorbed 50 per cent more iron from the food than the Swedish women did. Which means forcing yourself to eat things you don't like in the name of health isn't as good for you as you think it is.

At this point, some nutrition knowledge might be useful, but beware of 'health' advice that's sneakily tainted with diet culture, anything that's focused on calorie counts, fat-burning, weight loss, or promotes an overly restrictive intake isn't really about health at all, it's about dieting.

Health at Every Size contains some useful, unbiased nutritional information. Bacon's top piece of advice for healthful eating is to 'enjoy a variety of real food, primarily plants', she goes on to explore the effects of different food groups on physical health without using shame or scare tactics. Some people might benefit from consulting a HAES-friendly nutritionist (there is a growing number of non-diet dietitians out there who follow a weight-neutral approach).

Again – you are not required to prioritise healthy eating until your intuitive-eating mindset is secure, even then it still isn't a requirement or measure of your worth as a person. Some of you aren't in a position to bring that nutrition focus into your eating yet. If you're currently in recovery from a restrictive eating disorder, for example, anything that might stop you from finding true food freedom and mental recovery just isn't worth it.

I think what Evelyn Tribole and Elyse Resch wrote in *Intuitive Eating* about nutrition sums it up: 'We define healthy eating as having a healthy balance of foods and having a healthy relationship with food'. In other words, pursuing physical health should never come at the cost of mental health. Health isn't just about what you put in your body and how you move, it's how you feel and how you think about those things, too. Plus how you feel and think about yourself.

IT'S NOT ABOUT WEIGHT LOSS

No really, it's just not. Unfortunately there are plenty of programmes that turn intuitive eating into another 'how to get thin without dieting!' weight-loss method. But focus on weight loss will only hinder the process of getting back in touch with your body. It's hard to trust that your body knows best while you're still actively trying to shrink it, you won't be able to shake off food guilt for good or honour your hunger non-judgementally. This isn't about changing how you look, it's about healing your relationship with food and getting the mental freedom that you deserve.

Intuitive eating respects that every person has their own individual set-point weight, the weight that their body naturally prefers and functions best at. If you've spent years eating in a way that's disordered, restrained, or completely out of touch with your innate hunger and fullness signals, you might not be at your set-point weight.

Some people who have consistently eaten past the point of satiety might end up losing weight from getting back to eating intuitively. Others might gain some, others will stay the same. It's important to remember that your body knows the weight that's right for you, trying to force it outside of its set-point range will only work against you in the long run.

EMOTIONAL EATING

It's normal for food to have some emotional significance. We use it to celebrate, we use it to reminisce and to comfort ourselves. Like I said, food is not just fuel. However, for some of us, food and emotions get intertwined in a way that becomes problematic, like if food becomes the only form of comfort we can turn to in our lives, or if we regularly use it to numb what we're feeling.

Along with dieting, emotional eating separates us from our physiological hunger signals and stops us from eating intuitively. You're not a bad person for eating for reasons outside of physical hunger, but it's still something that you might want to address if you're healing your relationship with food.

First of all, never ever beat yourself up for emotional eating, because guilt will only keep the cycle going. You're not a glutton, you're not a failure, you're just coping with life in the best way you know how. Maybe your mental health isn't great right now and food gives you a little something to look forward to. Maybe when you're feeling anxious or like you can't control the events in your life, food is something that's reliable and soothing. Maybe eating something tasty even when you're not really hungry for it relieves boredom or becomes a way of rewarding yourself. Whatever the reason, food serves an emotional purpose in your life. It's probably not the best solution, but sometimes it might feel like the only one.

A little while ago I was speaking to someone who used to self-harm, and slowly replaced hurting herself with feeding herself. In her mind food was the best solution, and became a reliable source of comfort that she could turn to when the emotions arose that used to make her do other, more self-destructive things. The people around her didn't understand when she started gaining weight, but she was thankful that food could fulfil the need for emotional distraction when life got painful or overwhelming.

It's okay if food has become something that makes your life feel less overwhelming, but it might be time to address the underlying emotions and find new ways to cope. If you're not ready to do that yet, no pressure. If you are, read on.

When the drive to eat hits you, ask yourself what you're really feeling. If it's not actual hunger, what is it? Are you anxious? Irritated? Sad? Bored? Stressed? Do your best to decipher the emotions, and remind yourself that you're allowed to feel them. Be gentle with yourself. Practise mindfulness – allowing yourself to sit with your emotions, in the moment, and acknowledge how you feel in a, you guessed it, non-judgemental way. It's easy to think that negative emotions will sweep us away unless we drown them out with something else, in this case, food. But you can handle more than you think you can.

If you can get hold of the emotion behind your need to eat, is there a way of addressing it more directly and having your needs met without turning to food? Can you get an extension on that work deadline? Try to talk to that person who annoyed you? Or just cry it out? If there's not a solution to the feeling, just try to sit with it and remind yourself that as difficult as it might be, you're still here. You are withstanding. It's okay if you start to feel like the emotions are too much and you need distraction, nobody can feel every one of their emotions all the time. We'd never get anything done. Try to find other outlets so that food isn't the only thing for you to fall back on.

Most importantly, keep practising self-care and treating yourself with the kindness you deserve. Buy yourself flowers just because you like them. Take yourself on a date. Set aside some time for yourself to do that thing you love but never get a chance to do because life gets in the way. And do not feel guilty for making that time – your needs deserve to be met. Keep checking in with your mental health and never feel like you're not allowed to reach out for help when you need it. You are allowed. You are valuable. And what you're feeling matters.

NORMAL EATING

Intuitive eating will look different for everyone, and nobody else can decide how it should look for you. I used to wish all the time that I could just go back to thinking about food the way I did before the dieting started. Before I knew all the numbers. Before I felt all the guilt. When food was just food. Most people who've never had their relationship with food disrupted by dieting eat intuitively naturally, they eat what they want to eat, stop when they've had enough and don't spend all their time obsessing over each bite.

I've realised that while I can't un-know all the toxic ways dieting taught me to think about food (I'll probably never forget those numbers), I can stop giving those lessons any authority, and instead learn a new way of seeing food and the act of nourishing myself.

I knew that my relationship with food was healing more and more the less I thought about food. Which doesn't mean I don't enjoy my food or look forward to my favourite meal, it just means that it doesn't take up the mental space that it used to. Food is a delicious part of my life, but it's not my main focus, my main source of happiness, or comfort. It also doesn't have the power to push me into a black hole of guilt and shame any more. Intuitive eating helped me find freedom from the obsession that had started with that very first diet. I really hope that it helps you, too.

Here are a few things I want you to remember as you go on your journey back to intuitive eating: be patient with yourself and do not beat yourself up when things don't go smoothly, remember – this is not a diet! It's okay to not always eat in perfect harmony with your hunger and fullness signals. It's okay to eat beyond satiety sometimes. It's okay to eat without hunger sometimes. It's okay to focus on nutrition, or not to. It's okay for food to hold some emotional significance in your life. The ultimate goal is just to eat normally. And if you ever forget what normal eating is, you can always come back to this amazing definition by Ellyn Satter:

Normal eating is going to the table hungry and eating until you are satisfied. It is being able to choose food you like and eat it and truly get enough of it – not just stop eating because you think you should. Normal eating is being able to give some thought to your food selection so you get nutritious food, but not being so wary and restrictive that you miss out on enjoyable

food. Normal eating is giving yourself permission to eat sometimes because you are happy, sad or bored, or just because it feels
good. Normal eating is mostly three meals a day, or four or five,
or it can be choosing to munch along the way. It is leaving some
cookies on the plate because you know you can have some again
tomorrow, or it is eating more now because they taste so
wonderful. Normal eating is overeating at times, feeling stuffed
and uncomfortable. And it can be undereating at times and
wishing you had more. Normal eating is trusting your body to
make up for your mistakes in eating. Normal eating takes up
some of your time and attention, but keeps its place as only one
important area of your life.

In short, normal eating is flexible. It varies in response to your
hunger, your schedule, your proximity to food and your feelings.
So, one more time for the people in the back: YOU ARE
ALLOWED TO EAT.

I'LL DO IT 10 POUNDS FROM NOW

How We Let Our Bodies Stop Us from Living

'Our culture often expects women in general, and fat women in particular, to confine and limit ourselves. We are often discouraged, in many different ways, from moving freely, playfully, and happily in the world. We're not supposed to take up space and be visible and spontaneous and dynamic, colorful or loud or boisterous or rambunctious. Heaven knows we're not supposed to be fierce, physically unafraid, and fully aware of our physical power. To which I say: screw that'

– Hanne Blank, *The Unapologetic Fat Girl's Guide to Exercise and Other Incendiary Acts*

'I have faith that you want more out of life than a tombstone that says "All she ever wanted was a tight ass"'

– Summer Innanen, *Body Image Remix*

Or 15 Pounds, Or 20, Let's Make it 30

As I'm writing this, the first of the spring sunshine is breaking through the winter months and promising to make everything warm again. Not too long ago those beams of light would have meant one thing: summer is coming. The annual siren would be set off in my mind: MUST START DIET NOW IF YOU WANT A SUMMER. A summer wasn't something that just happened, a summer had to be earned by working hard enough to win the ultimate diet-culture prize: the bikini body.

And so the spring routine began. I would dust off the exercise DVDs, buy a dress two sizes too small to hang somewhere visible, spend one last day polishing off all of the food I wasn't allowed to eat again, and metaphorically lock the door.

I say metaphorically, but I quite literally shut myself indoors for months at a time to sweat myself smaller until I could emerge, butterfly-like, with a 'New Body New Me!' bang in the outside world. Year after year, I submitted to a life as a bikini-body hermit. Instead of actually living, I got by on the fantasy of how much happier I would be once my thighs were streamlined and encased in a piece of fabric with a single digit on the size label. Then I could really live.

Each time I set the goal to be bikini ready by the end of the summer, then go on holiday somewhere hot with a wardrobe that I could only fit in once a year and an overwhelming fear of the buffet. One of the summers that I lost the most weight ended with a trip to Egypt. I woke up on the first day, did 100 crunches on the bathroom floor and asked my boyfriend to take a picture of me before we could go to breakfast (in my mind, as soon as I had that first croissant it would attach itself firmly to my stomach and everything would be undone). The summer body fantasy came crashing down as soon as I looked at the pictures and still didn't see the photoshopped idea of perfection I'd been striving towards for all those months.

Just like that, the whole summer had gone, yet again, and I still didn't have a body deserving of the sunlight. I'd turned down days out with my family, said no to trips with friends, quit my job, pushed down all non-body-related ambition and put my entire life on hold. I'll do it once I've lost the weight. I'll do it all one day but not in this body. I traded in everything I could and it still wasn't enough. Just like that, all the summers went.

I'd love to say that I'm the only one who bargained away so much life just to make themselves smaller, but I'm not. Most of you will know exactly what I'm talking about, you might even be doing it right now. People everywhere are buying into the 'When I've Lost The Weight' fantasy and putting their lives on pause.

We spend our days waiting to live until our bodies are good enough. The only problem is, then our days are spent. And it's not just those few extra pounds that we believe are holding us back, it's the muscle we need to build, the nose we need to get fixed, the skin we need to keep hidden, the breasts we need to enhance. There's always something to change before we can really start living the life we want.

The list of things we put off is endless: holidays, dating, hobbies, career opportunities, meeting friends, making memories with our kids, having kids, buying new clothes, getting married, being in photographs, sex, food, lifelong dreams, and, of course, bikinis. All because we believe that we're not worthy of these things in the body we already have. We're not worthy of being seen in the world, living.

We learned a long time ago that happiness, adventure, style and romance only ever happen to people who look the part. The media perpetuates that myth every day; anyone who doesn't fit the image doesn't get the role. People whose bodies are the most marginalised – fat people, queer people, disabled people, people of colour, older people – often don't even get a speaking role, let alone a happy ending.

Somewhere along the line we forgot what our bodies really are: extraordinary vehicles that let us live. Instead, how our bodies look comes first, and what our bodies allow us to do in the world gets put back in the drawer with the too-small jeans, packed away for another time. Instead of going on adventures, we venture to our local weight-loss group. Instead of cultivating fulfilling relationships, we put all of our emotional energy into the act of not eating too much. Instead of chasing dreams, we chase a smaller size so that maybe one day we'll be worthy of those dreams. Our bodies feel more like prisons than vehicles.

We're told that the only way to release ourselves is to get rid of as much of ourselves as possible, to change and mould our bodies into something new. A new body will transform us into the person we've always wanted to be. A person who smiles at their salad and cackles maniacally while standing in one leg of their old trousers. A person who's successful, loved, outgoing, daring, and of course, happy.

It says a lot that in the 'When I'm Thin' fantasy we don't just have a different body, we are a completely different person. We really believe that reducing the amount of flesh on our frames has the power to change every single thing about ourselves that we don't like. Kudos, diet industry, genius marketing plan, but also, screw you.

Here's a thought: what if we refused to let the way our bodies look stop us from living our lives? What if we just started living them? Because the truth is that life isn't happening 10 pounds from now. It's here. It's happening. And every day that we spend obsessing over how to make our upper arms jiggle less is a day that it's passing us by. I know, I know, easier said than done. How do you go out into the sunlight when you've spent so long thinking that you're not deserving of it?

To start with, we need to stop believing that our bodies exist in the world just to be looked at by other people. Our bodies are not lifeless objects, we're not inanimate pieces of art hanging in a museum for people to gaze at and critique. Our bodies are for doing. How they look on the outside isn't the purpose of the design.

When we go to the beach and bare our skin we're not there to be visually appealing to others. We're there to feel the sand, hear the waves, smell the salt, take in the view. We're there to make memories. The dimples on our thighs or whether another beach-goer disapproves of our size is irrelevant. It's not why we're there. Being aesthetically pleasing is not the purpose of our existence.

The lesson that we learned so long ago, that how we look is the most important thing about us, is wrong. We are not a number on a scale or the texture of our skin. We are not a list of disposable body parts that need to be changed. We are not the judgements that other people make about our outer shells. We are more. Always were, always will be. We've just been made to forget it.

This chapter is filled with guest essays from people who stopped believing that their bodies determined their right to a full life. The parts of themselves they've reclaimed go beyond size and into other aspects of identity that our culture tries to teach us to be ashamed of. I hope that after reading about their body positive journeys, you'll realise how capable you are of starting your own. But first let me tell you something that I wish I'd heard all those years ago: however your body looks, you are so, so deserving of the sunlight.

> i want to apologize to all the women
> i have called pretty
> before i've called them intelligent or brave
> i am sorry i made it sound as though
> something as simple as what you're born with
> is the most you have to be proud of when your
> spirit has crushed mountains
> from now on i will say things like
> you are resilient or you are extraordinary
> not because i don't think you're pretty
> but because you are so much more than that
>
> – Rupi Kaur, 'milk and honey'

Tankini to Too Many Bikinis
Michelle Elman

It was an early Sunday morning as I made my way over to the breakfast table.

'A new bikini? What is this – a fashion show?' My mum asked.

It was the tenth bikini I had worn in the space of a week, each morning appearing from my room in a new two-piece that made me feel more beautiful than any other outfit I had ever worn.

I had half a mind to reply with a quip: 'Yes. Yes, it is a fashion show and I am the star of the entire show.' After all, I had earned it . . .

Each bikini felt like a medal of honour, bravely baring my body to the world unapologetically. Each morning, I would peruse my wardrobe and instead of having my brain bombarded with thoughts about how to hide my body, all I could think about was which one would result in the least tan lines. I had come a long way from the girl I used to know ...

Less than three years ago, going on a summer holiday would bring all kinds of anxiety about what I was going to wear and how I could subtly disguise myself so that I didn't offend anyone. All these thoughts would have consumed me in a way that would ruin the entire holiday. Weeks beforehand, I would scour the Internet in search of a kaftan or sarong that could hide my cellulite, stretch marks and lumps and bumps stylishly. I would spend the entire time in the pool or on the beach tugging at my tankini to ensure that not a single piece of flesh on my abdomen was revealed, in fear of exposing my deep dark secret that was lying underneath, sketched across my midriff.

Those secrets were my scars. All 15 of them. These lines are what made me decide at age 10 that bikinis were simply not for me. I've had scars since I can remember, my first one being placed on my skin before the age of one and slowly building up a collection that is unparalleled to many others. I've had 15 surgeries, a brain tumour, a punctured intestine, an obstructed bowel, a cyst in my brain and a condition called hydrocephalus, and all the evidence from these surgeries mark my stomach like an incomplete game of noughts and crosses. So with such a decorative piece of art on your abdomen, it seemed obvious that people like me can't wear bikinis.

Bikinis are often seen as a status symbol, a trophy at the end of an achievement, a marker for #bodygoals. But with each mark that was etched into my skin, this goal became more and more unobtainable. They are the kind of scars that make a person stare, double take or at the very least, make them curious. My scars induce pity and shock in people, and I always believed the solution to this was hiding them. I wouldn't make people uncomfortable that way, and I would never have to talk about it.

I made that decision young, not realising the consequences on my own body confidence. I lived in a body that I believed should be kept *hidden, I treated my scars like a secret and my surgeries like a past life that I never wanted to be associated with. Until one day in 2013, aged 19, I landed back in a hospital bed. My bowel had obstructed and had left me bedridden again for the first time in eight years, and it was in this moment, with the ability to walk, eat and even shower taken away from me that I realised how much of life I had been missing out on. I had been sitting on the sidelines of my own life because I was too scared. It was in this bed that I made a promise to myself: I was going to live my life on behalf of the people who couldn't.*

This began a year-long journey where I said yes to everything that scared me. It started with simply going to a dance class. I worried through the whole class about how I looked dancing or whether anyone was judging the fat girl in the corner. But I went and, more importantly, I stayed. I would never go on hikes with my friends just in case I slowed them down, but for the first time in my life I did. Over the next year, my body stopped being the reason to not do things, and before I knew it all my favourite activities were back in my life – from horse-riding to paddle-boarding and wake-boarding. I had started appreciating my body for its ability to keep me alive and in turn had found body confidence out of mere gratitude and respect for a body that was doing its best for me.

I loved my body for what it could do, but I still had to learn how to love it for what it looked like, scars and all. That's how wearing a bikini became my last step. The first time I put on that bikini, it wasn't easy. The stares were still there, the looks of pity and surprise too, but the difference this time was that I didn't care. I had such a deep fundamental appreciation for my body still working and being around long enough to keep me alive to do these things that no look, no stare, no comment could affect my body love. My bikini body was for me.

The same scars that marked my body and once hindered my body confidence became the fuel for my fire for body positivity. I took a photo that day and posted it on @scarrednotscared as the start of my campaign Scarred Not Scared. My scars are what caused me to be so invested in helping people realise that their bodies are so much more than prize possessions or objects to be adored. My scars will never be seen as pretty or attractive and I would never wish them on anyone else, but they are beautiful. They are beautiful because they show the magic of having survived, lived and thrived.

Wearing that bikini and being unapologetic about it was about more than just two pieces of material. It was about removing the limits that society had always placed on me about what my chronically ill, scarred body was capable of. It was about choosing my happiness over other people's opinions. Wearing that bikini was about recognising that I had a choice.

You can't wear a bikini if you don't own one. Thankfully, I own 10.

Photographs

Make sure you stand behind someone else. Always wear black. Don't smile too wide. Hand on your hip, shoulders back. For the love of god, suck it in! I don't do photos. How many rules do you have about having your picture taken? Seeing ourselves in photos can take away our self-esteem in an instant. It's why so many weight-loss fairy tales start with 'I saw a photo of myself and I couldn't believe I'd become that big! I knew it was time to do something about it …'. Despite seeing our bodies every day, there's something about having them caught in a snapshot that can make us hate every part of ourselves faster than a flash going off.

Part of the problem is that when we see pictures of our own bodies, we're comparing them to the glossy, airbrushed pictures of bodies we see every day. It might not even be a conscious comparison, but the parts of ourselves that we see as glaring flaws are only standing out so much because we're not used to seeing them elsewhere (unless they're in a 'before' photo). So when our holiday pictures pop up on the screen and we don't look like the cover model on the swimsuit edition of *Sports Illustrated*, we see something disgusting and vow to never be caught on camera again.

But unless you actually are doing a professional modelling job, it really doesn't matter how you look in pictures, it just matters that you're there. Your family holiday photos don't have to compete with a spread in *Vogue* because that's not what they're for. Photos are taken to capture a memory, that's all. They're supposed to be keepsakes to remind us of a moment, not opportunities to pick ourselves to pieces.

When you next see a photo of yourself, instead of zooming in on all the parts you think are wrong, try to remember the moment it was taken. Think about that sight, that smell, that experience, how you felt. Instead of focusing on how your teeth look when you smile, remember the joy.

Every photo is a moment that you can't get back, so cherish the memory – I realise that sounds like a Kodak advert but it's not, I swear. Just get in the damn picture and smile as wide as you want. And for the love of god, don't suck it in!

Someone Else's Skin
Brianna Butler (@sassy_latte)

For the first 12 years of my life, I'd always dream I was a white woman. I remember being around the age of five or six, and looking at myself in the mirror and not understanding what I saw. I saw this black thing, not even a girl. I saw kinky hair that was usually kept in braids, not long flowing hair. I saw a broad flat nose that reminded me more of an animal than a human. I saw muddy brown eyes, rather than colourful ones. And I saw two big lips that couldn't be reduced or hidden. Every time I saw myself, I felt ugly, undesirable.

I didn't know Black was Beautiful. I didn't know I could've been descended from queens and kings. I didn't know how to be a strong, black woman.

But I knew how to be a white woman. I knew white history better than my own. My history began as a slave. I had it memorised, and my identity as an American was wrapped in a history of people who had little to do with my own. I knew white women had options. On TV, they were fashionable, wealthy, business owners, getting attention. Black women were rarely seen … I knew I wanted to be seen, beautiful, important. I wanted options. And so every night, I'd dream that I was a petite, thin, white woman.

Around the age of 12, as my breast tumour reached its peak size, my heart broke. It was an inescapable truth that I wasn't a beautiful white woman with options. After having my first surgery, my mastectomy, something within me clicked. I came out of my comforting dream of white privilege. Something about waking up scarred and heartbroken, having to redefine myself forced me to see clearly who I was for the first time.

For the first time, I couldn't move beyond the reality of what I saw. I couldn't close my eyes and see anything other than my scars and stitches. The dreams of being a white woman did nothing to ease my physical pain that was rooted in reality. I saw myself and felt myself exactly as I was, a little black girl. And I wasn't empowered. I was sad and scared.

These memories that flood me in this moment aren't about anything other than the simple fact that REPRESENTATION MATTERS. For years, I struggled with living in reality and being truthful to who I am. It wasn't until I became a mother to a black child that I knew I had to face these issues. I had to learn to critique the effects of mass media. I had to understand the cause and effect of living in a capitalist society. I had to learn the complicated and painful history of African Americans. Education is power, and leaving my history out of school books, films, and advertising keeps me powerless. There is a profound beauty and confidence that comes from knowledge and there is power in creating a safe space, where you can represent yourself and speak on issues freely.

I want my daughters to know their history. I want my daughters to know how to navigate a world that leaves them out of a lot of important conversations. I don't want them waking up alone one day to figure out their place in the world. I want to create cracks in a system that keeps us segregated, and marginalised people silenced. I want Every-BODY to find worth and value, Outside of being thin, white, able-bodied, and heterosexual.

I want my daughters to see bodies and lifestyles normalised so that, as my little ones develop a sense of self and mould their identities, they know they are beautiful exactly as they are in any given moment of their growth and development. I also want them to see their immediate value and know they are vital members of society with options beyond their wildest dreams, without ever having to pretend they are walking this earth in someone else's skin.

Birth, babies, and getting your body back

People who experience pregnancy and childbirth are prime targets for the weight-loss fantasy. Instead of 'When I've Lost The Weight' it's 'When I've Got My Body Back', which is a bizarre phrase considering your body didn't actually go anywhere. It's not as if your pre-pregnancy body went away on a luxury holiday and left an imposter in its place.

Still, the headlines make it clear that the number-one priority after giving birth should always be shrinking yourself back to your former size: 'Celebrity Secrets to Losing Baby Weight', 'Amazing Post-Baby Bikini Bodies', 'Body After Baby: Star Moms Who Bounced Right Back'.

The message is clear: life won't restart until your body looks how it looked before. The 'When I've Got My Body Back' goal isn't optional, it's required. So what happens to the people whose bodies change permanently? Why are we being taught that pregnancy ruins a body, and that if we don't 'bounce right back' like elastic then we've failed?

There's definitely a lot of money to be made from teaching people to fear the inevitable physical changes that come with pregnancy. Making post-pregnancy bodies a problem is a diet-industry dream – the stretch-mark creams, the baby body weight-loss plans, the tummy tucks and breast surgeries. The pressure becomes one more thing that stops us from living until we've whittled ourselves down to size.

For the people who become mothers, that means missing irreplaceable moments with their children because they believe that their body isn't deserving of them. It breaks my heart every time a new mother tells me that they can't take their baby to the pool and be seen in swimwear. They can't play with their child in public because their body jiggles. They can't be happy because now they have stretch marks and loose skin and baby weight, and according to the 'When I've Got My Body Back' rules, these new parts of themselves are unacceptable. So instead of being in awe of what their bodies are capable of, they feel like they have to erase every sign of pregnancy as if it never happened.

Just think about that for a minute. The person who endures so much, who grows and changes physically and emotionally, who learns and adapts, gives endlessly and sacrifices so much, is then convinced that they have to erase all visual signs of that experience. All because of how something that is nothing less than miraculous has made their body look? How fucked up is that? Why shouldn't those visual signs be celebrated? Why shouldn't those bodies be valued and admired as much as they deserve to be?

To all the new mothers who've been made to believe that they need to get their body back: you already have a body, and it's extraordinary. It's powerful and resilient and it brought a human life into the world. Don't let anyone convince you that the signs of that are shameful.

And to all the people who experience pregnancy without childbirth: you are just as powerful, just as resilient, and just as valuable. You are so much more than how your body looks.

Go to the pool, play, keep living your life and don't miss out on a single thing waiting for your pre-pregnancy body to come back. You've outgrown it, in so many beautiful ways.

To Those Looking For Happiness
Gia Narvaez

Have you ever asked yourself, 'What is happiness?' According to Google, 'Happiness is a mental or emotional state of well-being defined by positive or pleasant emotions ranging from contentment to intense joy. Happy mental states may also reflect judgements by a person about their overall well-being.'

When I was around 10 years old, I was taken to a Jenny Craig facility in Menlo Park, CA. My mother pulled into the parking lot and

I innocently jumped out of the car and followed her through the 'clear and promising' glass doors. I remember anxiously waiting next to my mother, dazed and confused as to why we were there. Soon enough, we were called by one of the practitioners and we followed her into her office.

As we sat down, she handed us two binders that contained our rigorous diet plans. Endless sheets outlining times, foods, calories, red stickers for bad foods and daily lists that would allow us to keep track of the food we consumed. At that age, I didn't understand the negative effects that a weight-loss programme could have on a child, I had only been told that I needed to 'choose the right size and weight' if I wanted to be happy. As much as I wanted to do so in order to live a happy life, I struggled.

In my mind, food and my weight were my enemies. This toxic relationship encouraged me to use other methods of weight loss, including a painful tummy belt that would send 'fat-melting' electricity waves into my abdomen. Other nights, my guilt and shame of eating would push me to purge. A sense of praise came with vomiting, because I truly believed it was for the best and that I was doing myself a favour.

When I was 16 years old I began competitive cheerleading, and things quietly worsened. I would go to practice on an empty stomach so that I could burn fat and not food, only allowing myself water to feel full. I would work my body to exhaustion, to the point where I would come home after practice and fall asleep on the living-room floor. And still, happiness never came.

You know when happiness came? Once I stopped believing people's bullshit misconceptions about what defines beauty. Once I stopped shaming my body and denying myself the love that I needed. It came once I realised how oppressive society is to people who are different, people who don't fit into the various binaries, the status quo.

Happiness came when I surrounded myself with positive people who want to progress how we think, how we approach everything that we've been taught in life about what is normal and what is beautiful. Happiness came when I held myself tightly at night while apologising for the years that I abused me.

Happiness came when I accepted myself, my fat, my brown skin colour, my identity as a transgender woman, and all of my unique qualities that society once made me believe were not worthy of acceptance.

You are beautiful. Regardless of how different you may be, you have to believe in yourself the way I did in myself. You have to break free from the oppressive ideals that society imposes on us, the ideals that hinder our ability to see our own beauty.

I promise you that if you do, you too will find happiness.

Wrinkle and Disappear

Where have all the women over the age of 50 gone? According to what we see in the media, they've either disappeared, or stuck around and miraculously managed to keep all visible signs of ageing at bay.

Think about it: how many positive representations of visibly older women do we see? How often do we see grey hair being celebrated? How many wrinkles can you spot in any magazine that aren't the 'before' picture in an anti-ageing cream advert? How many times has Hollywood cast their latest blockbuster and relegated the older female actor to playing grandma, while male actors the same age still get to play the mature love interest to the twenty-something leading lady?

Even the most successful older women aren't allowed to wear their years on their face. On the rare occasions a female over 50 is featured on a magazine cover she's still made to look like she did when she was 30, the lines are smoothed, the cheeks are lifted, the years are disguised. They'll say it's so that she looks her best, but why does 'best' have to mean younger?

Naomi Wolf wrote in *The Beauty Myth* that 'to airbrush age off a woman's face is to erase women's identity, power, and history' – this isn't just about making a picture look smoother, this is, once again, teaching us who deserves to be seen in the world and who doesn't.

Everywhere we look we see evidence of the visible ageing double standard. The older male news anchor is joined by a co-host half his age. Older men are called silver foxes while older women are convinced that grey hair is shameful and has to be covered like a dirty secret. We're told that lines on our faces are hideous flaws and our bodies' natural changes over time are our own moral failings.

As our representations of female beauty seem to fade away with age, we're convinced that there comes a time for us to disappear as well. And you can guess what the main motivator is for teaching us to always equate beauty with youth: money.

In 2015, the anti-ageing industry was valued at over $140 billion globally.[52] That includes Botox injections, anti-wrinkle products, chemical peels and hair restoration treatments. Every week a new miracle serum promising to turn back time on skin hits the shelves, the adverts are filled with scientific jargon and a model who looks about 15 shows the supposed results. So many of us buy into the hype despite knowing, deep down, that there is no way to reverse the ageing process. Especially not by putting overpriced gunk on our faces. But as long as ageing is shameful and beauty is equated with youth we have to keep trying.

Not a single person in the world can live in their bodies and not age. Turning visible ageing into a problem and selling the solution might be the greatest marketing scheme of all time (even more reliable than selling weight loss, since some people are naturally thin, but nobody is naturally young for ever).

Wrinkles are inevitable. Grey hair is unavoidable. Body changes are inescapable. Teaching women to fear those things does more than make money, it convinces us that we're less valuable, less powerful, and less worthy of a full and vibrant life as we age. But that couldn't be further from the truth.

As we age we only get more powerful, more knowledgable, more resilient. The lines on our skin show that we've lived, laughed, cried, kissed, felt. With every new fleck of silver we've seen more, done more, been more. How could that be anything other than beautiful? Erasing all signs of life from a face isn't an improvement, it's a deception, and we're old enough to know better. Visible signs of ageing are not shameful, and they sure as hell shouldn't stop us from living out loud in the world.

In 2015, Carrie Fisher showed us all how to deal with sexism and ageism while generally not giving a damn. After the latest Star Wars film was released, there were plenty of morons on the Internet ready to criticise Fisher for not ageing as well as her male co-stars. Remember: 'ageing well' for a woman means not ageing visibly at all, which is impossible.

Fisher shut down the criticism with this iconic tweet: 'Please stop debating about whether or not [I] aged well. Unfortunately it hurts all 3 of my feelings. My body hasn't aged as well as I have. Blow us'. Followed by this – 'youth and beauty are not accomplishments, they're the temporary happy bi-products of time and/or DNA, don't hold your breath for either'.

So, in the words of Carrie Fisher, don't hold your breath. Stop hiding. Stop being 'age appropriate'. Stop believing that the new textures and colours that your body takes on with time are flaws, because they're not. Don't let our society's obsession with youthfulness convince you that life ends after a certain age. Be proof that it doesn't.

The Dancer

Whitney Way Thore (@Whitneywaythore) author of *I Do It With the Lights on* and *Ten More Discoveries on the Road to a Blissfully Shame-Free Life* and star of TLC's *Whitney: Fat Girl Dancing*

'Are you comfortable?'

I twisted, trying to stuff my fat underneath the armrests of the make-up chair in the Today *show studios in New York. It wasn't working. I could already feel indentations forming from the metal jabbing in my sides, forcing my 380-pound body into a mould designed for a much smaller person.*

'Absolutely!' I answered, flashing a big grin. 'Totally comfortable.'

It seemed the enquiry was more of a formality rather than a real question, and the make-up artist began shuffling through stacks of foundation, eyeshadow, and blush spread out on the counter in front of us. She picked up several brushes, rattling a metal can as she dropped the ones she didn't want back into it. Then she rotated my chair toward her, the lucky brush poised in mid-air.

'Are you the dancer?'

The question surprised me. Am I the dancer? I thought to myself. Surely I was the only person scheduled to appear on today's programme who was dancing, but surely, I wasn't the dancer. What even was a dancer? I wasn't positive I was a dancer at all; calling myself 'the' dancer seemed presumptuous at best and ludicrous at worst. It had been over 10 years since I'd referred to myself as a dancer, and even then I'd had my doubts.

The dance world is vast and home to millions of bodies. Bodies that leap, pirouette, and stretch themselves into motion over music. Bodies that are expressive, malleable, and magical. They are flexible, dynamic, perfectly muscled, and thin. And I was never thin – even as a 10-year-old child weighing one hundred pounds, I was made fun of for my thick thighs and soft stomach. Even though I was the star dancer in my teacher's in-home studio, it was the size of my body, not my talent or ability, that kept me from feeling like a 'real dancer'.

As I got older, I was swept into the hurricane of bulimia and restriction, and still I could never starve or purge my teenage body smaller than 120 pounds. In my extracurricular competitive dance company, I was moved from the front row to the middle, behind the thinnest girls and in front of the ones who would still need to watch me to remember the choreography. I won the 'Best Dancer' award at my performing arts school, choreographed professionally in the community, and even taught classes at my studio, but my less-than-perfect body labelled me a fraud. It caused me supreme embarrassment: my body had become my biggest enemy, even when doing what I loved the most.

By the time I was halfway through my first semester in college, my body had swelled to nearly 200 pounds. None of my clothes or leotards fit, and showing up to dance class and its endless line of mirrors felt like standing in front of a firing squad. I quit showing up after that, failed the class, and was swiftly put on academic probation. By the end of my freshman year, I had gained 100 pounds and a new layer *of shame that only a visibly fat woman can experience. I didn't dare dance after that. The years that followed were full of depression, self-hatred, a PCOS diagnosis, and an intense wishing for my old body. Those years were devoid of joy, of love, and of dance.*

When I graduated college, I was directionless. The fat that coated my body had robbed me of my identity. I was no longer a dancer, a pretty girl, a valid person; becoming fat had turned me into a bitter, lonely, and marginalised person. With my dreams of pursuing an acting and dancing career completely demolished, I set off for Korea, where I taught English for the next several years.

Korea presented a set of new problems. Not only was I foreign, but I was the largest person many Koreans had ever seen in real life. My body was a huge neon sign parading through a country of homogeny. My body was a target for unwanted touch, laughter, and insult every time I left my apartment. One day as I was walking to work, a middle-aged man began peddling his bike too slowly beside me. I made eye contact with him and he called me a pig and then spat on me. When I got back to my apartment that night, I sobbed – a common occurrence during my time there. I had so many feelings: the anger, the indignation, and the shame circulated every inch of my body with electric energy.

I picked myself up off the floor and felt the bottoms of my feet flat against the fake hardwood. And then something happened – I began to move. My body swayed, my knees bent and straightened, and before I knew it, for the first time since I was 18, I gave myself permission to dance. My tears of rage transformed into tears of release, and after a few minutes I collapsed on to my bed, breathless and aching for the feeling of being free.

It would be three years before I'd ever dance again. I was living back in my hometown in North Carolina and working as a radio personality when I called up my friend Todd, who had been my dance partner when we were teenagers performing in community theatre and paying for special dance classes with quarters. By this time, 2014, I was still fat, in fact, I'd lost a hundred pounds and gained it all back and more. I was the fattest I'd ever been. I still didn't think I deserved to call myself a dancer, but something was different.

The years of abuse had made me stronger underneath all of my jiggling softness. I was a feminist, I was angry, and I had begun to get turned on to an almost erotic new idea that I didn't yet have a name for: body positivity. Todd and I filmed some videos for a YouTube series called 'A Fat Girl Dancing', and I danced my heart out for the first time in a decade. One of the videos went viral and that's how I found myself twisting in that uncomfortable chair on the set of Today *being asked if I was 'the dancer'.*

I looked at the make-up artist and allowed myself to say four words I thought would never leave my mouth again.

'Yes,' I told her. 'I'm the dancer'.

In that moment, I knew my life was changing and I had the power to direct it, to claim it, and to live it. There were many more appearances after that: Good Morning America, The Steve Harvey Show, CNN, Inside Edition, Dr Oz, The View. *There were press tours in America and Europe. There was my memoir called* I Do It with the Lights On *and even an international TLC reality show called* My Big Fat Fabulous Life in America *(Whitney: Fat Girl Dancing, in the UK), now in its fifth season that chronicles my life as a fat woman who dances.*

Life is still hard now; it's not all sunshine and body positive rainbows. Being on a global stage means I am exposed to the best of people and the worst of people, but each day I navigate through the fatphobia and the misogyny, and take solace in the arms of my sisters who are doing the important work: championing eating-disorder recovery, intersectional feminism, and the visibility of all bodies regardless of race, age, gender, or ability. And today, I know that dance changed my life. It fosters the unspeakable connection between the mind and body, the intimacy experienced through looking at one's own body, through touching it, through moving it, through letting your soul guide it, sometimes gently and sometimes fiercely, into motion.

Dance is a delicious metaphor for all the ways I know I was meant to live. My body is fat, but it is valuable; it is pulsating with love, vibrating with newfound confidence, and always expressing its truth, whatever that is in any given moment. Today, I know that dance saved my life.

I can't wear that

There are few things in this world that can make someone feel as bad about their reflection as a clothing store fitting room can. The fluorescent lighting, the five-way mirrors that show your body at every single angle, the pressure of what size to try on, the sales assistant waiting to ask 'any good?' as you leave. Most of the time we end up feeling like the clothes were fine, it's our bodies that aren't any good. If something doesn't fit, it's not the fault of the fabric, it's on us.

How many crash diets have been embarked on after a zip won't close in one of those rooms? How many times have we left near tears and torn ourselves to pieces on the way home? Some of us have felt the fitting-room shame so often that we've just stopped going. It's easier to grab something safe and stretchy and hope for the best, even if it's too tight, we'd rather be uncomfortable than see the number on that label go up. We put so much value into that number, as if a lifeless bit of material is worth more than our self-esteem.

As far as fashion choices go, flattering is the only word that matters. And flattering is usually just code for 'makes you look thinner'. We've been trained in the art of disguising our problem areas, skimming over our flaws, enhancing our assets and cloaking the rest. For the record, there's no such thing as problem areas, our bodies are not flawed, and our greatest assets have nothing to do with our outsides, but you'll never hear that from the fashion police.

We've all internalised the rules of what people with our body type are allowed to wear. If you're a plus-sized woman you probably feel like you might explode if you're told another wrap dress is the flattering choice for your figure. And no matter what size or shape you are, we all know that cinching in our waists is more important than life itself!

Clothing stores the world over echo with chants of 'I can't wear that at my size', 'I'll have to tone up a bit first', 'Maybe if I had curves in the right places', 'I'll wear clothes like that once

I've lost the weight'. Why should we have to wait until our bodies are different to feel fabulous in what we choose to wear? Why should we be limited by made-up rules and the ridiculous idea that dressing should be about pleasing other people's eyes before pleasing ourselves? Here's the only fashion rule you really need to remember: YOU CAN WEAR WHATEVER YOU WANT TO WEAR.

Even shorts? Uhm … yes. What about bright colours? Hell yes! Bold patterns? Yep. Tight dresses? Of course! Bikinis? Did you read the first guest essay? But surely not … crop tops?! CROP ALL OF YOUR TOPS IF THAT MAKES YOU HAPPY. But what if it doesn't suit me? If it makes you happy, it suits you. But what if other people don't like it? You're not dressing for them, you're dressing for you. But what if it's not flattering? Forget everything you've been taught about flattering. From now on whatever makes you feel the most you, is what's flattering.

My 'I can't wear that' item was always bodycon. I was convinced that I could never wear anything tight-fitting until I had a flat stomach, a rounder arse, perkier breasts, and could buy a size 10 or smaller. But funnily enough, no matter what size I shrank myself down to, I still wouldn't let myself wear it.

When I found the body positive community, I was suddenly seeing people of every size and shape rocking bodycon. They were even embracing their non-flat stomachs and highlighting their visible belly outlines (VBOs for short). Before 'they shouldn't be wearing that' could pop into my mind, a different thought appeared instead: 'They look fucking fantastic … maybe I can wear that, too'.

So I did. I bought my first bodycon dress and challenged myself to wear it – at first just in my room, then in front of a camera, and then in public. And you know what? Nothing happened. The world didn't implode because I'd broken the fashion rules of what I was supposed to be wearing for my body type.

Little by little, I broke more, until there weren't any left. Sometimes even now when I catch my reflection in a shop window I'll get a flash of 'this isn't flattering', until I remind myself that flattering is whatever I want it to be, and I strut on feeling like a body positive queen. Wear whatever you want to wear, buy the size you actually need, and forget the fashion police. You look flawless.

The Body Standard, Masculinity, Self-Love, and Style

Kelvin of Notoriously Dapper (@notoriouslydapper), author of *Notoriously Dapper: How to Be a Modern Gentleman with Style, Manners and Body Confidence*

When people think of body positivity they automatically think of women who are powerful and voice the feminist right to love each and every inch of their body. It's rare that men ever get a chance to be thought about when it comes to body insecurities or emotions. As a man, I can admit I have suffered from depression, anxiety and eating disorders. The societal standard for men has always been that we're supposed to be masculine and not show emotion. Men don't cry, boys don't cry. Why is it not okay for a male to cry?

Men make up almost 79 per cent of suicides and that is a scary number. When you think about it, it all makes sense. Due to the societal standard of masculinity, men have been told to be quiet about their emotions and insecurities, they've been emotionally suppressed. Women for so long have been breaking the societal standard of what being feminine is. Women have shown that just because these ideals were somehow made doesn't mean they are right, nor should they be followed. Now more than ever women all over the world believe they can be anything, anywhere at any given time, and that's a beautiful thing.

I can remember my first time seeing my dad cry when he was explaining to me how his father passed away. I felt pure emotion, I felt his heart and mind. I could understand his pain and it made me realise it is okay to cry. My father never told me that men don't cry, he never shut me out and told me to not be emotional. He embraced who I was and loved me for being me like any parent should. Still, there was that societal standard telling me to be strong, tough, and don't ever show emotion, especially as a black man.

Being a black man in America can be a difficult experience. We are stereotyped everywhere we go and still have to fight to be seen as an equal in most circumstances. I can honestly say as an Instagram influencer/model I feel like I have to work a bit harder to be seen as something important. In the black community we aren't supposed to be emotional in any way, and if we are we're perceived as being weak. We are supposed to be confident, strong and tough in every way.

But how can you be body confident if your body isn't valued, or is seen as less important than others' bodies? How can you feel comfortable in your own skin when you are always profiled because of your skin? How can you love yourself when the media puts so much hate and fear on the idea of a black man?

I can honestly say that my confidence took a back seat when I watched numerous news outlets report unarmed black men being gunned down. It just happened one after the other and it's hard to worry about body confidence when your body doesn't matter. It's hard to feel comfortable in your own skin when you get gunned down because of your skin. People can deny this all they want and say that I'm just using this as a ploy (or pulling the race card). I live in this body, I know what it is like to be treated differently simply because of your skin tone or the way you are dressed.

The truth of the matter is that a suit is armour for a black man. We are viewed as a priority and important in a suit. If we are seen, or if we approach someone while wearing 'regular' clothing we can easily be perceived as a threat. I view my clothes as my saviour and my armour. Style has helped me become more confident in life and my style has also helped me be viewed as less of a threat to society. I feel confident in what I wear; when I style an outfit I feel invincible and it helps me exude confidence. It's sad that we live in a world where you're more valued in a suit than you are in a hoodie. Whether I'm in a blazer or hoodie I am still the same confident, positive individual I was when I got dressed. Still, my journey to being a body-confident black man has not been an easy one.

I have learned to love myself through being true to who I am. I have a wonderful support system of friends and family who embrace me for the original person I am. I have learned over the years of personal experience how to care for my mental and physical health. My style is me and I am my style. I think it's vital to wear what makes you feel happy and surround yourself with positive energy. It makes the bad body days good and the good body days better.

Everyone has a struggle we don't know about, so always be nice to people even when they are mean to you. Kindness can change the world, and when you are kind to yourself and others you can truly make the world a better place. Be sure to care for yourself, take a mental health day from work, and do something to make you happy. We often forget about ourselves in this busy life we have. It's easier to love others when you love yourself.

Fellas, remember that you define what masculinity is, not society. If you want to be a fashion designer do it, if you want to be a ballet dancer do it, or if you want to be a computer engineer do it. Don't let the societal standard stop you from following your dreams or caring for your well-being.

Masculinity and society

Body confidence is for everyone, every race, every gender and every age. We can never forget that men suffer from these issues, and giving them an outlet to speak about their insecurities and emotions will help breed brave men for future generations. We all deserve to feel safe, loved and celebrated, not feared, hated and ignored. So, spread love and awareness to your friend, boyfriend, husband, brother, dad, uncle and nephew. Show them that it's okay to make their own definition of masculinity in today's society!

Dating, sex, and love

I'm going to keep it simple and break this section down into the lies we've been led to believe about romance, sex, love and our bodies, and what the truth really is.

Lie: You have to lose weight, be prettier, or change your personality before someone will be interested in you.

Truth: We've been tricked into believing that we are unlovable, unattractive, and unwanted as we are. Teaching us that love is the prize at the end of the big transformation means that we'll keep buying things to transform ourselves. We'll keep believing that our romantic happy ending will come just as long as we stick to our diets, wear the right perfume, own the right clothes and splurge on the right make-up. The truth is that we've never needed any of those things in order to be worthy of love, to own our sexuality, or to have our happy ending.

There are countless people in the world who will be interested in you, physically attracted to you, and would fall head over heels in love with you given the chance. As you are. I know that's hard to believe if you've spent a lifetime believing that you're unlovable. You might have also had some shitty experiences that have left you even further convinced that you're the problem. If you just looked different it would have worked. If you just weren't as ... you, then it could have worked. But you can only be you, and you are good enough.

Let's say you do manage to force yourself into something that you're not for the sake of making another person fall for you. You shrink yourself down, you fake a different sense of humour, you change your style and put on a whole new persona. The people who never gave you a chance before start falling at your feet, but is it really you who they want?

What good is making people interested in a version of you that doesn't exist? And who wants to be with anyone who doesn't appreciate them for their true self anyway? I always thought that once I lost the weight I'd find the perfect man ... I realised that an actually perfect man wouldn't give a damn how much I weighed anyway.

You don't need to fit an idea of what you think other people want you to be. Because it's just that – an idea. You will be wanted in all of your real, messy, one-of-a-kind glory. You don't have to compromise any part of yourself in order for someone to be interested in you. You're a catch as you are.

Lie: Unless you fit conventional standards of beauty, you should be grateful for whatever you can get.

Truth: You deserve it all. You deserve fireworks, passion, safety, communication, laughter, trust, companionship, romance, butterflies and more. You never have to settle for anything less than that, no matter how that glorious body of yours looks. Again, there will be people out there who love and appreciate every inch of you, and treat you like royalty.

Lie: As soon as they see me naked they'll run a mile.

Truth: I know this is a wild idea, but maybe if a person has seen you with clothes on, has expressed an interest in you, and has said or shown that they're sexually attracted to you, you should believe them? Unless what you've got going on underneath your clothes is more mysterious than Mary Poppins' handbag, that person already has a pretty good idea of what they're in for when the layers come off. They definitely already know what size you are, and if you've got to this point, they definitely don't have a problem with it.

You know what really ruins sex? Obsessively thinking about what the other person (or people) is thinking about how your body looks, instead of being present in the moment. Worrying about what's jiggling, how many chins they can see in that position, or how you measure up to their last partner sucks every drop of enjoyment out of getting it on. And I can guarantee that they are not thinking the same things as you are about your body. Most of the time they're probably just thinking 'I'M HAVING SEEEEEEEEEXXXXX!', or worrying about how their own bodies look to you. Wouldn't it be so much more fun if we focused on what we're actually doing instead of how we look doing it?

If you ever do have a sexual partner who dares to say anything negative about your body, then they don't deserve to even be in your presence, let alone in your bed. The next time they comment critically on how you look, tell them that they can go and fuck themselves, and not you.

> **Lie:** Nobody will love you until you love yourself.
> **Truth:** I see this lie being used a lot as a motivational tool for getting people to love themselves. The problem is that it leaves people who fall short on self-love feeling unlovable all round, which just isn't true. You are worthy of love even if you don't see it, even if you're insecure, even if you hate your body. No matter how you feel about yourself, you are worthy of love.

Always Red
Melissa Gibson

I like to joke that red lipstick changed my life. I'm fat. I was a fat kid, a fat teenager, and now a fat adult. And trust me, it was never just 10 pounds that 'I needed to lose'. I spent most of my life as a perpetual work in progress. I had my first gym membership when I was 9 years old. I learned that the purpose of my body moving was so that I would become smaller. Movement was no longer about joy, about adventure, about play. Movement had to yield results. Over the years, I increasingly felt disconnected from my body.

I was never very successful at losing weight and when I did, it still was never good enough. The weight loss was never a victory, but felt more like the price I had to pay to be able to be included and to start living a life beyond dieting. I was a problem, an embarrassment, not worthy of the life I was meant to live, the life that my thin peers were privy to. I really bought into this! I bought into the stigma, the narrative, the lies about what it meant to have a fat body. That was until an image of a confident fat woman in a bikini flashed across my screen one night with the byline talking about body positivity.

I was uncomfortable with it at first, I didn't have to hate my body? I think I was jealous; I didn't believe I could ever feel positive about my body. Positivity was reserved for thin bodies, yet I couldn't shake those images aside and I began seeing my own experience in my body differently. This is where the red lipstick comes in.

I was plain. I thought I had to be. I wasn't supposed to stand out, I had always done everything possible to bring the attention away from my body. I had on hand a red lipstick that I wore once many years before for my senior prom. One day I got it out and put it on. Was I really going to wear this out? How was I going to wear this out? I knew if I didn't own it, I would just feel silly. It became a challenge, just like the bodycon dress was a few weeks later, and then going out without a sweater, and so on. Each challenge demanded more confidence. And with the confidence I felt empowered in my body for the first time as an adult.

I wanted to move, I wanted to be seen, I wanted to be heard. Using my body made me feel powerful. I began experiencing life in my body; I truly felt what I touched, tasted what I ate, saw beauty in the world around me. I slowly stopped planning weight-loss goals and began making travel plans, life-changing plans, future plans that were not contingent on me being a certain size.

I took joy in how my body moved, in developing my own style, in feeling sexy, classy, and fabulous. I started dating. Dating for the first time in my life on my terms. I took joy in navigating this new experience for me with a fresh mindset and confidence. And when it came I relished being able to share my body in intimate moments with new partners. I had always been a sexual person, but felt ashamed for feeling that way. I was supposed to be undesirable; I learned I was not.

In my own awakening, body positivity gave me a space to explore my friendships, my dreams, what I valued about myself. Life was exciting. I loved being able to share my joy and excitement with people. My mom had always encouraged me to flirt more. 'Melissa, I see how boys look at you, you just have to let them know you like them back.' I hated that. I didn't want to flirt. I was sure I was always going to be the girl that those boys settled for. I never wanted that. And still don't, but now I know that I'm not the type of girl guys settle for, I'm the one they want. I had always been.

My new confidence opened a whole new dating world to me. A world where I got to explore what I wanted out of a relationship with a man and didn't simply have to change to be what they wanted out of a partner. Where sex became an experience, a shared experience where my partner and I got to use our bodies to work towards and with each other for our mutual pleasure, pleasure my body was designed to give me. Where I was valued not for the acts that I could do in bed, but for the simple fact that it was me in all my fat, sexy, confident glory in that bed, couch, car, park, ambulance with them. I explored my sexuality, I valued it, and I kept falling in love with my body.

While our bodies aren't all that we are, so often our negative feelings towards them stop us from believing that we deserve the life we want to live. Those feelings quieten us, we begin trying to become smaller physically and mentally. We learn to take up less space in friendships, in relationships, in our own minds. We learn that we are not worthy of our own desires and our bodies so often become our very own prisons.

Body hatred, born out of a fatphobic society, keeps us from being able to look outside of ourselves, keeps us from flourishing, keeps us from being in the moment. Our bodies are ours. They are our tools to feel and be and dance and love and move. I once said, 'Unreserved, unapologetic joy is the greatest gift the body positive movement has given me.' It taught me to connect to and experience life not only in this body but beyond it. To live in the moment and to stop seeing myself as a work in progress.

In the beginning, it felt good to see myself as beautiful, to understand that I don't have to just see my beauty as inner beauty, but also that I could see my outer beauty in all its glorious uniqueness as well. Coming into body positivity for me meant that I could explore so many new parts of myself. My passions, my goals in life, my relationship to sexuality, and lip colour all changed. Symptoms of being able to spend my time aware of the world around me and my relationship to it, symptoms of me feeling connected to my own body and my own life again.

Cake

A little while ago I asked people online to tell me how their lives have changed since they found body positivity. The next day I woke up to over 1,500 comments filled with all the amazing things people have been able to do since making peace with their body.

One comment read 'I was actually in my own vacation photos for the first time last year', another read 'I wore shorts for the first time (since I was 14) this summer ... I'm 35 now and through body positive reminders, I'm not sweating to death in fear of my own and others' judgement'. And another comment said it all: 'I am finally enjoying my life again, not counting calories, but collecting beautiful memories. I've realised that I only have this one life!' The overwhelming message was clear: finding body positivity had allowed people to start living.

It turns out that when you stop believing that you exist just to fit an impossible physical standard, you're free to live the life you deserve. To do that thing you've always wanted to do, to wear that outfit you've always wanted to wear, to go for that job, visit that place, try that activity, talk to that person. To finally stop putting 'When I've Lost The Weight' conditions on your dreams and go out and get them instead.

For far too long we've believed that the key to being able to do all of those things is changing our bodies. We've believed that our real lives would only start once we looked different. We were wrong. The key to starting the lives we want isn't hiding in a number on our bathroom scales. It's already in us. It's reclaiming the space our bodies take up and learning to exist in them, unapologetically.

We need to stop telling ourselves that we're not worthy of happiness as we are. We need to start taking our happiness now.

After reading all of those comments online there was one that hit me the hardest. It was from a girl called Carrie who was battling anorexia, and through finding body positivity was able to keep fighting, she shared this victory: 'I'm finally in recovery and on 28 August I will eat my birthday cake'. She sent me a picture of the cake, too.

So, my loves, eat the cake, do the thing, live now. Because life isn't waiting on those 10 pounds, and neither should you.

#seenwithoutshame
Rebekah G. Taussig

When I was four years old, I was convinced I was a Disney princess. My sister and I would twist our T-shirts into makeshift sexy Princess Jasmine tops, put on sweatpants, and lounge across the sofa like exquisite replicas of royal femininity. When we went to the pool, we'd take deep breaths, plunge under water, then burst out into the open air singing, 'Part of Your World!' We'd whip our tangled, soppy manes over our heads, imagining our hair blowing in the wind like real-life cartoon mermaids. In those days, I wiggled and flailed and crawled and lazed about in my body – I enjoyed my body – without noticing that my paralysed legs moved and looked quite differently from those around me.

I was paralysed by a pair of tumours wrapped around my spine when I was three. Maybe it sounds strange, but it took me some time to notice my transformation into 'a kid with a disability'. At first, I didn't feel that different, but when I started kindergarten, I took my first trip on the short bus. I'd never been surrounded by so many people with disabilities, and it shocked me. These kids didn't look anything like graceful princesses, but I had been assigned a seat on their bus. Did I look like them? Move like them? I had been so sure I flitted like Belle, lighter than a violet, when I made my way across the room, but as I looked at them I could see – as if for the first time – my own clunky metal braces hugging my calves and thighs with brown Velcro, my scarred and swollen feet, my awkwardly fitting clothes.

Eventually, it became less about how I felt in my body and more about what other people saw when they looked at me. Their faces confirmed my suspicions that something was wrong – their eyes and mouths were marked by pity and heartbroken pride. I learned to tune my senses to these external markers of acceptable and unacceptable bodies.

As I got older, Disney movies were replaced by rom-coms and sitcoms and soap operas and ads for anything from tampons to beer. They weren't cartoons, but the fairy tales were the same. Slowly, steadily, I came to understand certain Laws of the Universe: attracting men was of vital importance to women, but men only chose beautiful women, and 'beautiful' was very narrowly defined.

I was hopelessly outside the boundaries of that cut-out paper-doll standard. How does a girl survive a set-up like this? If you're like me, you take pictures that crop out your deformed lower half, you cover your legs with tights or socks (even in the summer), you try to pretend you don't have a body, and you marry the first boy who likes your body, because you're sure his attraction is only a fluke, and you'll be alone for ever if you don't go with this one. For years, I swaddled my body in shame with ritualistic consistency. Like prayers that never left my lips: your twisted trunk is grotesque, hide those hideous feet, don't let people see you struggle to stand.

I wish I could point to the day when I finally realised that this shame was built on fiction, but it turns out unlearning shame is a long, complex process, and one I'm still in the middle of. Maybe the binds of shame first started loosening when I left my husband. Not because he was an awful man, but because the marriage existed for all the wrong reasons, and my misery in it convinced me that someone looking at my body as a beautiful object to consume wasn't the end-all be-all gig I expected. So I left.

I moved into a little apartment by myself and got used to moving through rooms naked – familiarising myself with the soft folds of my belly, my purplish limp feet, and my bony knees. I started to listen to my body – I paid close attention to the way my skin felt in a warm bath – like the mornings my mom would wrap me in hot towels fresh from the dryer – safe and alive. I listened when my body told me I was anxious, acknowledging my beating heart and tense shoulders. Strangely enough, the more I saw my body as an ally – a tool to guide me, a source of pleasure, a conduit for connection – the less I saw it as a shameful object. How can a body that tastes and breathes and cries and laughs and pumps blood and makes up jokes and feels empathy and gives hugs be ugly?

I started a public Instagram account that celebrated my disabled body, because I wanted more images of strong women with different sorts of bodies in the world – because the opposite of shame is coming out of the dark and connecting with others. The first few pictures I posted to my Instagram account @sitting_pretty focused on my floppy scarred feet and shrivelled legs, and I talked about my history of shame for these parts of myself. I started using the hashtag #seenwithoutshame, because I wanted to get back to the childhood bliss of experiencing my body without the weight of evaluation. I didn't know if anyone would care about these posts – did this kind of shame even affect anyone else?

What I found surprised me. While there were people who made comments about my disproportionately big arms or fetishised my paralysed feet, the loudest song came from people chanting, 'Me, too.' So I shared even more personal experiences with my body – the pang I feel when people applaud my boyfriend for dating me, disabled body and all – the immense discomfort I have letting people watch me take laboured steps with a walker – the unique vulnerability of being a teacher to college students when you're a woman with a visible disability.

As I shared in this virtual space, I found so many sorts of bodies fighting shame together – bodies with disabilities, bodies with scars and stretch marks and cellulite, bodies labelled too big or too queer or too bumpy or lumpy or unmanageable. It was almost like being part of a stadium of people shouting a fight song together. For much too long we have been dominated by a narrow-minded vision of what bodies are acceptable, and collectively, we have rallied our voices to cry: we are here to end the reign of body-shaming – we will see and be #seenwithoutshame because #allbodiesaregoodbodies and #allbodiesarebeautiful.

I never quite returned to that place of seeing myself as a Disney princess with my sister in the pool. When I go to the pool now, I am well aware that my hair sticks to my forehead, the sunscreen makes my nose shiny, my belly swells larger on one side. I think, though, that I've landed somewhere better than those early days. When I was little, I thought being seen as a pretty princess was the grand prize. It took time to recognise that pretty princesses are stuck in a two-dimensional world – they aren't allowed to grow or age or scar, which means they aren't allowed to go about the business of living.

As I've stepped into the three-dimensional world, I've begun to see that from the moment I used my lungs to screech – I'm alive! – I embodied the grand prize. My racing, flailing, ageing body is inherently beautiful. It was stunning when I was a soft lump of pink baby, it was beautiful when the surgeon sliced open my back to extricate the tangle of tumours, it was radiant when my newly paralysed body crawled on all-fours until my knees were covered in bright red scabs, it was exquisite when I sat in my wheelchair for my first school dance and awkwardly attempted to sway with the music next to my date, it was beautiful on my wedding day and my divorce day and graduation day and all of my birthdays, and it will keep being magnificent as it wrinkles and sags and scars. This beauty isn't passive or here to be consumed. My body is beautiful because it's bursting with the stories of living, because it has the power to interact with the world around it, because it carries me to life on life on life. This kind of beauty has the strength to flip planets.

NOT SICK ENOUGH
And other Eating Disorder Myths

The first time that I heard of anorexia, it was from one of my mum's magazines. There, in the 'Real Life' section, were all the tell-tale signs of a media eating-disorder story – the shocking low-weight pictures, the disturbingly sparse food diary, the numbers all written in bold. I was fascinated and horrified, just as the audience is supposed to be.

Over the next few years I read several more of those stories, and it started to seem to me that eating disorders were things that only existed inside women's magazines. Nobody in the real world was talking about them. I'd never been taught anything about them at school. They were clearly just unpredictable tragedies that struck the unlucky few. One thing I do remember thinking above all else: it could never happen to me.

A handful of years later when I was diagnosed with anorexia nervosa I still didn't know anything about it. In my mind, I was just losing weight the way the world had taught me to. How could there suddenly be such a huge problem when 15 pounds ago people were so impressed with my dedication and willpower? I just couldn't see the issue. (I learned along the way that not seeing the problem is characteristic of anorexia.) I didn't see it when my clothes all become too big. I didn't see it when I was pulled out of school. I didn't see it at any of the weekly weigh-ins and therapy sessions. I didn't even see it when I was admitted to a residential psychiatric unit.

The first time that I was forced to realise how big of a problem it had become was when I was hospitalised. And still, I didn't understand anything that was happening to me, other than that it was bad. I didn't know where it had come from. I didn't know how it had got to the point it had. What was this thing that seemed to creep up out of nowhere and steal me away from my own mind? How did it have such a hold on me? How had I become one of those stories without even realising?

It was obvious that every single person around me knew as little about it as I did, even the ones who were meant to be professionals trained in how to help. Which meant that we were lost. Since that diagnosis 10 years ago, I'm reminded daily that our culture still doesn't have a fucking clue about eating disorders.

Eating disorders have the highest mortality rates among psychiatric disorders.[53] Beat, the UK's leading eating-disorder charity, estimates that more than 725,000 people in the UK are affected[54] (other estimates are over 1.6 million[55] or even more, since statistics are based on those who are diagnosed and receiving treatment, so many people never seek treatment or make it into the figures). NEDA, a leading eating-disorder charity in the United States cites that 30 million people in the US alone will experience an eating disorder at some point in their life.[56] These are illnesses that turn people with all the potential in the world into empty shells. They are more devastating than words can describe, and yet our main picture of them is still a pretty rich girl throwing up her lunch, or the latest female celebrity who's taken her diet too far.

The myth that I heard the most of during that time painted every anorexic as The Attention-Seeker, which is a misconception that's existed ever since anorexia was first recognised as an illness 150 years ago. According to Joan Jacobs Brumberg in *Fasting Girls*, her history of anorexia nervosa, the illness has been belittled by medical professionals as female foolishness from the start. Samuel Gee, an English physician of the time declared that 'anorexia nervosa seems to arise from a morbid excess of that craving for sympathy which is common to all mankind, as is especially strong in the female sex'. Yup, you got me, Gee, just wanted a bit of sympathy!

CELEBRITIES SAYING IGNORANT SHIT ABOUT EATING DISORDERS

'I wasn't strong enough to have an eating disorder ... I tried to go anorexic for a good three hours. I ate ice and celery, but that's not even anorexic. And I quit. I was like, 'Ma, can you make me a sandwich? Like, immediately.' - Meghan Trainor

'I never suffered from this problem because I had a very strong family base ... The parents are responsible, not fashion.' - Gisele Bundchen

'I tried being anorexic for four hours, and then I was like, I need some bagels.' - Kat Dennings

Along with The Attention-Seeker, other eating disorder myths include: anorexics are people who just don't like food, you can't have an eating disorder unless you look sick enough, and that eating disorders are a choice. At best our assumptions turn into ignorant jokes that ignorant people still find funny (anyone who's in recovery recognises the instant gut punch feeling of enjoying a film that suddenly busts out an insensitive anorexia joke and people actually laugh at it). At worst, our widespread misunderstandings could turn into the reason why someone never seeks treatment – who wants to be seen as self-centred, vain, or as the punchline to an all-too-obvious joke?

Pursuing medical treatment for any mental-health issue is a courageous act in the face of the current stigma attached to mental illness, and since stigma is largely based on misconception, I think it's about time we break down some of those eating disorder myths.

Let's get one thing clear straight away – this isn't a rare spectacle contained within the pages of women's magazines. Eating disorders are not a phase or a diet gone too far. They are an epidemic. And we should be doing everything we possibly can to understand and prevent them.

IMPORTANT: This chapter is filled with details about my experience with anorexia, including content that could be triggering for people who are currently battling eating disorders. If you're in recovery at the moment and you feel that content on the reality of eating disorders will be harmful to you, then please skip this chapter. If you'd like to read on but skip past parts that contain graphic detail or any mention of numbers, then look out for one of these:

— — — — — — — — — — — — STOP 🎀 READING — — — — — — — — — —

You'll see one at the start of any potentially triggering content, and another one when that section is finished and it's safe to keep reading that looks like this:

— — — — — — — — — — — START 🎀 READING — — — — — — — — — —

The first one is coming up at the beginning of the next section. Your mental health comes first, so protect your recovery above all else (P.S. keep kicking arse, you're amazing).

The majority of this chapter focuses on anorexia nervosa, as that's where my experience lies, but a lot of it will apply to other eating disorders as well. This is all based on my personal history, and I definitely don't know all there is to know about eating disorders. I'm still learning, too. I hope that from reading this anyone who knows someone currently struggling with an eating disorder will gain some insight, and anyone who's been there will know that they're not alone, and that they never were.

— — — — — — — — — — — — STOP 🎀 READING — — — — — — — — — —

What it was really like

When I think back to that time I remember the clichés. The coldness. It isn't the same kind that people talk about on a blustery evening walk, it's a coldness that starts in your bones and travels through you. The dizziness. Feeling my blood pressure plummet when I stood up and wondering whether that was it, lights out.

I remember when I started to lose my hearing, and the whole world sounded like it was underwater. I remember sitting down on a hard plastic chair and feeling lightning bolts up my spine through my hip bones. I remember hair and nails as thin as crepe paper and giant boulders knocking together where my knees used to be. I remember feeling as light as air, and more indestructible with every piece of me that fell apart.

But all those physical things are meaningless. None of them capture the madness. None of them show how painful it is to exist for even a moment in your own mind. They don't show how minutes feel like weeks, how you wonder whether time is really moving, whether five o'clock will ever come – the only time you'll allow yourself to start eating that one apple, the one you make last until 6:30 p.m. and think about for the rest of the night.

The coldness doesn't capture the battle that rages in your mind night and day, where fleeting glimpses of reason and rationality slowly disappear into nothingness: 'The doctor says if I don't start eating I could die, maybe he's right … no … NO … he's not right … he's trying to trick me like everybody else … he has no idea what he's talking about.'

Nothing on the outside could show the voice that takes over everything. The voice that counts, and calculates, and accuses, and rips you into shreds every second of every day. The voice that eventually replaces your own until all that plays are reminders of your worthlessness on repeat, and nothing else gets in.

That voice is a forcefield. I didn't speak for months beyond a muffled 'yes' or 'no', I didn't dare, I wasn't allowed my own voice any more. Losing weight doesn't compare to gradually losing everything you thought you were, every opinion, every passion, every joy in life slipping away until all that you are, and all that you have, is that voice, and what it allows you to do.

There are moments of bursting clarity, when the weight of all that pain pushes down on your fragile lungs and you can't believe what you've done ... Then just as fast those moments go and the 'you' that thought them goes too.

I remember feeling the whole world moving past me. All those lives blazing into the future, moving on, changing, growing, leaving me chained in a prison that nobody else could see. When my family came to visit me, I wanted so badly to be there in that room with them. I wanted to reach across and feel their warmth; all I'd felt was cold for so long. I wanted their love to be enough to pull me out of this hell and teach me who I was again. But it was never enough. So they left, without me. To go back to their lives, to try and forget, just for a little while, the pain that seeing me caused. They left, and I stayed. Thinking how nothing would ever be enough.

Until one day, something was. You see my rock bottom wasn't my lowest weight. It wasn't being pulled out of school or losing my friends. It wasn't even when the doctor told my parents that I might only have a few hours to live since my organs were slowly shutting down. It was a little while after that, when I saw my dad cry for the first time in my life.

START 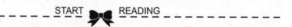 READING

My solid oak tree of a father, eternally patient, forever trying his utmost to understand, broke. And in words that spilled out with his tears he told me that he couldn't do it any more. He couldn't keep living like this, I couldn't, we couldn't. Before he left the room he took the single tissue he was clutching and threw it down where I sat, silently. He'd saved up so much sadness, so much frustration, and anger and hopelessness, and it all came crashing down on me in that one tissue. I felt it all. But most of all, I felt anger.

I was suddenly furious about all the time that was stolen from me. All the years I should have been becoming who I was, wasted on becoming less and less every day. All the impossible dreams I should have been dreaming, starved into oblivion. All the adventures I never realised were happening. All the foolish teenage mistakes and bad first kisses. All the moments that are meant to colour the most vivid years of your life, faded into the greyness of anorexia.

I was enraged at how much hurt this thing had caused. This thing that took my hand and dealt blow after blow to everyone I loved most in the world. This thing that took root inside me and set me aflame, making me sit back and watch as everyone who came close was burned along with me. For what? For thin? For control? For fear of ever changing? Fuck that. And fuck anorexia.

That rage fuelled me. It gave me the power to take that first bite. It gave me the power to defy that voice. It made me see all the lies – how doing what that voice told me to do wasn't control at all, it was losing control, and now I had to get it back. Years later it would be the same rage that powered me into body positivity, that made me refuse to hate myself for a second longer. It's the same rage that I want every one of you to feel, when you think of all the time wasted on self-hatred.

Now I know that even though I'm not that girl any more, everything I am is built on her. When I remember it isn't a sharp pain of shame and fear but a dull ache, a slow sadness for all the things I never deserved. It's realising that no matter how far I get, no matter how much I grow and learn and heal, I will be forever changed by that time. I was forged in those flames. For a long while, I thought that recovery was simply pretending that nothing happened, hiding the leftover wounds and treating that girl like she was someone else entirely.

Now I realise that everywhere I go I'm carrying her with me. I imagine scooping up her tiny frame, letting her rest on the softness of my well-fed stomach, and showing her everything she accomplished. I show her how she fought her demons and won. I show her the dreams that were waiting for her. I show her how she turned it all into something worthwhile, how her pain was for something. I show her that it was inside her all long – the power to overcome. The power to recover. It was all in her.

And most of all, when I think back now, I know, and I believe, that it wasn't her fault. It wasn't my fault. I fell at the hands of forces so much bigger than me, we all do. None of us asked to live in a world that sells starvation in a million different ways and then ignores the cries of the ones who learned the lesson too well. And even though the pain we're taught takes root in us all in different ways, whether it grows into an eating disorder or not, we have one crucial thing in common: we don't hold any of the blame for planting the seeds.

'I can say finally, for myself at least: at 13, to starve half to death? Not guilty. Not that child. There is certainly a charge of guilt to be made, long overdue. But it doesn't belong to me. It belongs somewhere, and to something, else.'

– Naomi Wolf, *The Beauty Myth*

A diet gone too far

If you've read this far, you already know how I feel about diets. You've seen how diets can be dangerous, how they don't work, and how they make us hate ourselves even more than we did before we started them. And if you still need convincing about just how toxic they are, then look no further. Diets and the culture that surrounds them play a huge role in the development of eating disorders. In fact:

- Adolescent girls who diet even moderately are five times more likely to develop an eating disorder than those who have never dieted.

- Adolescent girls who've dieted severely are a terrifying 18 (EIGHTEEN!) times more likely to develop an eating disorder than those who have never dieted.[57]

What better way to ruin young girls' relationships with food and their bodies than dieting? Diets don't just encourage disordered eating, they are disordered eating. Just think about the things that any common diet might encourage: counting every calorie, cutting out entire food groups, weighing and measuring food, keeping track of your intake in a food diary, weighing yourself daily, taking your measurements weekly, working out every day, tracking how many calories you burn, eating very slowly, chewing each bite 20 times before swallowing, taking unapproved supplements to aid weight loss, only consuming liquids, intermittent starvation (only starving yourself for 2 days of the week, which is harmless, apparently), only eating fruit before 5p.m., not eating after 5p.m., the list goes on and on. Is it just me who sees that that list could be identical to a list of behavioural symptoms for recognising whether someone has an eating disorder?

So where's the myth? Diets are clearly the start of eating disorders for so many people. However, the problem with saying that eating disorders are diets that have gone too far is that eating disorders are not diets. Even if they started as them. When someone crosses that line between dieting and developing an eating disorder, a whole new beast is born. One that is so much hungrier, and so much more dangerous than before.

Someone on a diet might count their calories, but they're not likely to have that number emblazoned in their minds for every one of their waking hours. Someone on a diet might plan their meals ahead of time, but they probably won't be so consumed by the planning that they can't focus on any conversations, events or activities in the meantime. Someone on a diet might be desperate to lose weight, but they don't believe that their very existence depends on it. And most notably, someone on a diet will probably be able to tell if they've gone 'too far', for someone in the grips of anorexia, there is no such thing.

The space between dieting and having an eating disorder is mental health. Anorexia, bulimia, binge-eating disorder and OSFED (other specified feeding or eating disorder) are mental illnesses. Extreme dieting damages your mental health, but it doesn't compare to what goes on in the mind of someone with an eating disorder. Diets might lead into eating disorders, but once someone is in that disordered mindset, they've gone so much further than any diet ever could.

Diets are so often the final stepping stone before falling over the edge into the depths of an eating disorder. The restriction of a diet comes with feelings of success, a high at the sense of control, a taste of how addictive denying your hunger can feel. Restriction also causes physiological changes in the brain, which, when sustained for long enough, could play a significant role in developing a full-blown eating disorder. My stepping stones were made out of the diets I'd started when I was 10 years old, each one more restrictive and more essential to my sense of self-worth. But my final stepping stone was getting ill when I was 13.

STOP READING

It was a standard kind of sickness, a little bit of the flu, a few days of headaches and sluggishness that sent me to the sofa instead of school. At first, I even lost my appetite, and I was overjoyed about it. I imagined going back to school 10 pounds lighter and basking in the compliments.

While I was lying there I thought a lot about how I was surviving on only a bit of fruit a day, and what an amazing weight-loss technique it would be if I could only live that way all the time. When my appetite came back, I denied it for as long as I could. Although I didn't dive head first into starvation straight after that, I never went back to eating normally, either. I'd felt how intoxicating the denial could be.

START READING

When I started to restrict more and more after that illness there was one thing that was undeniably different. It's the one thing that truly separates a diet gone too far from an eating disorder: it didn't feel optional any more. I couldn't slip off track or break the rules by indulging in something 'naughty' and feel bad about it later. Pure restriction was obligatory, non-negotiable. It didn't take long before it really did start to feel like my very existence depended on that restriction, and not in a hyperbolic 'I'll just die if I have to go out looking this fat!' way, in a real, scary, no turning back way.

Susan Bordo describes how diets can easily form the basis of a restrictive eating disorder in *Unbearable Weight*:

> Usually, the anorexic syndrome emerges, not as a conscious decision to get as thin as possible, but as the result of her having begun a diet fairly casually ... having succeeded splendidly in taking off 5 or 10 pounds, and then having gotten hooked on the intoxicating feeling of accomplishment and control.

I was hooked. Addicted. Gone. I might have got into the car and turned on the engine myself, but not too far down the road something clicked and before I knew it I wasn't the one steering any more. I was left in the passenger seat hurtling towards a destination that I knew nothing about, one that I certainly hadn't decided on before I got in.

I can't say at what point exactly, how many pounds in, how many more calories down, but there came a time when it wasn't a choice any more. Choice only exists if the second option seems viable, and seems possible. Getting myself out of that car once it had started moving was impossible, the doors were all locked and after a while I forgot that they were supposed to open at all. That's the real difference: someone on a harmless diet can choose to stop, someone with an eating disorder loses all sense of choice.

Why don't you just eat more?

Any of my fellow anorexia survivors out there will have heard this one plenty of times. Those well-intentioned, but completely clueless people handing you the magic answer to recovery – just eat! Gee, thanks Brenda, I'm all better now! Ta-da! Well-intentioned or not, saying those words to someone with anorexia is like telling a person who's desperately flailing in choppy waters to just swim out.

---------------------- STOP 🎀 READING ------------

The most memorable time those words were said to me was when I was in a residential psychiatric unit. It was the scariest time of my life. My parents had realised that despite their unrelenting support and unconditional love they were still losing me. Anorexia had turned me into a master of deception, hiding food, secretly exercising, faking my weekly weigh-ins to make them think I was 10 pounds heavier than I was.

When my dad walked downstairs one morning to find me running laps around the house they realised that it was time to go. They couldn't supervise me 24/7, they wouldn't be equipped if I suddenly collapsed. So they took me to live in a building opposite a hospital, filled with around 15 other mentally ill young people. A variety bag of messed-up teenagers, monitored by a bunch of people with no idea how to take care of us.

The first thing I noticed when we got there was how many weeds were growing through the crevices of the concrete car park. I hoped so hard that they would wrap round my ankles and pull me down into the cracks. Maybe I could leave my body behind entirely and just sink underneath the earth. I stood watching the weeds and wishing my existence away until my dad put his arm around my shoulders and guided me towards the door.

We went through the reception area, down an endless corridor and into a room with green chairs to meet the man in charge. The man in charge admits you, and decides when you get to leave. He wore bright magenta socks and smiled in the most patronising way I'd ever seen. After an assessment where I said nothing, I was taken through to my room, where everything was grey. My belongings were checked – no sharp objects, no mobile phones, no illegal substances. I begged my parents to take me away from this place that I didn't belong in, not with these people, not by myself …

Then they left. I think it must have been the most difficult time they've ever had to leave me. I've never cried as hard as I did that first night, deep, racking sobs that left my brain short of oxygen and my whole body aching. Every hour someone came round with a torch that shined through the panel of my door and reminded me exactly where I was.

In the days we did arts and crafts in a crumbling shack apart from the main building. I thought at first that our drawings and papier mâché creations were being taken away somewhere to be analysed, scoured for the hidden reasons behind what was wrong with us all. Actually, they were just left in a drawer or the corner of the room to gather dust – there was a lot of dust in that room.

The others went out – bowling, cinema trips, swimming. I wasn't allowed to do any physical activity so I stayed behind scouting out secret areas I could exercise in instead. I found an abandoned step to jump on and off of. I skipped down the never-ending corridors with the walls that felt like they were tilting inwards, stopping to a slow walk past the doors to the offices and staff rooms.

Occasionally I was allowed out into a grey courtyard that the sun found its way into for a little while every afternoon. I would take a book and when my mind was too clouded to focus on it I'd close my eyes and try to sink into the orange light soaking through my eyelids. I spent group therapy sessions staring at a single red thread in the grey carpet as I listened to the other kids argue with the staff over whatever happened the day before. All day long I lived in fear of the next mealtime being announced, when everyone would pile into the dining hall and swarm around the buffet table in the corner.

I sat at a grey table while the staff member assigned to me brought me a plate of food. Then I spent the next 45 minutes with my eyes aimed at the floor while they tried everything they could to make me eat it. If it was someone nice they would try to talk to me, make me relax a bit, get me out of the swirling abyss in my mind. The not-so-nice ones quickly moved on to orders, threats about not being allowed to see my parents, cold comments about wasting their time and disdainful looks.

Some days I couldn't stand saying no any more or bearing the guilt of ignoring someone looking at me so pleadingly, so I dragged my shackled hands and with every drop of resistance I had, took a couple of pitiful bites of that day's sandwich or breakfast cereal. Afterwards, I retreated back to my room for as long as I was allowed, dancing frantically and jumping on and off the bed. A man in a red checked shirt saw me once and opened my door – 'How do you expect to gain any weight if you keep jumping around like that?' – why would I be trying to gain weight?

That was generally the level of understanding that all of the staff had. I remember sitting on the faded blue sofa in the lounge and being brought my 8p.m. snack of juice, an apple and two digestive biscuits. The woman who brought them seemed genuinely surprised that I wasn't willing to touch the biscuits. As if I'd personally checked myself into this place with the intention of eating everything I was allowed, having taken my weight loss just a bit too far and decided to put a bit of meat back on my bones.

On a daily basis they reaffirmed all of my feelings about being a burden, about being worthless. They interpreted their role as being my feeder. The people who coerced me into eating by any means necessary, none of them seemed to consider that anorexia is about more than just not wanting to eat. I was a refeeding chart. I was a weekly weigh-in. I was never, ever, a person worthy of getting to know beyond the anorexia.

The 'therapy' I received all centred around 'why didn't you eat this week?' in an accusing tone, or attempts to pin the blame on members of my family. I stayed with my eyes fixed on the floor, never once feeling safe enough to talk to any of them. Why would you open up your rusted emotional locks and spill all of your pain out for people who don't even treat you like you're a human being?

One day I was asked to help prepare dinner in the kitchen, another grey room with tiny windows for the sunlight to creep through and illuminate the dancing particles of dust. I was allowed to just watch once I mumbled that I didn't know how to peel potatoes or dice carrots. Really, I thought that I might suffocate under all that food, piling on top of me until everything went black. I must have frustrated the woman in there with me because she stopped peeling, turned to face me and said 'Do you really think you're the first anorexic we've had in here? You're not. We've had worse.'

Okay, the voice of my eating disorder said, I'll give you what you want then, I'll give you the worst.

I started brushing my teeth for 30 minutes at a time. I sat on the hard plastic toilet seat and brushed until someone knocked on the door, while I pored over the old women's magazines that my mum had brought me from home. I find it ironic now how the self-harmers had all of their sharp objects taken away to stop them from hurting themselves, but I was given free reign over those glossy pages filled with diet plans and photoshopped bodies that still seemed so much thinner than my own. I wore down those pages until they were flecked with white and my gums were red from brushing.

I watched the people I was living with from my silent corner. There were the girls with swollen purple scars running all the way down their arms. The girls who had to sit for an hour after meals so they didn't run straight to the nearest toilet. The girl whose mood would oscillate violently without warning. The girl who you could hear shouting in the night. And there was one boy. One tall, sandy-haired boy who wrote me a terrible poem and kissed me on the forehead when I was discharged. Apparently, not even being in a mental institution could kill his need for female attention.

One evening he told me he liked me and I asked him whether he thought I was too thin like everybody else. Only a little bit, he said. I probably weighed about 75 pounds at the time. Only a little bit. He left a few days after that just to be readmitted the next day with a broken hand from punching a wall. Such a shame that romance never had a chance to blossom, we could have been the Beyoncé and Jay Z of mental health issues ... I remember a conversation we had in the dining hall after anorexia had won another round over lunch. It went something like this:

'Do you want to get out of this place?'

I nodded in response.

'Then why don't you just eat more?'

And there it was. Why didn't I just eat more? I'm pretty sure that he wouldn't have liked me once I did anyway. Not once I'd nearly tripled my body weight and spent countless hours gorging until my stomach swelled to the point of bursting and I was left in a tear-stained bundle on the floor. That probably would have tarnished the fantasy of the feather-light damsel in distress. Of course, him liking me had nothing to do with me not eating more, I didn't even like him very much myself (his poetry really was terrible).

I managed to find the poem after I wrote this, apparently I hoard things from horrible times in my life. Brace yourself:

> That girl I like has eyes of a beautiful brown,
> Amazingly, I have never seen her frown!
> All I ever see her wear is black,
> It makes her glimmer like the midnight sky,
> Her eyes shine with beauty like the moonlite sky.

All about those similes. Also, I'm almost certain he would have seen me frown at least once, since we were, y'know, locked up in a psychiatric facility. But I'll grant him poetic licence on that one.

The reason I didn't eat more was because it simply felt impossible. It was the most absurd suggestion I'd ever heard – why would I eat more? I still had so much weight to lose, so many rules to follow, so many calories to burn. There was no way I could do anything other than those things. There was no choice.

My friend Rachel, who is in recovery from anorexia as I write this, told me once that it feels like a real person follows her around wherever she goes and places a hand over her mouth whenever she attempts to eat. As if it is literally not her in control of the decision of whether to eat or not.

That's why people with eating disorders refer to their illness as 'Ana' or 'Mia', the disorders are personified because they feel like real people dictating what you're allowed to do, with real voices to instruct and real hands to cover mouths. So when I answered Lord Byron's question of 'why don't you just eat more?' with a feeble 'I can't', I was telling the truth. At that point of my eating disorder the light hadn't broken through the darkness yet, there was no other path than the one I was on.

 START READING

Asking anorexia patients why they don't just eat more misunderstands restrictive eating disorders in every way. Most notably because it implies a level of conscious choice that was left behind a long time ago, but also because it fails to grasp that eating disorders are about so much more than food.

Anorexia means 'absence of appetite', which implies that someone with anorexia has just gone off food, or just isn't feeling very hungry. But as Susan Bordo writes 'anorexic women are as obsessed with hunger as they are with being slim. Far from losing her appetite, the typical anorectic is haunted by it ... and is in constant dread of being overwhelmed by it.'[58] If someone is that obsessed with hunger and food, don't you think that they would eat if they felt like they had the choice to?

Food, exercise and weight simply become the things that mental illness can take shape in for so many of us. They are the things we can grasp on to, the things we can control, the things we can put our pain into in the hopes that it might hurt a little less.

I'm still learning about my pain, and why it took shape in anorexia. I'm not a medical professional, I don't have a degree in psychology and I'm pretty sure I still have a lifetime of learning ahead of me. But from what I already know, eating disorders are never just about food. They're more complicated than just wanting to be thin. They are things that grow deep inside of us, they might bloom in ways that display themselves on our physical bodies, but their roots are far, far, further down than what meets the eye.

My roots were made out of many things. Parts of who I am as a person, parts of what the world is like and parts of what starvation itself gave me.

Whose fault is it anyway?

Every therapist I've ever had has reeeeally wanted to point the finger. They treated my eating disorder more like a game of Cluedo than an actual mental illness (the culprit is the magazines! In the bedroom! Or the parents! In childhood! By George, I think I've got it!). Of course, it's crucial that we find the cause of these illnesses, but it's nowhere near as simple as finding one thing to blame all that suffering on and calling it a day. Eating disorders are far more complicated than that.

WHAT NOT TO SAY TO SOMEONE IN ANOREXIA RECOVERY

'You look so much better now!'

'Boys like curves way more than they like sticks.'

'Before you were scary skinny but now you're just good skinny.'

'It's so much easier gaining weight than losing weight.'

WHAT YOU COULD SAY INSTEAD

'I'm proud of you.'

'I'm so thankful that you're here.'

'You are one badass, powerful human being!'

'If you want to talk about anything at all, I promise to listen without any judgement.'

And unless the person you're talking to is a someone who you share a close bond with, don't say anything at all. Don't comment on their body or their eating habits, just treat them like a normal human being. Because y'know, that's what they are.

When people talk about eating disorders being multi-dimensional, there are three parts that dominate the conversation – the psychological, the socio-cultural, and the physiological.

The psychological explanation focuses on what makes the minds of some people latch on to eating disorders while others can spend their lives dieting and disliking their bodies while remaining on fairly stable ground. Traits such as perfectionism, attention to detail, and the tendency to set impossible standards have all been linked to the development of eating disorders. I've been an all-or-nothing person for as long as I can remember, there was never going to be a safe middle ground for me.

The psychological is also where all the talk about 'control' comes from. The anorexic controls how much they eat. The bulimic controls how much remains after they eat. The orthorectic controls the type of food they eat and how much is burned off. Binge-eating comes with more of a sense of allowing yourself to lose control, but it's still a similar feeling of release to the restriction and purging of the others. The element of control symbolises the things in that person's life that they feel they have no control over.

When I started slipping into anorexia I was just finishing Year 9, there was lots of talk about moving to the upper-school campus, making decisions about what to study that might impact the rest of my life. There were sleepovers with hushed midnight talks about who would get boobs first and which boys would want to touch them. The games of our adolescence and our loyal childhood toys had all been packed away, and hormones were making sure that my days of being a happy-go-lucky girl were long gone.

Change, change and more change. I was terrified. I had no idea what was going on and I didn't want a single thing to change. But at 14 everything was – my school life, my family dynamics, my friendships, my body. A lot of people with anorexia have a deep need to stay exactly where they are, or even to turn the clock back to a time when things felt more under control. Female anorexia is so common during puberty because it starves the body of the natural changes of entering womanhood.

There is a reason why eating disorders are still overwhelmingly female (commonly cited statistics put around 90 per cent of cases as occurring in females,[59] a number that's been fairly steady for decades). There is something undeniable in the essence of what it means to be a woman in our culture that makes us turn towards eating disorders in the numbers that we do. Womanhood is messy. Womanhood is filled with things that we can't control. Womanhood is filled with people telling us who we're supposed to become, and rules dictating how we should look, live, act, and be.

Womanhood is being valued for the physical above all else. Womanhood is sexual pressure and sexual danger. Womanhood is still not existing on an equal social, political and economic plane as men but being told that we have it all, and that we're being extreme when we express our feelings of being treated as 'less than' in all of those ways. Womanhood is realising that the control has been given to somebody else. So we take control of what we think we can – what we eat and the number on the scale. Actually, we're not taking control at all considering that we're still following the rules handed down to us by our culture.

The socio-cultural explanation for eating disorders is about what's going on in the world around us, i.e., everything I won't shut up about in this book. It's diet culture and body ideals. It's food guilt and the fear of fat. It's all the little ways we learn that weight loss is the ultimate achievement, and all the body dissatisfaction we're taught from a young age so that people can profit from our self-hatred.

All these ways of seeing bodies and food that are so entrenched in our culture provide the perfect breeding ground for eating disorders. Put someone in it who's psychologically susceptible (perhaps a perfectionist who feels like the world is moving too fast for them to hold on to), and really, they never even stood a chance.

Sometimes I imagine all the powers that be gathering together around a sprawling black table where decisions about the world are made. One day the agenda for the meeting was deciding what kind of world would be the most efficient at creating eating disorders. After much pondering, and colluding with the diet, beauty, fitness and food industries they put a plan in motion to give birth to this eating disorder utopia.

The world they came up with is the one we are living in today. If you had to create a culture that could most efficiently contribute to people developing eating disorders (while still being elusive enough to convince billions of people that there isn't a problem), this would be it. We are in it. It's a miracle that any of us make it out alive.

The socio-cultural plus the psychological puts someone in prime position for an eating disorder. And once they're on the way down, another factor comes into play to make damn sure that they stay down: the physiological. That is, the physical effects on the body that come with starvation, purging, or binging. In particular, the neurobiology of the brain.

According to the Anorexia and Eating Disorders Information and Resources (ANRED) website 'both undereating and overeating can activate brain chemicals that produce feelings of peace and euphoria, thus temporarily dispelling anxiety and depression'. The sense of release I mentioned earlier that comes from restriction or binging is a real alteration of brain chemicals. What better way to keep someone coming back and gradually forming an addiction to their disordered behaviour?

An important physiological aspect of restrictive eating disorders in particular is that the brain is literally starved, to the point where it isn't functioning normally any more. Think back to the Minnesota Starvation experiment, remember the effects that semi-starvation had on a group of mentally healthy men: obsession, reduced concentration, anger, loss of sex drive, development of disordered food rituals, constant preoccupation with food, dreams of cannibalism, literally chopping off their own finger with an axe!

Mentally healthy men. Without the unrelenting pressures of diet culture. Without a history of dieting. Eating 1,800 calories a day. I'm reluctant to say how many calories I was eating at my lowest points, since I don't want anyone currently struggling to latch on to that number, but let's just say it was far less than that. How do you think the level of starvation that anorexics undergo affects someone's brain? As Em Farrell writes in *A is for Anorexia*, 'starvation brings its own madness in its wake'.

Our final picture is the perfectionist who's never felt good enough, who's been completely poisoned by the toxic messages of the media and her culture about bodies and worth, who gets hooked on restriction and eventually starves her brain so much that she becomes a shadow of who she was, lost in the depths of anorexia and unable to see any way out. That is the reality for so many people at this very moment. That was my reality. And if that isn't enough to convince you that eating disorders are about more than not liking food or wanting to lose a few pounds, then nothing will be.

Even then there are countless other contributing factors being discovered and researched every day. Our picture doesn't include the role of the family and how dynamics within the home can shape eating disorders, genetic predispositions to eating disorders, or an actual physiological cause that eating disorders may initially arise from (rather than the effects of starvation that become a perpetuating factor). So as far as blame and fault are concerned, the world is overflowing with potential culprits, we just need to open our eyes and take responsibility for the ones that we can actually change.

Not sick enough

One of the most insidious myths about eating disorders is that you don't deserve help until you're 'sick enough'. In most cases, this translates to 'thin enough'. People who reach out for medical help are actually told to come back when they've lost more weight, enough weight to be taken seriously, because apparently a mental illness just isn't real enough unless you can see it.

In the UK an adult has to have a BMI of 17.5 or below in order to be diagnosed with anorexia nervosa, meaning a woman who's 5 foot 6 inches tall needs to weigh 109 pounds or less to be taken seriously. Let's say that same woman weighs 140 pounds.

STOP READING

It used to be 190 pounds but over the last year weight loss has been her main preoccupation. In fact, every waking moment is consumed by thoughts of weight, food and exercise.

Every day becomes an opportunity to eat less than the day before. Monday: porridge, green salad, chicken breast, two apples. Tuesday: porridge, green salad, chicken breast, one apple. Every bite etched into her mind and calculated over and over again. She skips meals out and goes to the gym instead, she runs for two hours on the treadmill until nausea sweeps over her and black spots creep into her vision. Her fellow gym-goers praise her dedication. She drags herself home and tries to sleep through the pain of the hunger she's been ignoring for so long. Every pang is her body crying out for help, for sustenance, but she doesn't need it – she's not even underweight. She dreams of devouring the world, and wakes up again in her mental prison, where calories, pounds and inches play on a non-stop loop.

What is that woman? On a diet? Harmlessly pursuing a better version of herself? Thirty-one fewer pounds on her body and she'd be diagnosed in a heartbeat: anorexia nervosa. But even if she finds the resistance against her eating disorder to make that doctor's appointment – and it's a big if, considering one of the most prominent features of eating disorders is denial, and her denial seems to be echoed by everyone around her assuming that she's fine – what awaits her?

— — — — — — — — — — — START ✖ READING — — — — — — — — — —

If she's extremely lucky she might have a doctor with enough knowledge to diagnose her with atypical anorexia nervosa, which is characterised by having all the features of anorexia without the low weight. But atypical anorexia is still a relatively new diagnosis (The DSM-5 added it as a specific subtype of OSFED (Other Specified Feeding or Eating Disorder) in 2013), and it seems that many medical professionals are reluctant to use it.

The number of people online who share their experience of nobody taking their issues seriously because of their weight are a testament to how strongly we still believe that weight is the be all and end all of eating disorders. So many people reach out for help and are told the same thing: come back in six months, your BMI is too high.

Telling someone with an eating disorder to lose weight is like giving a pyromaniac a flamethrower and asking them to see how much of the house they can burn down. Maybe our woman does burn herself down. Maybe she loses enough weight that people gasp at her when she walks down the street. She finally gets that diagnosis and is scheduled for outpatient treatment. How much less likely is she to recover having already spent 18 months spiralling down into anorexia?

It's widely acknowledged that the longer someone spends falling into that darkness, the harder it becomes for them to get back out. The National Institute for Health and Care Excellence state in their National Clinical Practice Guideline that 'there can be serious long-term consequences to a delay in obtaining treatment ... People with eating disorders should be assessed and receive treatment at the earliest opportunity'[60] ... but apparently only if they look worthy of it when that opportunity arises.

Of course, there's the possibility that she won't lose enough weight to look worthy. For some people, even semi-starvation won't make them supermodel thin or drop their BMI below 17.5. There are people with eating disorders who will never lose enough weight to be taken seriously according to diagnostic standards. Unless they find a medical professional who understands that eating disorder weight requirements are bullshit, they'll just keep spiralling.

Everyone, please stand back while I drop a truth bomb on this eating disorder myth: you can have an eating disorder at any size. Eating disorders are mental illnesses, not body types.

Putting a weight requirement on eating disorder diagnoses is downright dangerous. Praising one woman for her dieting efforts, and diagnosing another with anorexia when the only thing that separates them is weight is a complete misunderstanding of mental illness. Telling the woman who weighs 140 pounds to lose more weight before she's allowed treatment would be laughable if it wasn't so horrifying.

To anyone who's ever had their pain invalidated because they don't fit the narrow stereotypes of an eating disorder sufferer – I see you. Your experience is valid. You deserve to have your struggles acknowledged, and treated with the appropriate respect and urgency. Your recovery is important. It doesn't matter what your lowest weight was, it doesn't matter how far down you fell. You are worthy and capable of recovering, and you shouldn't have to fight that battle without anybody else on your side.

The Invisible Unbelievable Secret Of A Fat Girl
Danielle Galvin (@chooselifewarrior)

I am 16, I am sitting in the bathroom of my family home. It's 1a.m. and the house is so quiet. I've always hated the darkness and shadows but I am so numb tonight I hope they simply swallow me whole. My parents and little brother are sleeping; they have no idea who I am. I'm sitting on the lid of the toilet with a 12-inch kitchen knife wrapped in a towel that I got from the kitchen 10 minutes earlier. The buzzing fluorescence of an outside light is making the knife's blade shimmer. It's actually beautiful watching the light it reflects, unlike the person holding it.

-------------------- STOP ✤ READING --------------------

I'm staring at my size 14 thighs, the smallest part of me for sure, but still so big I can't imagine a pretty girl would ever have them. Pretty girls don't have big anything, except maybe big breasts. I stare into the mirror in front of me, so disassociated with the girl I see. It is as if I'm not even looking at myself. I'm not at this place with the knife because I'm depressed, well, no, I am, but I'm depressed because of the secret.

The thing I cannot talk about, the thing no one believes because my secret, they say, isn't real. The world tells me that I am making it up. So I have learned to not speak about it, to avoid it. Unfortunately, sometimes I explode about it to friends who I think maybe care. I'm trying to do that less.

Everyone is distracted. Always. My big fat thighs distract them from it. My belly. My size. All of it doesn't communicate what really happens. How hard I really try. How desperately I want it. That's why I have the knife. I can't live in my brain any more. I can't take it. I can't bear to live.

-------------------- START ✤ READING --------------------

I am 24 now and that secret above is something that nearly killed me, but also completely shaped me into the person I am today. My big secret was that I had an eating disorder. A festering, dangerous, scary eating disorder, and yet for the majority of my life I have been overweight or obese. My twisting demon of a disorder started when I was a chubby 11-year-old, encouraged to lose the pre-pubescent puppy fat off her body. Not for health but for beauty. Not in a healthy way but by any means necessary.

This obsession with beauty and being the smallest size I could be haunted that young 11-year-old's life. Slowly but surely I gained an addiction to exercise and gym culture. I believed the weight-loss prophecy – that becoming thin would be the greatest and biggest achievement of my life. But the prophecy never came true. This obsession mixed with personal traumas resulted in a fully fledged eating disorder by age 14. Control and self-punishment served as an extremely easy outlet for a lot of the pain in my life.

Yet I was still fat and therefore my illness was invisible – I was still fat so I was lying. I was lazy. I devoted my adolescence to giving my all to be 'perfect', 'beautiful' and 'worthy'.

I was convinced I didn't have an eating disorder, living life on the least calories possible, while guzzling down information on eating disorder websites that told me 'Try Harder Fatty. You Aren't Like Us, You Don't Have The Willpower, You Don't Want It Bad Enough'.

This was echoed through reinforcements from people around me who spat the words 'phase' and 'attention-seeking', as if this psychological illness would somehow weed itself out of the tangles of my cerebral cortex. It didn't – some days it still feels like it hasn't completely.

I was a young girl who was smart, talented and sociable. Yet I felt like I was living a double life. My insecurities strangled my self-worth at every twist and turn. My eating disorder raged and controlled me until at 19 a friend of mine gave me an ultimatum: either the next time I said suicide she would call an ambulance and have me admitted to a mental health ward or I could voluntarily go to therapy.

Five years later and I have begun telling my story in an extremely public way. Sharing the hardships and struggles of being an eating-disorder sufferer who never did fit the weight criteria needed for anorexia or bulimia. It has been an extremely difficult road still to accept and deal with the fact that yes indeed I suffered from a dangerous, life-threatening, happiness-sucking mental illness – which without treatment would have killed me. This idolisation of being gifted the diagnosis of anorexia as the 'worst' eating disorder contributed to the time I spent not seeking treatment.

My feelings of invisibility (yet hyper-visibility) were so hard to manage, I constantly felt like everyone was staring at my fat and I wanted to scream that I had worked out for hours and eaten so little. The already sneaky and deceitful eating disorder held me captive and *dragged me back down with every person I told I needed help, but who doubted me due to the extra fat on my hips.*

I was a prisoner of invisibility and being invalidated every step of the way. I was a young girl warped by goals that no person should be held to. I was afraid and alone, fat and forever apologising for my existence. I was invisible – I was 'unworthy' of help. I was not trying hard enough. I was a failure, simply because of my fucking BMI.

The validation and processing I received through therapy saved my life and made me passionate about telling my story. No person held by a mental illness should strive to get sicker before the world validates them or before the world believes them.

While the woman I am today is very different from the 11-year-old girl I was, I will carry that 11-year-old girl with me every single day of my life because she deserved a voice and finally I can be that for her.

STOP  READING

Recovered v. weight restored

During my final counselling session I sat, as I had sat every week for the past 18 months, silently looking down at my nails, unresponsive, unwilling, afraid to say what I was really feeling. I'd probably said no more than 15 words over the entire course of my 'treatment'. What I was really feeling was relief, not that I'd 'recovered' or regained my health, but that soon I could go back to destroying myself without anyone trying to stop me. I'd complied, I'd gained weight (a lot of it in a very short amount of time), and I was pronounced no longer anorexic. Recovered at last!

Truthfully, I'd made a few desperate stumbles towards recovery. I hadn't learned how to eat without fear or stop obsessing over every calorie every second of every day. I'd learned how to devour. I'd learned how liberating it could feel to eat everything I could get my hands on after so many months of starvation. But my eating disorder hadn't gone anywhere, only receded into a smaller space, ready to emerge again when I was the most vulnerable, the most stuffed. From the outside I was recovered, I didn't fit the skeletal image of anorexia any more so off I went. Back to school, back to normality, back to starving myself at the first opportunity and then eating until I couldn't move.

The years I'd spent fading away were glossed over and ignored. It was easier for everyone to pretend that had all happened to some other girl, not this one with the ever-growing thighs and full cheeks. I played the part, I only starved until somebody got worried, then I went back to devouring and my weight went right back up. During a family holiday I refused to go out for meals and swam endless laps in the pool instead, I lost 10 pounds in 11 days. As soon as we got home I headed to the bakery, I put those 10 pounds (and more) back on before I'd finished unpacking my suitcase.

My new chubby body meant that I could disguise extreme restriction behind 'dieting' and exercise addiction behind 'keeping fit'. Everyone around me seemed completely convinced that I was fine. Parents of friends commented on how well I'd 'filled out', others hugged me and exclaimed what a relief it was that they didn't have to see me that way any more. Friends went right back to talking about their diets and pointing out how fat their arms were in front of me. It was like I'd flicked a switch and none of it had happened, for everyone else anyway.

----------- START ❧ READING -----------

Thinking that being recovered and being weight-restored are the same thing seriously underestimates the power of eating disorders. In order to gain weight only a small part of me had to recover – the part that allowed to me eat. There were still a million more broken parts that nobody else wanted to acknowledge. I hadn't healed my feelings about eating, or food, or my body, or my self. One of the first used 'cures' for anorexia in the late nineteenth century

Don't worry about your body.
It isn't as small as it once was,
But honestly, the world needs more of you.

– Clementine Von Radics

was wrapping the patient in cotton wool and forcing her to eat, if she gained weight, she was cured. I wrapped up all my pain in cotton wool and I ate. I wasn't cured.

I wish so badly that there had been someone at that time to tell me that it was okay. That it wasn't supposed to all go away when the hand settled higher on the scale. That all the pain I'd felt had cut deeper than I realised it had, and there's nothing shameful about that. There should be no embarrassment, no need for denial. Acknowledging all the parts that are hurting doesn't mean that you aren't healing, too.

If you're in recovery and reading this right now, I want you to know that it's okay to feel that pain. You do not have to put on a costume every day and pretend that it's all fine if it isn't. You don't have to convince yourself that you're recovered if you don't feel it, no matter how long it's been. You are not a failure if your body is changing faster than your mind and it's really fucking scary. You are a person fighting the hardest fight of their life. Don't let anybody invalidate that or make you feel like you have to hide your pain away for their comfort. Be kind to yourself. Be patient with yourself. And keep going. I believe in you.

STOP READING

Is recovery possible?

When I hit my physical rock bottom I was admitted to hospital. I don't remember much about the series of events that led to the decision, but I remember the day I went. I remember the emergency consultation with my therapist, hearing his words float through the thick air around me and jar against the fishbowl I was living under, explaining that I'd become a danger to myself and that my life was at risk.

I remember having to walk the 200 metres from his office to the car, I could feel my veins pressing against my skin, my heartbeat slowing to a crawl as I dragged myself down the quickly fading pavement. It was the first time in all those months that I genuinely believed that I might die, right there on that pavement on my way to the hospital. It felt as if my body had finally decided to give up.

I entered the hospital in a fog, I must have been taken to the children's ward in a wheelchair. I'm not sure what was happening outside of my mind but I remember anorexia mustering up the energy to tell me that I needed to burn more calories before I got there. I was taken to a small, stark room where I was asked to change and step on the scale.

I don't know what the hospital scales said, but I know what the bathroom scales at home had said the day before, the third, fourth, fifth time I'd weighed myself that day: four stone eight; 64 pounds. I'd thought standing over them that I probably only needed to lose another seven pounds or so. It didn't occur to me that it would never be enough.

After that I was sat on a plastic chair in the corner and jolted back into the world by the sandpaper sensation of a tube scraping down my dry, voiceless throat. Just until I started eating, the nurse said. I was taken to my bed while I waited in terror for my liquid calories to be fitted.

I stayed up all night sure that I could feel it pouring into my stomach, instantly turning into lumps of fat on my legs and arms. I was told the next day that I was only given 200 calories, slowly dripped in over the course of 10 hours, nothing that I possibly could have felt. I didn't believe them. I spent the next night throwing myself around in my bed, crying out like a wounded animal. A nurse came over and snapped that I had to stop because I was scaring the other children.

During the day, I did the school work I'd insisted that I was well enough to keep up with. I made project portfolios and read entire science books. I was getting straight As throughout my whole illness, despite not having attended a lesson in months. I thought that if I could prove that I hadn't lost my concentration or dedication then there would be no reason that I couldn't go back. The staff didn't expect that a girl who'd nearly starved herself to death would be analysing Shakespeare and memorising scientific formulae.

I spent hours coming up with logical arguments why I needed the tube to be taken out – I don't know now what logic that could have been but if any of the nurses left themselves open to questioning I was ready to wear them down with debate. I got a reputation for being difficult. I pretended to sleep and overheard conversations about me needing to be in a specialised eating disorder unit, not here. I glimpsed my notes where it said I was deceptive and cruel. And I was – these people were all trying to make me fat, trying to make me gain all the weight I'd worked so hard to lose. I fought back in all the ways anorexia taught me to. Sharp-tongued words and dangerous secrecy.

Everyone was in disbelief when I still wasn't gaining any weight. They hadn't figured out that I was going to the bathroom three times a day to do star jumps, sit-ups, and hold planks for five minutes at a time. The floor in the bathroom smelt of disinfectant and salt. It was grey with tiny sparkles that swirled round your vision if you stared for long enough. There was a mirror above the sink but I don't remember ever seeing my reflection in it, only the visions in my mind of my swelling stomach and wobbling thighs. When I started feeling like I was going to die again I stopped my bathroom workouts; I could barely lift my limbs in and out of bed to sit at the window and watch the grey British autumn go by.

Everything I consumed became a bargaining move. If I eat this potato, I need less liquid feed tonight. If I drink half of this juice, I get to walk down the hallway once. Getting rid of the tube became my main goal, it made my throat sore and it took my autonomy away. I started eating again on the promise that they would take it out, and I kept eating when I realised that it was the only way I was getting out. I told myself that I could always lose the weight again once I left.

START 🎀 READING

One day in the hospital my least favourite nurse was on duty; she always watched me like a hawk while I ate. That lunchtime, in an attempt at conversation, she said that I would never fully recover. She told me that I would struggle with eating for the rest of my life and that I would just have to learn how to push through it.

She probably thought she was handing me a helpful piece of recovery wisdom, but I think she misunderstood it herself. What she was supposed to say is that eating disorders become more manageable over time but may never go away completely, that they'll always require conscious effort to fight against and can resurface in difficult times. Instead she made it sound like I would have a panic attack every time I was presented with a meal and live in agony for the rest of eternity – not helpful.

Just like many alcoholics consider themselves to be forever 'recovering', a lot of people who've experienced eating disorders identify in the same way. They believe that recovery is a lifelong battle. It's not necessarily an eternal struggle, as my nurse so gloomily put it, but it is a conscious effort, a daily reassertion of the strength it takes to recover. A lot of people take comfort in the idea of recovering for life, it certainly does justice to how hard breaking free from an eating disorder is, and reassures people whose struggle lasts for years, decades, or even lifetimes.

But I think it's dangerous to tell people who've only just started recovery that they'll never reach the other side, or even that there is no other side. As I was lying in that hospital bed, finally feeling a glimmer of strength as I managed to eat two or three pieces of food each day, being told that I would never recover shattered the little hope I had. Why even bother starting to fight the hardest battle of my life, if there was no chance that I could win?

It's hard to even imagine what full recovery means in a culture where disordered eating is considered normal and harmless anyway. The person who's pronounced recovered goes right back to living in a world where obsessing over calories is commonplace and burning off the food you eat is encouraged. After using so much of their inner strength to quiet the voice of their eating disorder, they re-enter a reality where those familiar words are splashed across magazine covers and overheard in female changing rooms where women tear their reflections to pieces and vow to eat less and less. Is recovery possible in that setting? Or is the best-case scenario that the eating disorder simply becomes less extreme and learns to camouflage itself in the values of self-hatred and restriction that are still totally accepted in our society?

That's where body positivity comes in. I was diagnostically 'recovered' for over five years before I found body positivity. In that time, I didn't have any counselling, I didn't learn about eating disorders or reflect on my experience. I simply tried to distance myself as much as possible from that time in my life. I pretended that girl wasn't even me. I starved, I binged, I exercised until I passed out, I spent every, single, night, crying my eyes out over my disgusting, fat body.

I thought that was what my life would look like for ever. I thought that was as good as recovery gets. And then along came body positivity. It barged in with its facts and figures, with reasons why we hate our bodies and explanations of how we got here. It taught me about diet culture and being a woman. It told me, for the first time in those five years, that what had happened wasn't my fault. It let me explore those days, navigate that pain, and reclaim my experience as my own.

Of course, body positivity isn't going to cure every eating disorder in the world, some eating disorders don't stem from body-image issues at all. But it needs to be taken seriously as part of a comprehensive treatment plan for anyone in recovery. The deepest discussion on body image I ever encountered in my anorexia treatment was my middle-aged male therapist asking me which celebrity's figure I was trying to obtain by losing all this weight. I replied nobody's, and that was that. It took me finding body positivity on my own, five years later, to realise that it was what I needed all along, way before my eating disorder even began to develop.

I've said in the past that body positivity saved my life, and I mean it. If I hadn't have stumbled upon it when I did I would have kept popping multiple diet pills each morning, working out for countless hours a day, and living on so little food until either my physical health or mental health gave up. Either way, I was on a slippery slope back to that hospital bed. Back to that disinfectant-smelling floor. Back to not seeing myself clearly in that bathroom mirror. Body positivity saved me from that, and allowed me to finally, fully, recover.

Whether someone chooses to identify as recovering or recovered is a matter of what helps them the most; both are valid and neither should be discredited – no one person owns the rights to eating disorders or gets to decide how everyone else feels. But to the question of whether it's possible to recover, my answer goes something like this: fuck yes.

It is possible for all of us. It is possible to banish the voice of your eating disorder. It is possible to heal your relationship with food. It is possible to eat without guilt or fear. It is possible to accept your body however recovery has made it look. It is possible to overcome your addiction to exercise. It is possible to leave behind the urges to binge or purge. It is possible to live your life without having to count each bite, each pound, each minute until the next meal or workout or weigh-in.

It's possible to reach a point when the pain from those days doesn't hover over everything you do. One day you might stop and realise that it's been a while since you even thought about that time. And when you do think about it, you know that those demons don't have the power to tear you apart any more. It is possible to recover.

Three years ago, I found body positivity. And it has been exactly three years since I've cried about the state of my body. Three years since I've restricted, over-exercised, or weighed myself. Three years free from disordered thoughts or behaviours. Three years without any struggle over food. I'm not arrogant enough to think that that could never change. Nobody can predict their mental health for ever, or know what might creep up on them in the future. But I know that right now I am recovered. I am free. If only that nurse could see me now.

5 WAYS TO HELP A LOVED ONE WITH AN EATING DISORDER

1. Be patient. I know how frustrating it is to feel power-less when someone you love is hurting, but it's important to remember that this isn't something that they chose. It isn't something that can be easily over-come, either. Things that seem simple and insignificant to you can feel like the most terrifying things in the world to them. So try to be patient, even when you don't understand.

2. Listen if they're willing to talk. And leave all of your preconceptions about eating disorders behind. Let them know that you will listen without judgement and that'll you'll always be there for them.

3. Do what you can to understand – research, read, use the resources at the end of this chapter. There is so much information about eating disorders out there, even now I stumble across things that I wish someone could have told me back then. Remember to be wary of taking everything you read as fact, every eating disorder is different, and the best way to find out whether something you've read applies to your loved one is by talking to them about it.

4. Make sure they know that you believe in them. Unrelentingly. Even if the odds are against them. My dad always used to say that he had no doubt that I would pull through, even when everyone else had lost hope. He said that he knew me well enough to know that I would do it, and he never stopped reminding me what I was capable of.

5. And most importantly, keep reminding them of who they are underneath the eating disorder. Talk about your memories together and how much you want to

> make more. Talk about your shared passions, even if they seem to have lost them now. Let them know all of the amazing things about them that have nothing to do with food or appearance. One of the most devastating parts of having an eating disorder is losing sight of the person you once were — don't let them lose sight of themselves.

Thank you to my brother, who did his best to bring me back to who I was, and who helped me forge the new version of me when the old one just didn't fit any more. Thank you to my mum, who sacrificed so much time and energy to make sure that I never felt like I was alone. Thank you to my sister, for never seeing me any differently. And to all of my friends who stuck around, tried to understand, and ate cookie dough and ice-cream with me to show me that it was okay to eat. Most of all, thank you to my dad, who taught me how to control the elephant. I wouldn't be here without you.

Eating disorder help

If you or anyone you know is currently struggling with an eating disorder, please know that help is out there. Every eating disorder is valid, no matter your size, age, gender, skin colour or ability. Everyone deserves recovery. Please reach out for the support you need, I promise you that you're not alone.

UK

B-eat (Beating Eating Disorders)

https://www.b-eat.co.uk/

Helpline: 0345 634 1414

Youthline: 0345 634 1414

Anorexia and Bulimia Care

http://www.anorexiabulimiacare.org.uk/

Helpline: 03000 11 12 13

Eating Disorders Support

http://www.eatingdisorderssupport.co.uk/

Helpline: 01494 793223

Seed (Eating Disorders Support Service)

http://www.seedeatingdisorders.org.uk/

Helpline: 01482 718130

MGEDT (Men Get Eating Disorders Too)

http://mengetedstoo.co.uk/

USA

NEDA (National Eating Disorders Association)

https://www.nationaleatingdisorders.org/

Helpline: 1–800-931–2237

ANAD (National Association of Anorexia Nervosa and Associated Disorders)

http://www.anad.org/

Helpline: 630 577 1330

BEDA (Binge-eating Disorder Association)

http://bedaonline.com/

N.A.M.E.D. (The National Association for Males with Eating Disorders)

http://namedinc.org/

T-Feed (Trans Folx Fighting Eating Disorders)

http://www.transfolxfightingeds.org/

Australia

The Butterfly Foundation for Eating Disorders

https://thebutterflyfoundation.org.au/

Helpline: 1800 33 4673

Eating Disorders Victoria

https://www.eatingdisorders.org.au/

Helpline: 1300 550 236

NEDC (National Eating Disorders Collaboration)

http://www.nedc.com.au/

Canada

NEDIC (The National Eating Disorder Information Centre)

http://nedic.ca/

Helpline: 1–866-663–4220

BANA (Bulimia Anorexia Nervosa Association)

http://www.bana.ca/

International

Mirror Mirror

http://www.mirror-mirror.org/

F.E.A.S.T. (Families Empowered and Supporting Treatment of Eating Disorders)

http://www.feast-ed.org/

'BEING OVERWEIGHT IS JUST AS UNHEALTHY AS BEING ANOREXIC'

And Other Lies about Health and Weight

'If shame could cure obesity there wouldn't be a fat woman in the world'

– Susan Wooley, PhD

But what about your health?

Every single day someone who I've never met before on the Internet makes a judgement about my physical health. Some say how great it is that I have a healthy body now. Others say I'll be dead by 40 because I'm obese. Some say what a relief it is that people are realising that curves are healthy. Others say that I'm clearly eating myself to death and need to lose weight to be healthy.

And the strange thing is, I don't recall ever meeting any of those commenters in real life, or spending enough time with them for them to monitor my lifestyle and decide whether it is, in fact, 'healthy'. I definitely haven't had any in-depth conversations with them about my daily nutritional intake or fitness levels. I don't believe any of them have access to my medical records, or have hidden cameras planted in my fridge. So how exactly are they all so sure about my physical health?

Sadly, the comments I receive are child's play compared to what people with bodies bigger than my own experience on a daily basis. These days, a fat person who dares to be visible in the world has to face a constant stream of fatphobic hatred. Fat people are accused of promoting obesity for merely existing in their own bodies. They face harassment ranging from mild abuse to death threats for nothing more than how their body looks.

They're treated as a burden on the economy and a strain on our health-care systems. They're denied competent healthcare and fair opportunity in professional spheres. They're the punch-line of endless jokes. They're seen as walking examples of every moral failing that could be attributed to a person: stupidity, lazi-ness, poor hygiene, lack of control, gluttony and every other tired stereotype that's been forced on other marginalised groups in the past. And ultimately, are seen and treated as less than human, just for being fat.

Fat people are the last remaining group that it's socially accepted, in fact, socially encouraged, to be prejudiced against. Plenty of people who wouldn't dream of bullying someone based on the colour of their skin or their level of physical ability will be the first to crack a fat joke and revel in their moral superiority.

In the conversation about equal rights, size discrimination gets left out, and fat people remain reviled and ostracised in our culture. Why? Because they're unhealthy. Because they are wil-fully and knowingly destroying their physical health by refusing to lose weight and change their outside appearance. At least that's what the headlines have taught us.

Unless you've been living in a media vacuum for decades you'll be well aware that obesity is killing us all. Fatness is to blame for every problem in society, and what Kate Harding and Marianne Kirby have dubbed 'THE OBESITY CRISIS BOOGA BOOGA BOOGA' has been firmly planted in all of our minds as public health threat number one.

On the other hand, physical health and wellness (or at least the appearance of it) has become the epitome of human achieve-ment; it's what we're all supposed to strive for and use to measure our value as people. And according to the rules of the health game, a single factor is sufficient in deciding whether someone is winning or losing: their weight. Thin is healthy; fat isn't. End of story.

What every one of these anti-fat messages add up to is a culture that is well and truly living in fear of fat. And no matter what size you are, you will feel that fear. If living in a body that doesn't fit the ideal image of beauty isn't enough to scare you into the next diet, being told over and over that your body fat will kill you is sure to do the trick.

The war on fat has been so over-inflated, and so drenched in scaremongering rhetoric, that it isn't just people whose weight falls in the upper end of the BMI (a.k.a Bullshit Made-up Irrelevant) categories feeling the fear, it's all of us. We've been led to believe that even the slightest bit of jiggle on our bodies is a sign of disease. We see our own harmless flesh as a toxic parasite pushing us towards certain death. How are any of us supposed to see our bodies as anything other than dangerous and disgusting in a culture that demonises fat to this extent?

And I hear you – health is important, right? I'm definitely not here to tell anyone that taking care of their physical health shouldn't be a priority, if that's what they feel is best for them. But what I am here to tell you is that health is so much more than the one-dimensional image we've been given by the media to aspire to.

The relationship between health and weight is not what we think it is, and the assumptions we currently hold are hurting us all, fat, thin, and every size in between. And lastly – whatever we might believe about size, fitness, weight and health, doesn't really matter when it comes to body positivity. Because physical health is not a requirement for self-love, respect or to be treated with basic human dignity. Those are things that we all deserve, regardless of how our bodies look, or how our bodies function.

I'm not a scientist or an academic researcher, nor do you have to be to recognise that there is something seriously wrong with how our culture currently treats fatness. Not only is it wrong on a moral level, but it's wrong on a factual level too, and there are plenty of resources out there that can show you that much better than I can (check the book list at the back!).

What I'm going to do is share some of the things that made me think about health and weight in a totally different way, and freed me from the fear that we're being force-fed every day. If there's one thing that I want you to keep in mind going through this chapter, it's this: self-hatred isn't healthy at any size.

Weight ≠ health

When I was about a year into recovery from anorexia I started taking birth control. I went to the three-month check-up with no problems to report, all I needed was a repeat prescription. The nurse asked me if I was a smoker, took my blood pressure, and of course, weighed me. I wasn't yet brave enough to request not to be told my weight, like I do now.

I sat back down next to her desk and watched her type the numbers into the system, anxious to leave and start planning the party I was having the next week. Then, with my medical history laid out on the screen in front of her, she turned to me and said 'it would be best if you could lose a few pounds, just to get you back within the healthy range', tilting her head and nodding at me knowingly.

I was three pounds over the cut-off point for the 'normal' BMI category, and by medical standards, overweight. Eighteen months earlier I'd been confined to a hospital bed and my parents were warned that it could be a matter of hours before my organs started failing from the starvation. Those three pounds must have been seriously hazardous for my health, for a medical professional to recommend that a recently recovering anorexic go on a diet. Those three pounds must have been far more dangerous than the risk of my mental health deteriorating again and me falling back into a complete relapse. Those three pounds must have literally been killing me!

There it was, straight from the people who are paid to take care of our health: being overweight is just as unhealthy as being anorexic (something that I'm frequently told by Internet trolls who care oh-so-much about my well-being). Unfortunately, that nurse is a perfect example of just how unhealthy we now believe fat to be – even a few extra pounds could kill you faster than an eating disorder will.

So what is the truth about health and weight? It's a topic that is so much more complex than cutting every single person on the planet into a handful of arbitrarily designed BMI groups and painting them all with the same health brush. But one thing is clear: it's definitely not what mainstream media has made it out to be. Let's start with the simple fact that you cannot tell how healthy a person is just by looking at them. There are people who are fat and healthy, and there are people who are thin and unhealthy.

BELLY LOVE TIP #3

ROLL WITH THE GODDESSES
Remember *The Crouching Aphrodite* sculpture whose belly rolls made her the ultimate figure of female beauty? Go find her, and all the other artworks from times gone by that capture the wonder of a rippling mid-section. Get postcards of them and stick them on your mirror – better yet, create a whole gallery of belly love. Find all the pictures you can of tummies in all shapes and sizes and look at them often. The more beautiful, rolling bellies you see, the less you'll see yours as a problem.

I know fat babes who are hardcore athletes. I know fat babes who run marathons. I know fat babes who can twist and contort their bodies into so many different yoga positions that anyone watching is left spellbound. I know fat babes who are vegetable-loving vegans, and guess what? They're still fat, despite their physical fitness or nutritional intake. It's almost as if their bodies are just meant to be that size ... bizarre concept, I know.

On the other hand, I'm sure we all know someone who eats a junk-food diet, never exercises, and stays thin no matter what. Yet we refuse to believe that the opposite could be true, that you can be fat, eat well, exercise, and stay fat. Most people think that if you're thin (but not too thin), you are healthy without question, even if you smoke, drink, do drugs, eat a nutritionally poor diet and rarely leave the sofa. Clearly, for a lot of people looking healthy is what counts, rather than actually being healthy. Then again, how can the countless news headlines screaming about the obesity crisis be wrong?

It seems like every day a new study about the hundreds of thousands of people dying from obesity gets splashed across another front page. The articles are almost always accompanied by what Charlotte Cooper has termed a 'Headless Fatty' image – a picture of a fat body cropped from the neck up, symbolically stripped of their voice, their thoughts, and their humanity.

No matter how extreme the numbers or exaggerated the title of the piece is, the 'facts' presented are rarely questioned because they fit perfectly with what we already believe is true. Somewhere along the line the theory that being fat carries health risks got turned into immutable truth, and every new piece of information that backs that up is taken as gospel. Why bother questioning something that is so deeply ingrained into our societal belief system? The problem is that we should be questioning it, all of it, and this is what we should be asking:

Who funded the study?

If you've read this far then you already know from the diet industry chapter that money talks, and when it comes to how we've been taught to see fat bodies, cash influences everything. If we look at the scientific research on weight and health, the same story applies.

Obesity research is almost solely funded by the weight-loss industry. Conducting studies is expensive, and government funds don't even begin to cover them all. Luckily, our good friend the diet industry is there to give millions to studies aiming to prove that fat is killing us, meaning that in turn their sales go through the roof as we all run, terrified, to our nearest weight-loss group.

Conflicts of interest are everywhere in the realm of obesity research, and often the very people we trust the most to tell us the truth about fat have a vested interest in twisting the truth. If you're not sure what a conflict of interest is, allow me to illustrate with an example about cheese (best sentence of the book so far, right?).

Not long ago I saw an article floating around my social-media feed with a title claiming a study has proven that full-fat cheddar is beneficial to our health. Now, I love full-fat cheddar, and it would be really handy if the amount of it I eat was, in fact, helping me live longer. As it turns out, the entire study had been funded by the dairy industry, i.e., the people who stand to make a lot of money if we all start believing that cheese is good for us and eating even more of it. And in a lot of people's eyes, that puts a pretty big dent in how trustworthy the information being presented is.

Medical research on obesity is littered with examples just like that one. Sometimes it's studies funded by diet companies, some-times it's obesity experts who own weight-loss centres on the side, patents for diet drugs or shares in diet companies. In other words, a lot of obesity experts are far from impartial, and they make a whole lot of cash from the world believing that fatness is as dangerous as we do.

A perfect example of this lies in the holy grail of health myths: the BMI chart. Not too long ago the cut-off point for women to be in the 'normal' weight range was up to 27.3 on the BMI chart. These days, the cut-off point is 25, what happened?

In 1997, the National Institutes of Health in the US brought together a task force of nine medical experts to decide whether the BMI categories should be lowered. Despite a lack of evidence that those with weights in the upper end of the categories experienced more illness or decreased life expectancy, the experts went ahead and lowered the cut-off points anyway.

The day before the ruling, 58 million Americans were considered overweight or obese by BMI standards, the day after the ruling that number jumped to 97 million. Which means that millions of people in the US had become medically fat overnight, without gaining a single pound.

So why were the cut-off points lowered? Two journalists from Newark-based *The Star-Ledger* shed some light on the question when they uncovered some serious conflicts of interest: 'Eight of the nine members of the National Institutes of Health task force on prevention and treatment of obesity have ties to the weight-loss industry, either as consultants to pharmaceutical companies, recipients of research money from them, or advisors to for-profit groups such as Weight Watchers'.[61]

Eight of the nine experts being entrusted to decide whether more people should be classified as overweight were profiting from people thinking they were overweight, and believing that their health was at risk because of it. You cannot make this shit up.

Marilyn Wann cleverly recognised that the new cut-off points meant that a woman who's five foot four tall and weighs 145 pounds is now overweight, and at the time, the average American woman (who the diet industry targets) was five foot four and weighed 144 pounds. In her words 'it must be nice, getting 30 million new customers in one day. The tobacco industry must be terribly jealous'.

I know this all sounds a bit like a conspiracy theory; I thought the same when I first started reading about it, but the examples of this happening are endless. Authors like Laura Fraser and Harriet Brown have filled entire chapters with evidence of how conflicts of interest within obesity research sway results and bend the truth.

There are tales of doctors endorsing diet plans and failing to disclose that they owned part of the diet company (the Cambridge Diet, for example, was a 320-calorie-a-day liquid-protein diet endorsed by Dr Alan Howard. At the time 58 people were already known to have died on liquid-protein diets, but Howard still promoted it without revealing that he had a huge financial stake in the company).[62]

There are the world's most well-known authorities on obesity treatment being sponsored by fistfuls of pharmaceutical companies peddling the latest dangerous diet pills.[63] Those pharmaceutical companies aren't above paying medical experts to sign off on research in support of pills such as Fen-Phen either[64] (yep, the one I mentioned on page 66 that killed people, yep, obesity experts supported it, and yep, got paid for doing so).

Even the 2013 ruling of the American Medical Association to classify obesity as a disease in and of itself reeks of vested interest – the AMA's own research committee presented extensive evidence against recognising obesity as a disease, but the AMA passed the ruling anyway.[65] Which probably has something to do with how much money medical professionals can make prescribing treatments for the disease of fatness. Diet plans, bariatric surgery ... who cares if the treatment doesn't actually work; if we're fighting against a disease, then it must be worth it!

There is a big problem with this picture. It means that the people we get most of our information on health and weight from are far less reliable than we think they are. Most of them will deny that conflicts of interest have any effect on the research, or the results. They might really believe it too, that they're only telling us the absolute truth.

But with this much money and power at play, the absolute truth can be twisted in whatever direction the cash-flow points.

Spend enough on studies that say that cheese is good for our health, while cultivating a society that shames, bullies and discriminates against people who don't eat dairy, and soon enough we'll all be running for the cheddar.

The next time you see a study supposedly proving the horrific health consequences of fatness, or a diet plan that's been 'approved by medical professionals!', see if you can sniff out the financial ties. Follow the money, be suspicious, and don't believe everything you read in the news.

Is fatness really the cause?

Have you ever noticed how all those headlines screaming that 'obesity CAUSES death' make it sound as if our fat is literally morphing like Flubber in the night and trying to strangle us as we sleep? As if our weight, and our weight alone, is directly responsible for killing us? Making it sound that way does produce a much snappier title than the truth: that obesity is often correlated with certain diseases, but that no direct causal link has been established.

All correlation really means is that there is a link between two things. In this case, there is a pattern where people whose weights fall into the higher end of the BMI chart seem to contract certain diseases more often than those whose weights are lower.

Because weight is one very obvious thing that the people who contract those diseases more often have in common, it's easy to point the finger at the scale and shout that excess weight causes disease. But just because the pattern is there, doesn't necessarily mean that one thing directly causes the other. Correlation does not equal causation. A lot of the time there are far more factors at play than what meets the eye.

A common example of this is lung cancer: there is a pattern where people with yellow teeth contract lung cancer more often than people whose teeth are whiter. If we take the same line of reasoning that gets applied to obesity, this must mean that yellow teeth cause lung cancer. We know that that's not true, and that there's a third thing that causes both: smoking.

The physical attribute of yellow teeth and the disease of lung cancer are correlated, but one doesn't cause the other. In the same way, the physical attribute of fatness and various diseases are correlated, but since our fat cells aren't literally toxic, we should be looking for the third thing that's actually the causal factor.

So what's the third thing? Kate Harding and Marianne Kirby have some options in their book *Lessons From The Fat-O-Sphere*:

> It could be a lack of physical activity. It could be a poor diet.* It could be the stress of constantly getting ostracised and berated for being fat. It could be a history of weight-cycling because we're so often told that one more diet will be the key to permanent thinness.

*Remember that neither of those things apply exclusively to fat people, or apply to every fat person!

The reason why this causation/correlation stuff is important is because the media just doesn't seem to understand the difference. Every time obesity gets blamed for ruining our health, the real culprits go unnoticed, and fatphobic prejudice gets reinforced instead. We get obesity tunnel vision, thinking that weight loss by any means necessary is the key to health, when actually it's healthful behaviours that the health conversation should be focusing on, regardless of size.

Is this straight up made up?

Did you know that some of the most widely held 'truths' about health and weight are just plain made up? And that even when some 'facts' about obesity turn out to be completely inaccurate, they're still printed in news media and stuck in our minds as truth? I thought we could take a look at some of the most ridiculous facts we've been fed about fatness that actually aren't true at all. Because who doesn't love catching diet-industry profiteers with pie on their face?

If you've ever tried to engage an Internet troll in a discussion about fat acceptance then you've probably witnessed something like this: 'STOP SAYING FAT IS OKAY DON'T YOU KNOW OBESITY KILLS 400,000 PEOPLE EVERY YEAR YOU DISGUSTING FAT WHALE'. Now, whales are majestic and graceful rulers of the sea so being compared to them is definitely not an insult. But it's the other part that gets me, the 400,000 deaths from obesity part that still pops up all the damn time despite being debunked over 10 years ago. The following information is largely from Abigail C. Saguy's brilliant book, *What's Wrong with Fat?*

The actual study the trolls are referring to was conducted by the Centers for Disease Control and Prevention (CDC) and published in 2004. The study attributed 385,000 (revised to 365,000 the following year) excess deaths to overweight and obesity in 2000. As it turns out, the study was seriously flawed on many levels, and reportedly failed to properly apply a statistical correction factor to the data used.

Plus the media missed the causation/correlation memo and instead of focusing on a lack of healthful behaviours as potential causal factors in mortality rates, just went straight for the FAT KILLS EVERYONE angle that sells so well. Before we knew it, we had a new home truth about obesity: 400,000 fat Americans eat themselves to death every year. Pretty shocking, and also highly inaccurate.

A second CDC study published in 2005 found that the number of excess deaths associated with being overweight in 2000 was actually just under 26,000 (112,000 for obesity, concentrated mainly in BMIs over 35, and 86,000 fewer deaths for overweight, as in overweight actually helped people live longer!).

The CDC released a statement revising their estimations to fit with those of the second study, stubbornly adding that overweight is still a health risk (despite the evidence suggesting otherwise). And if you're thinking that 26,000 excess deaths associated with overweight and obesity seems like a lot, bear in mind that in the same year 34,000 deaths were associated with underweight – where are the screaming headlines about that?

Saguy goes on to explore why the 400,000 figure was so widely accepted and faced far less scrutiny than the revised 26,000 figure. Despite being such an extreme number, it fit perfectly with what we already believe to be true about fat, which is why it spread so far and got taken as fact so easily. It was just another piece of the fat-demonising picture our culture has painted, why question it? The lower number however, was questioned, and doubted, and picked apart, despite the CDC itself crowning it the better study.

Of course it helps that 400,000 KILLED BY THEIR OWN FAT makes a really snappy newspaper headline. It really does grab people's attention and get that shock-horror reaction journalists crave. They could have made it even better by throwing in some stuff about lasers, unicorns or aliens too. I'm only half-joking – some of the headlines about the obesity epidemic really have been that ridiculous, and that overblown.

Remember when everybody and their grandma were saying that thanks to obesity, children of this generation will be the first who don't live as long as their parents? It was a statement that spread like wildfire, being recited by news media, medical professionals, respected authorities on health, celebrities; even Michelle Obama and the former US Surgeon General got in on the action.

Soon enough, this shocking prediction became fact in the general public's mind. It even mutated, so that some people believed that parents would literally outlive their children and see them die because of obesity. This surely must have been based on some rock-solid evidence, considering the amount of fear that was put into the public over it?

One of the main sources responsible for first making the claim reportedly admitted that it was only 'based on intuition'.[66] Another, who authored a whole study adding fuel to the fire is quoted as saying that their predictions were just 'back-of-the-envelope, plausible scenarios' and 'were never meant to be portrayed as precise'.[67] In other words, they made it up. One of the most commonly repeated 'facts' about obesity is made up. It's also well-documented that life expectancy rates in the US and UK continue to rise, which means that while obesity has supposedly been killing us all, we've been living longer than ever … huh.

Shocking headlines about fat are gold dust in journalism. Sensationalism sells. And obesity experts use the same tactics to get people on board with their message, using the language of crisis, doom and disaster to evoke panic in the public (even calling obesity an epidemic is a misuse of a term that used to be reserved for actual disease running rampant in a society). Take a look at some of the most blatant examples of fear-mongering that have been used in the obesity debate:

- '"Tsunami of obesity" threatens all regions of world'[68] is one headline echoing a statement from an expert who compared obesity to 'a massive tsunami heading towards the shore-line'.[69] Nothing like the threat of natural disaster to get us all running around like headless chickens.

- 'Unless we do something about it, the magnitude of the dilemma will dwarf 9-11 or any other terrorist attempt'[70] is a statement made by a former US Surgeon General who called obesity 'the terror within'. Not only do comparisons to war and terrorism scare us senseless, they give us a righteous sense of duty to 'fight the flab' and 'battle the bulge' (but nobody's telling the majority of diet soldiers that there's a 95 per cent chance they'll lose the battle).

- 'There's a rapidly spreading epidemic afflicting all regions of the country, all ethnic and economic groups, and all ages. Children are especially vulnerable … It's not SARS, West Nile virus, or Lyme disease. It's obesity'.[71] Or in other words 'NOBODY is safe, our CHILDREN are going to DIE from a killer DISEASE worse than any other DISEASE. Did I mention it's a DANGEROUS. DEADLY. DISEASE!'

Infection, plague, doom and disaster. It's understandable why concerned trolls barge into fat positive spaces and fight against them so zealously, they really do believe that they're helping to save the human race from certain death by fatness.

With this much fear-fuelled anti-fat rhetoric flying around, how is anyone supposed to form an opinion that isn't rooted in terror and misinformation? Even if you do stumble across the idea that the obesity epidemic isn't actually all it's cracked up to be, how could you possibly take the argument seriously? We're at war, for Christ's sake!

There's something very important about this whole thing that far too few people realise. That this 'war on fat' isn't one against inanimate objects. We're not fighting independent adipose cells or advancing on a lifeless enemy. Make no mistake, this is a war against fat people. People with feelings, and humanity, and value, regardless of the size of the body they inhabit.

For those who've been influenced most by the fatphobic narrative, the goal isn't to eradicate a disease, but to eradicate an entire group of human beings based purely on what they look like. The whole issue of fatness is so wrapped up in health and morality clauses that we don't see this for what it truly is: a witch hunt. A justification for the last remaining socially acceptable prejudice. And no matter what we believe about weight and health, we should all be very, very concerned about the lengths our society has taken to dehumanise half its population for not conforming to the rules that have been set.

So what's the other side of the story?

I hear you! So far it probably seems like I've trashed a lot of the conventional wisdom on health and weight without giving you any kind of alternative. How are you supposed to stop believing that your fat is a death sentence without any proof to the contrary? Luckily, there is proof. It's just that most people never hear about it because of the whole money/fatphobia/sensationalism thing.

A sensible headline about health being far more complicated than how much we weigh isn't going to get a lot of attention. Not to mention that some very powerful people stand to lose a lot if we stop buying into their media scare tactics and weight-loss schemes. But I think it's only fair that we know there's another side to the obesity story. That way we can make up our own minds and do what we wish with our own bodies. After all, our bodies and our health are our business, and nobody else's.

Believe it or not, there is no consensus within the scientific community that fatness is always bad for our health. In fact, there are studies by respectable figures within obesity research that suggest fatness can even sometimes be good for our health. I know that goes against every message the mainstream media feeds us about weight, so let's take a look.

In 2013, the *Journal of the American Medical Association* published the results of a study that aimed to find, once and for all, the link between mortality rates and BMI[72] (a.k.a is our fat really killing us?). The study was led by Katherine Flegal, an epidemiologist at the National Center for Health Statistics, and her colleagues.

After analysing 97 studies of mortality rates and BMI that included almost 3 million people, Flegal found what's known as a 'U-shaped curve'. At the top ends of the curve, where death rates were the highest, are people whose BMIs categorise them as either severely underweight, or severely obese. At the lowest point of the curve, where death rates are the lowest, are people whose BMI falls within the 'overweight' category. Meaning that statistically, people who are overweight according to BMI had the lowest risk of death.

Following the U-shaped curve, people whose BMI fell within the 'mildly obese' category had no higher risk of death than people within the 'normal' category. The increased mortality rate came at the extremes, either side. This wasn't the first discovery of this pattern either, Flegal had previously found it in 2005, and others had noticed it as early as the 1980s.[73] Flegal concluded that 'Grade 1 obesity overall was not associated with higher mortality, and overweight was associated with significantly lower all-cause mortality'.

You can probably guess how some diet-industry-affiliated obesity experts reacted when Flegal's research was released. It. Kicked. Off. Other prominent researchers scrambled to discredit the work. One was so invested in tearing it down that he organised an entire symposium just to convince people that the research was wrong. He's also quoted as calling the study 'a pile of rubbish' that 'no one should waste their time reading' – those are some pretty strong feelings for someone whose career requires a neutral analysis of the facts in order to find the truth. It's almost as if he had a vested interest in burying the findings.

Harriet Brown documented the backlash in *Body of Truth*, quoting one spokesperson for the UK National Obesity Forum who said 'It's a horrific message to put out. We shouldn't take for granted that we can cancel the gym, that we can eat ourselves to death with black forest gateaux' ... which isn't what Flegal was suggesting at all.

She wasn't suggesting that people gain weight, lose weight, eat more, or eat less. In fact she wasn't suggesting anything; she was just analysing data and showing the results. As she said in an interview, her data are 'not intended to have a message'.[74] They're just the numbers. And unlike many of the people opposing her, she had no conflicts of interest from the diet industry, or any other industry, when undertaking the research.

Another body of research within the obesity debate suggests that fatness is the wrong thing to be focusing on altogether when we think about health. Steven Blair spent years as the Director of Research at The Cooper Institute for Aerobics Research, and has worked on multiple studies showing that it's fitness, not fatness, that counts (and if you're still thinking the two can't exist together, hold on ...).

The Cooper Institute is the home of the largest database of fitness in the world; their Cooper Center Longitudinal Study has been running since 1970 and has collected data on almost

209

100,000 individuals, including their fitness levels, their overall health, and their death rates.

The results of Blair's studies have shown again and again that when it comes to health and longevity, it's better to be physically active and fat, than physically inactive and thin. The evidence shows that 'the death rate for women and men who are thin but unfit is at least twice as high as their obese counterparts who are fit'.[75] In other words, thin doesn't always mean healthy, and fat doesn't always mean unhealthy, but fitness levels do mean something.

You don't have to be the Olympic athlete kind of fit either. Thirty minutes of moderate activity five or more days a week showed a 50 per cent reduction in mortality rates, and importantly, there is no weight loss required in order for health to improve. Blair himself is living proof that no matter how fit you are, some people just aren't meant to be thin: 'I was short, fat and bald when I started running ... after running nearly every day for more than 30 years and covering about 70,000 miles ... I am still short, fat, and bald'.

You can be fit, and fat, and healthy all at the same time, take THAT diet industry! There's also an entire movement called Health at Every Size (HAES), which is dedicated to promoting healthful behaviours like physical activity and nutritious eating habits, without the unnecessary focus on weight as the only indicator of health. A HAES study led by Linda Bacon showed that against traditional methods of dieting, people who focus on healthful behaviours without striving for weight loss keep them up for longer, have higher self-esteem, and benefit from long-term health improvements. Unlike the dieters in the study, who experienced weight-cycling, lower self-esteem, and didn't show any sustained health improvements.[76]

I'm not trying to tell you that Flegal's, Blair's, or anyone else's research is right without question. The reason I'm telling you this is just so that you know another side to the 'obesity epidemic' story exists.

I'm willing to bet that all of us are familiar with the fatness = death argument; we hear about it most days and are constantly

inundated with this study or that research backing up the prejudice and cultural disdain for fat people. We don't hear the other
side. We're not told that the issues are still very much up for debate
and that what we 'know' about obesity isn't solid-gold truth.

There is so much more to health than weight and weight
alone. This is just me giving you a heads-up that more information is out there. Whether you choose to go and research it and
come to your own conclusions is up to you, but at the very least
I hope that you stay sceptical, you sniff out the bullshit, and you
stop believing that your fat is trying to strangle you in the night.

The real effect

Has anyone else noticed one glaringly obvious thing that the
war on obesity hasn't done? It hasn't made us any thinner.
Which probably has a lot to do with the fact that the most
commonly prescribed 'cure' for obesity is weight loss through
dieting. And as we've already seen, diets don't work and often
make us fatter in the long run than we were when we started.

But what about health? That's what this war is supposedly all
about, after all. Has our culture's fight against fatness made us
any healthier? I guess that all depends on what your definition
of health is; is it based purely on what can be counted, weighed,
and measured ... or does mental health count too?

Without a doubt, what the war on obesity has created the
most of, is stigma. It has turned fatness into the ultimate moral
sin, and given the public a medically motivated reason to bully,
harass and discriminate against someone based on their size. The
amount of hatred this war has inspired is disgusting. And the
effect it's had on any person who falls outside the rigid definition
of 'healthy-looking' cannot be underestimated. That effect might
not be something that shows on a bathroom scale or becomes the
subject of nationwide campaigns, but it is there, bubbling under
the surface and destroying people. In our effort to fight for health,
we seem to have forgotten that mental health is health, too.

If you are currently living in a fat body, you'll know all too well how much hurt this war has caused. You'll know what it's like to face an endless stream of slurs, dirty glances, judgemental comments, threats and abuse, just for daring to leave the house and exist in the world. You'll know how it feels to have every morsel you eat and every piece of clothing you wear scrutinised and opened up for public debate. You've probably felt the fear of hearing a nearby camera click and wondered whether your image is going to be plastered online for people with small minds to find humour in your humiliation.[77]

You'll know what it's like to live in a world that literally will not accommodate you: aeroplane seats,[78] restaurant chairs, cinema rows, theme park rides, medical equipment, public transportation and more. You will have felt the weight of being blamed for every political, economic and social problem that you could possibly be blamed for. You might have personally experienced the type of workplace discrimination that leads to fat people being overlooked for professional opportunities[79] and being paid less than their thinner colleagues.[80]

You've probably been affected by society telling you that you're unworthy of romantic or sexual relationships, while simultaneously being fetishised and told that anyone who's attracted to you has some kind of sick perversion. You'll know how it feels to not find your size in most clothing stores, and to have to pay triple the amount in specialised stores that carry it.

You'll know what it's like to look at the mainstream media and only ever see bodies like yours as 'before' pictures, headless targets of hatred, or punchlines to tasteless jokes. You will have experienced a level of prejudice that's thought to be absolutely unacceptable when aimed at any other marginalised group, and you've probably internalised a lot of shame from people refusing to recognise that prejudice and blaming you for your own mistreatment. For all that and more, I am so, so sorry.

I could never accurately depict all that you've experienced, my body grants me an amount of thin privilege that means I'll probably never have to endure what you've endured. And

I can't even begin to imagine the toll it has taken on your mental health.

If you are reading this and you are not currently living in a fat body, listen up. People of all sizes experience body-image issues. Every single person's body-image issues are valid and important. Mentally, the struggles of a thin person can be just as damaging as the struggles of a fat person. But in the outside world, fat people face a different reality than thin- or medium-sized people do, and we need to recognise that. I've spent years hating my body, struggling with eating disorders, and believing that I was too big. But the outside world didn't treat me the same way I treated myself.

Yes, body positivity is for all bodies, but those of us with privilege have to acknowledge it, and recognise that our struggles are not the same. If you have not personally experienced any of the above examples then you are benefiting from thin privilege. That's not to say you haven't been through hell and back hating the size of your body, trust me, I know that you have. But the outside world has not hated you for the size of your body on top of it all.

Recognising that doesn't diminish your experience, but it does let us appreciate the fight that our fat sisters are up against, and help us to be allies in the fight. We have to remember that body positivity is born out of radical fat acceptance, and was first powered by fat, queer women of colour. Only then can we work together to dismantle the roots of our collective body image issues.

Acknowledging the lived experience of fat people in the world shows us one thing loud and clear: this is not about health. When people verbally attack fat bodies out of 'concern' for that person's health, they don't care about health at all. They're just using health as a socially condoned veil for their prejudice. If they really did care they might consider the impact that their hate has on fat people's mental health.

They might realise that humiliation and shame cause people to harm themselves far more often than it causes them to treat themselves well. They might acknowledge, as I asked you to remember at the beginning of this chapter, that self-hatred isn't healthy at any size. They might open their eyes and see that crusading for 'health' while ignoring and hurting people's mental health is a lie. And nothing but a convenient cover for their bigotry.

A war on obesity that teaches people to hate themselves in the name of health is useless. Campaigning for health while ignoring the harm the campaign has inflicted on those who it's supposedly trying to help, is senseless. And aiming to improve people's physical health with methods that actively destroy those people's mental health, is so obviously backwards that I have no idea how people aren't seeing it.

Let's put mental health to the side for a minute and think about whether the war on fat is helping our physical health. We already know that most of the people trying to fight their way out of enemy territory will do so by dieting, and when 95 per cent of them regain any weight lost they'll experience the negative physical effects of yo-yo dieting described in the Lose Weight For Good chapter.

If they realise that dieting isn't enough they might try some of the other dangerous diet industry scams like pills, teas and potions. I'm sure we don't need a recap on how bad those can be for physical health. And if they've internalised enough fatphobia they might just follow up on that thing their doctor keeps mentioning, and pay thousands for someone to cut into their healthy flesh and irreparably damage their organs so that they lose weight.

Bariatric (weight loss) surgery is increasingly common and incredibly dangerous. The adverts featuring carefree, smiling models make it seem like a safe quick fix to all of your health issues, and because people believe that weight loss by any means necessary is good for your health, business is booming. Four hundred and seventy thousand bariatric procedures were performed worldwide in 2013,[81] but the truth about the surgeries are much darker than the ads and even most medical professionals let on (again, money is a big motivator here; bariatric surgeons are some of the highest paid medical professionals in the world and want to sell as many procedures as possible).

Linda Bacon exposes some of the rarely mentioned side effects of weight-loss surgery in *Health at Every Size*, listing a shocking 82 symptoms including lifelong vitamin deficiency, loss of bowel control, consistent vomiting and excruciating pain after eating, hormone imbalances, infection, kidney and liver failure, nerve and brain damage and often, weight regain. Bacon sites further studies that found that 4.6 per cent of bariatric surgery patients died within a year.[82] She argues that weight-loss surgery 'would be more appropriately labelled "high-risk disease-inducing cosmetic surgery" than a health-enhancing procedure'.

Just think about it: we are so convinced that our fat is the problem that we will pay people to cut us open and permanently mutilate perfectly functional organs in order to lose weight. Many patients go into the surgery with no actual health problems (that is, they're metabolically healthy), and come out with lifelong, debilitating health problems. All because they've been convinced that weight is the be all and end all of health. They believe that losing weight by any means will help them lead fuller and healthier lives, and they end up compromising the length and quality of their lives.

Beyond the effects of dieting, dangerous weight-loss products, and bariatric surgery, there's one more major way that the war on obesity is hurting fat people's physical health. That is the fact that our cultural fatphobia is so all encompassing, that it even affects how medical professionals do their jobs. And when the people who are entrusted with our well-being can't see past size, you can sure as hell bet that fat people's health doesn't improve.

Diagnosis: fat

When we go to medical professionals, we're all entitled to respect and proper treatment regardless of how we look. You might think that doctors are able to filter through the anti-fat bullshit the rest of us take in and deliver unbiased care. Think again.

In a society that hates fat this much, there is no such thing as neutral. Medical professionals exist in the same society we do, they're influenced by the same cultural attitude of fatphobia that we all are. They may even be more susceptible to anti-fat prejudice, since they're surrounded by so much information pushing the 'obesity epidemic' agenda in their professional lives.

For a lot of fat people, going to the doctor is hell. Because no matter what issue they've gone in to have checked, the prescription will always be weight loss. Migraines? Lose weight. Depression? Lose weight. Allergic reaction to an insect bite? Lose weight.[83] Those are just a few examples from a blog called First Do No Harm: Real Stories of Fat Prejudice in Health Care. And they aren't the worst ones, by far. When doctors can't see past the fat to the actual person, it isn't just irritating, hurtful or dehumanising, it's dangerous.

Diagnoses of potentially fatal conditions get missed because doctors can't see anything other than weight. The complaints of fat patients are dismissed, symptoms are ignored, and illnesses get worse and worse.

One example comes from Rebecca Hiles, who wrote a blog post that went viral about her lung cancer going undiagnosed for years while medical professionals focused on her weight instead. Every time she sought help for a new symptom, she was given a different diagnosis and told to lose weight – five years later her lung had to be removed (it could have been saved if the cancer had been found all those years ago). In her own words 'My doctors treated my fat, rather than investigating the real reason I was sick and it could've killed me'.[84]

Others stop going to the doctor altogether to avoid the constant stream of condescending lectures and diet recommendations. Several studies have shown that fat women are less likely to attend screenings for breast and cervical cancer. Gynaecological cancer screenings are delayed for reasons including 'disrespectful treatment, embarrassment at being weighed, negative attitudes of providers, unsolicited advice to lose weight, and medical equipment that was too small to be functional'.[85]

Who would want to face that every time they needed to go to the doctor? And this isn't just the experience of an unlucky few – one survey found that 54 per cent of doctors believe that the

NHS should have the right to withhold treatment from patients unless they lose weight.[86]

Another survey of physicians in the US showed that over half thought that their obese patients were 'awkward, unattractive, ugly and noncompliant', and a third even described them as 'weak-willed, sloppy, and lazy'.[87] You know what tends to be really bad for people's health? Not feeling comfortable enough to go to the doctor when they have a medical issue.

Our culture cares sooooo much about the health of fat people, but not enough to give them competent health care or treat them like actual human beings when they seek medical guidance. It's almost as if we don't truly care about their health at all, and 'health' is just a really handy excuse to shame and harass people.

We like to think that if there's anyone who can see beyond the lies about health and weight, it's our doctor. And that's what we all deserve – truthful, unbiased, respectful health care.

We shouldn't simply be seen as walking BMIs. 'Lose weight' shouldn't be the go-to treatment plan for every single complaint. A doctor's office shouldn't be a place of alienation and shame. If the goal of the war on fat really is to make people healthier, making sure that fat people aren't treated as less than human by their health care providers seems like a good place to start, doesn't it?

Fear of fat

We are all living in fear of fat. No matter what size we are, it gets us. If we're fat we live in fear of what our bodies will do to us, or what the world will do to us because of them. If we're thin we live in fear that fatness will creep up on us. If we're in between we feel the fear just as fiercely, and spend our lives chasing weight loss to secure our safety. Ultimately, we all lose.

Teaching people to fear fat is often justified by the health argument – fear acts as motivation to get or stay healthy. But since we know that fat isn't the villain the media makes it out to be, there doesn't seem to be much justification for teaching us to fear our own bodies. Whatever positive effect it's supposed to have had is by far overshadowed by the damage that's been done.

Look around. Look at the devastation that fear has caused. Look how self-hatred has become the norm. Look how diet culture has engulfed us. Look how we hurt ourselves to become the impossible. Look how our mental health suffers. We are living in a world where 81 per cent of 10-year-olds are afraid of being fat, more afraid of being fat than they are of war, cancer, or losing both their parents.[88] We have to take responsibility for how that fear got there, and what it might grow into.

I spent a long time being a walking example of how far that fear can go. I was so terrified of fat that I tried to eradicate every ounce of it from my body, pound by pound. Ask someone with anorexia what their greatest fear is, and they will say becoming fat. Maybe that fear was first intended as misguided motivation to keep people healthy, but like it or not, it's grown into so much more than that.

There is an undeniable connection between the way our culture treats fatness, and the forever rising numbers of people suffering with eating disorders. You cannot separate the war on fat from the war we all launch against ourselves no matter what size we are. All those anti-fat messages have trickled down into our consciousness, and the real effect is clear to see.

We can't instil the fear of fat into a nation and then ignore the consequences of the people who've absorbed it who it wasn't designed for. We can't just say 'don't worry about it, it wasn't meant for you' when a young girl is cutting all fats out of her diet because every day she sees a new front-page headline about how fat is killing us.

We can't ignore that demonising fat means demonising our bodies, no matter what they look like – there's no such thing as a body without any fat, even our brains are 20 per cent fat. And once we see that ever-present part of ourselves as a problem, as ugly, as unhealthy, in comes diet culture to profit from our fear and send our self-esteem spiralling. For millions of us, that's where the eating disorder voice starts to take hold.

Zoom out to the big picture and you'll see that how we're treating fatness isn't benefiting anybody. The picture below shows how it's all connected, and how we can't support one, without supporting a rise in the others.

Let's break it down: the war on fat has been waged because fatness is apparently unhealthy. The weapons that this war has used – shame, scare tactics, fearmongering and dehumanisation – have helped to build a cultural fear of fat that affects us all.

That fear distils into fatphobia; the fear of fat isn't directed at some lifeless cluster of cells, the fear of fat becomes a fear of fat people. Or rather, a disgust for, hatred of, and prejudice against fat people. Once the stereotypes about fat people have been learned, it's all too easy to believe that fatness, in any amount, is ugly. Which is backed up by the media ideals we've been brainwashed by since we were children.

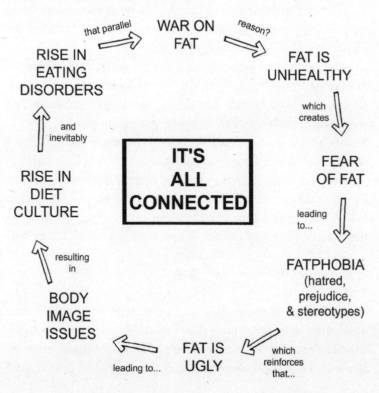

Our body-image issues grow larger, not just rooted in aesthetics but in fear for our health. We go searching for weight-loss solutions in Dietland, leaving with drained bank accounts, lower self-esteem than ever and disordered relationships with food.

For more and more of us every year, those things then form into fully blown eating disorders. And when we want reassurance that the voice of our eating disorder is right, that fat is ugly, dangerous and deadly and that weight loss is the ultimate achievement, all we have to do is turn to the world around us. If there's a war on fat, surely a completely fat-free body is victory. The cycle continues.

It doesn't just go in that order either; all of the steps are linked together in one giant, tangled mess. Whichever way you look at it, the war on fat is contributing to the actual epidemic of eating disorders that just keeps growing. In her book, *Fat Talk Nation: The Human Costs of America's War on Fat*, Susan Greenhalgh uses personal essays to explore how 'the extreme cultural and medical emphasis on getting rid of extra fat at any cost seems to be pushing some people down a slippery slope into full-fledged eating disorders'.

The link is clear to see, but it keeps being overlooked because fatness has been framed as the worst possible thing for our health. Far worse than starvation, obsession, addiction and madness, apparently. Which is why people on the Internet are forever telling me how great it is that I overcame anorexia, but I should probably still lose some weight if I want to be healthy ...

But recovering and embracing my body is the healthiest thing I've ever done; it might not be the kind of health that people believe they can measure from a picture on a screen, but letting go of the fear of fat saved my life. What could be healthier than that?

STOP READING

When I spent that summer in a residential youth psychiatric unit, there was only one other girl who'd been admitted for anorexia nervosa. She was a couple of months into recovery by the time I got there, but I was told that when she first arrived she was 'really anorexic, even worse than you' (way to fuel the competitive side of an anorexic mind).

One day I was sitting on the faded blue sofa in the common room, pretending to watch TV while the usual sharp-edged numbers filled every corner of my mind, and I overheard people talking about her. She'd done something. Something bad.

Those of us with clear records were allowed to borrow razors for the extent of our shower time, and instead of using hers to shave, she carved a word in screaming red letters down her newly softened forearm. FAT.

That girl was so disgusted with her reflection, so terrified of existing in a body covered gently with lifesaving fat cells, that she branded herself forever. Sure, it was by her hand. But it was our culture that moved it. It was everything that girl had been taught in her 14 years about weight, and worth, and food, and beauty, mutated into demons more fearsome than anybody ever told her they could be.

I don't remember her name. I don't know where she lived, or where she wanted to go when all of it was over. I know that she had dark-blond hair, ice-blue eyes, and milky pale skin. I know that every time she looks down she'll see that word there. Maybe she recovered, maybe she got out and dyed her hair and got a colourful tattoo that covered all that pain. But wherever she went, I hope with every part of me that she left the fear behind.

‒ ‒ ‒ ‒ ‒ ‒ ‒ ‒ ‒ ‒ START READING ‒ ‒ ‒ ‒ ‒ ‒ ‒ ‒ ‒ ‒

Promoting obesity

Let's talk about the number one criticism that's launched against body positivity: that it is promoting obesity, glorifying fatness, encouraging being overweight, and basically making the whole world unhealthy. You might have even wondered yourself whether it's right to support a movement that does those things, I know I did at one point. Thankfully, some wonderful people educated the crap out of me and I realised what a ridiculous concept 'promoting 'obesity' really is, and how using it is just a tactic to shut down a movement that people don't have the first clue about.

First of all, remember that fatness is not the terrible thing we've all been led to believe it is, in terms of beauty or health. Which means that even if body positivity did promote obesity, there would be no need for people to jump up and down shouting about how we're all going to die from loving ourselves. But the thing is, body positivity doesn't promote obesity, since 'promote' means to 'actively encourage' or 'further the progress of' something.

During my time in the body positive community, I have never encountered a single person whose message is 'HEY EVERYONE! THE SECRET TO SELF-LOVE IS GETTING A BODY LIKE MINE! NOT FAT ENOUGH? GAIN WEIGHT! I ACTIVELY ENCOURAGE YOU ALL TO SHIFT YOUR BMI TO "OBESE" SO THAT YOU CAN BE BEAUTIFUL TOO!' (although change 'fat' to 'thin', 'gain' to 'lose' etc. and it does sound familiar ...). In fact, that message would be the exact opposite of body positivity, and exactly what the movement seeks to destroy: the idea that happiness and self-love can only be found in a certain body type. I have, however, encountered hundreds of people whose message is about every single person being worthy of self-love and good enough as they are, no matter what their body looks like, thin, fat, and everything in between.

This is my body. I love it and I'm happy with it.

This is a statement that, to most, is harmless. But there is a small subsection of people who do not like me saying this. They tell me that simply by existing I'm promoting obesity and an unhealthy lifestyle and I should be ashamed. Actually the only thing I'm promoting is loving yourself as you are, that's it. I do not want you to live the lifestyle I live, eat the things I eat or exercise the way I exercise. I want you to do the things that you want to do and do them for yourself. I just want you to be happy. That's what body positivity is about – being happy with who you are as you are. And anyone who doesn't like that notion can go jump in the fucking bin.

– Amy Eloise

The reality is that we currently live in a culture that does promote one body type, but it sure as hell isn't fatness. Thinness is promoted everywhere we turn, it is literally sold to us as the key to happiness and self-love at every opportunity. Which got me thinking what it would really take for our culture to start promoting obesity. Maybe the concerns about encouraging fatness would carry more weight if these things started happening too:

- Fat bodies suddenly replaced all of our current images of beauty in the media: models were forced to gain large amounts of weight for fashion shoots; thin actresses lost their roles to fatter leading ladies; advertisers started using plump bodies to sell their toothpaste, handbags or cars; Photoshop became a tool for adding extra layers of flesh to all bodies to make them more worthy of the spotlight; cosmetic surgeons started specialising in lipo-inflation and flabulous became our new ideal body type.

- A multi-billion dollar fattening industry sprang up to replace our current slimming industry: weight-loss groups turned into weight-gain groups with names like Weight Boosters, Fattening World, Jigglefast and Chubbisystem; millions of miracle products flooded the market promising to add pounds in only four simple monthly payments; celebrities started advertising chemically enhanced extra-fat lard as the secret to their coveted physique; and pharmaceutical companies started investing billions in fattening pills and handing prescriptions out to all thin patients, even if the pills had dangerous side-effects and might even kill them!

- Prejudice against slimness and thinphobia started running rampant through society: stereotypes about slim people being untrustworthy, unhygienic, lazy and unintelligent spread like wildfire; suddenly everywhere people below a size 16 go they're berated and harassed with weight-gain advice and jokes about toothpicks; employers started discriminating against thin staff, paying them less and hiring fatter candidates regardless of qualifications; public spaces were renovated and tailored solely to larger bodies, making smaller bodies feel unwelcome wherever they go.

- The medical profession backed up the new fat ideal by convincing us that non-fat bodies are walking diseases, sure to drop dead at any minute: the fattening industry started giving billions to studies aiming to prove that obesity is the key to health; the mainstream media reported on the studies crying out 'THIN KILLS!' with every headline; thin people grew sick of their doctors always telling them to gain weight rather than treating their complaints and stopped going; nationwide public health campaigns like 'Fatten Up, America!' appeared, aiming to solve the problem of childhood slimness within a generation!

- The idea that only fatness will bring happiness, beauty and love seeped into our cultural consciousness and became fact: magazines started running weekly stories of people before and after weight-gain raving about how they got their life back; thin people fell to the bottom of the dating pool and became too scared to include their weight in online dating profiles; slowly but surely, millions of people stopped living their lives because they believe that they don't deserve happiness living in a slim body.

These are the type of things that add up to society glorifying and promoting a certain body type above all others. Currently, the body type being promoted is thinness, and has been in differing degrees for about a century. So to anyone who believes that body positivity is promoting obesity – I hate to break it to you, but it's going to take a lot more than a handful of fat babes loving themselves to create that kind of cultural shift (it's nice to know that you think fat babes are that powerful though!).

If all of the things above do start happening, then come back to me and we can talk about promoting obesity. I'll be just as worried as you are – not because of any bullshit health concerns, but because no one body type should be promoted above any other; that's just not what body positivity is about.

What body positivity does actively encourage and aim to further the progress of, is unapologetic self-love and happiness for all human beings, no matter what their size, shape, shade, age, ability or gender might be.

Body positivity promotes self-acceptance, and freedom from the oppressive ideals we've been bombarded with for so long. It works against the forces that try to tell us that only certain bodies are worthy of being seen and represented in the media, and it encourages all people to take their joy right now, as they are, not once they better fit the cultural standard of beauty. And it certainly doesn't promote any one body type as the key to those things.

As Jes Baker sums up perfectly in *Things No One Will Tell Fat Girls*, 'I believe in glorifying all bodies. All of them. Because every single person in the entire world deserves to feel good about and love themselves ... y'know what else I glorify? I glorify HAPPINESS'. What more is there to say?

Of course, the easiest defence against people who make accusations about promoting obesity is to say that fat people can be healthy too – the majority of this chapter serves as proof of that. You know by now that fat is not synonymous with unhealthy and you can use that knowledge whenever someone challenges your new body positive stance, but we also need to be careful about using health as a defence for body positivity. Because the 'fat people can be healthy too!' argument makes it sound as if only healthy people are worthy of self-love, when really, self-love is something we all deserve, regardless of our health status.

As long as you're healthy

Since body positivity became a media buzzword there are more and more people supporting the movement every day. But unfortunately for a lot of them, their support comes with a condition: as long as you're healthy.

The health requirement usually comes to light in comments like 'Go girl! As long as you're healthy that's all that matters!' or 'I'm all about body positivity as long as you're healthy'. Somewhere along the line, the health requirement has firmly attached itself to what people believe body positivity is all about, and in doing so, has twisted the meaning of the whole movement.

The problem with being 'all about body positivity as long as you're healthy' is that it's still casting judgement over who is and isn't worthy of feeling good about themselves. And it's still using people's bodies to make the judgement. Doesn't that sound exactly like the kind of thinking we're trying to dismantle here?

It's ironic that the very same people who support a movement dedicated to not judging people based on how their body looks, will still support a system that judges people based on how their body functions. As if that's any better.

If we only award body positivity to people whose physical health matches our standards, we're being exclusionary and ableist. Here are just some of the people who get left out when we buy into the idea that perfect physical health is a requirement for feeling good about yourself:

People who suffer from chronic illnesses such as cancer, cardiovascular disease, diabetes and asthma; people with autoimmune diseases like ulcerative colitis, Crohn's disease or coeliac disease; people with neuro-degenerative diseases such as Alzheimer's or Parkinson's; people whose physical health has been damaged by eating disorders; people with physical disabilities; people struggling with addiction; people who deal with chronic pain, and basically any other person who's ever been in poor physical health, for any reason, at any time.

I don't know about you, but I don't believe that someone experiencing any of those things is any less worthy of self-love than the healthiest person on the planet is.

And if you'd like to argue that fatness is different because it involves wilfully destroying your health through over–eating and under-exercising, I'd encourage you to 1) reread this chapter and 2) think about whether you'd apply the same reasoning to a smoker who developed lung cancer; would they deserve to feel good about their body still? In case you're unsure of the answer, it's yes. People deserve self-love no matter what their health stats are or how they got that way.

When we believe in the 'as long as you're healthy' requirement, we buy into a system of healthism where our human worth is ranked by how well our bodies function. Anyone who isn't a perfect specimen is made out to be morally defunct, a burden, a liability, useless, pitiable or just plain worthless.

Newsflash: you are worthy regardless of your physical health. You are valuable simply because you exist. Even if you are unhealthy. Even if you are fat and unhealthy. Nobody should be bullied, harassed and dehumanised based on their size or their health. We are more than BMIs. We cannot be defined by how many miles we can run or how many vegetables we eat. Our blood pressure doesn't dictate what kind of person we are. Our medical records don't determine whether we get to love ourselves.

So if you've been reading this chapter so far and wondering whether the condition of your health means that you're excluded from the magical world of body positivity, you aren't. And if you're someone who usually qualifies their support of body positivity with an 'as long as you're healthy' requirement, I hope that you can reconsider. There's room for all of us here, but there's no room for health-based exclusion.

#BODYGOALS

Ditching Fitspo and Reclaiming Movement

'Our society places the most value on a body that, without speaking, screams: HEALTH. VIBRANT HEALTH AND WELLNESS IS WHAT I EMBODY.'
– Jes Baker, *Things No One Will Tell Fat Girls*

#strongnotskinny

There is a clever magic trick being performed on our body image. The magicians in charge of the trick have promised to deliver the impossible: to make our insecurities disappear. In go our high hopes that thinness will make us happy. In go our obsessions with losing weight. In go our counted calories. A wave of the wand and voilà! We emerge no longer wanting to be as skinny as we can possibly be; now we only want to look healthy and strong! Sounds promising, right? Except it turns out that the rules for looking 'healthy and strong' are just as narrow as the rules for being thin.

Now we don't just want to lose weight, we want to be lean and toned and firm as well. We don't just count calories any more, we count macros, we monitor how clean our meals are, we track protein grams and calculate the exact numbers needed to starve our fat and build our muscle. We might have even fooled ourselves into thinking that the numbers on the scale don't matter, but only if the results are still visible when we flex in the mirror.

Sure we can gain some weight, but not if that weight is soft and malleable, only if it's sculpted like marble exactly where we've worked for it to be. And because we've been told that this new image is based in health, we don't see that it's still hurting us. We believe that these body goals aren't anything like the ones before, this isn't just about fashion or vanity! This is about living longer and feeling better!

Except it's not. It is still 100 per cent, absolutely and completely about how our bodies look; we've just been duped into thinking that there's more to it than that.

If you're on social media you will have noticed the smell of spandex in the air. You might have seen quotes flying around about not getting the ass you want by sitting on it, and how you have NO excuse not to be at the gym this very minute. And you'll probably have noticed (surprise surprise) that one body type dominates the images of fitness inspiration, a.k.a. fitspo.

The images usually feature a headless woman's torso, chiselled by the outline of protruding abdominal muscles, glistening with a dewy sweat, perfectly lit and posed for maximum impact. The message is clear: this is what a fit body looks like. This is why you should be working out. This is the goal. Forget moving your body in order to feel good; according to fitspo all that matters is how moving your body can make you look.

Fitspo itself isn't anything new; Jane Fonda was rocking those high leg leotards way back in 1981. For decades now, magazine covers have pushed headlines promising to show 'How YOU Can Get Fit, Lean & Toned!' Fitspo is not new, but the idolisation of fitspo bodies on social media is new, and it's dangerous.

Don't get me wrong, a new trend that actually was about feeling better and reconnecting with our bodies through the power of movement would be wonderful, but fitspo ain't it. This is another pawn of the diet industry, dressed up in sportswear and advancing on us.

Suddenly everywhere we look are the new rules of health and beauty and happiness. Some of us start playing by them thinking that we're only taking care of our health … how could that be a bad thing? But slowly the exercise that we started to increase our stamina or build our strength turns into a relentless obligation.

The chiselled, glistening bodies that represent how fitness should look follow us around, popping up on our social media, in our magazines, on our screens, and in our minds whenever we look in the mirror.

Since we still don't look like those bodies, we're obviously not being healthy enough. Cut the carbs, up the workouts, eat clean, train dirty. Keep telling yourself it's all about health when you'd give anything just to get your body-fat percentage lower. Keep logging on to find the images that spur you on to work harder, listen to the people telling you how dedicated you are, and how admirable it is that you care so much about keeping fit. Be healthy. Be healthier. But most importantly, look healthier.

There is nothing wrong with pursuing physical health or wanting to increase your fitness; the problem comes when we start to believe that health and fitness only look one way. Once we believe that fitness only comes in one form we create yet another exclusionary body standard that makes us all feel like failures for not matching up. Fit bodies come in a million different variations, and fitness itself should be about how your body feels, not how your body looks. Thanks to fitspo, we're forgetting that.

There are endless benefits of moving our bodies: exercise can make us feel empowered and strong, it can remind us what we're capable of and help us reconnect with our bodies, it can help us manage stress, feel more energised, increase our stamina and most importantly, bring us joy!

There are countless positive effects of physical activity that have nothing to do with how our bodies look. The fitspo trend is making us forget that movement is a celebration of what our bodies can do, and instead it's convinced us that fitness should be focused on the attainment of washboard abs and rock-hard glutes.

When I used to spend my days locked indoors doing exercise DVDs, I noticed that not a single bit of the motivation the instructors gave was about how the movement felt. Every comment was focused on looking smaller and firmer, burning fat, being able to wear tight-fitting clothes or finally having those 'beautiful ballerina arms' by the time summer came around. We no longer think about movement in terms of anything other than weight loss and body-sculpting. We use working out as a punishment for our bodies falling outside the fit ideal and by doing so, we've poisoned our relationship with exercise.

Do you remember how movement used to feel when you were a child? When you tried to run so fast that it felt like you were flying, not because you had to but just because it made you feel free. When hazy summer days were filled with frantic sports games in the sun, skipping and kicking and batting and throwing until you were too tired to move any more, but too filled with happiness to care.

When you spent all of those hours trying to conquer a forward roll in the grass or a handstand propped up against your bedroom wall. When your friends had birthday parties at the pool and the person who could swim the fastest or the longest distance went home filled with pride. When jumping on the bed and dancing to your favourite music was the best way to spend a rainy day, falling asleep in a blissful fatigue and then waking up excited for whatever activity came next.

You weren't thinking about how many calories you were burning. You weren't trying to work off a dessert or earn your next meal. You weren't trying to force your body into a smaller size and counting down the minutes until the required time was up. You were just marvelling in all of the amazing things that your body could do. What if you could get that back?

What if we could banish the guilt and the obligation and find the joy in movement again? Not only would we gain so much mental freedom, we'd benefit physically by turning exercise into something we actually look forward to and are more likely to do regularly. But we can't do that until we banish the idea that the purpose of exercise is only to change how our bodies look.

As I'm writing this there are currently 38 million posts on Instagram alone under the hashtag '#fitspo', there are 1.5 million tagged with '#bodygoals' and 4 million under '#strong-notskinny'. Floods and floods of gleaming muscles, low-calorie meals, photoshopped body parts and before-and-after weight-loss pictures. This is the toxic side of social media. One click can send you spiralling down a rabbit hole of comparison, diet culture and shame. It's no wonder studies show that time on social media can make our self-esteem plummet.[89]

We need to take fitness back from fitspo. Because encouraging people to ignore their mental health and use exercise as a way to punish themselves to perfection, isn't actually very healthy at all.

Burn

Exercise addiction? Wait … isn't that just being healthy? At what point is the healthy part of physical fitness no longer healthy? When it starts to take up that bit too much mental space? When it becomes a distraction? How about when it becomes an obsession? When you start feeling that creeping sense of guilt when you miss a workout? When you start arranging your entire life around it? When you start missing social events because of it? When every other thought goes back to a tally of calories burned, reps lifted, miles clocked and progress achieved?

The difference between fitness as a passion and fitness as an addiction is mental health. As soon as our mental health is compromised in the pursuit of physical fitness, our new healthy body isn't that healthy at all.

Every time that I've lost a significant amount of weight in my life it's come with a hefty serving of obsession, especially around exercise. And every time my body started to change in came the comments of praise – 'You look so much better, what's the secret?', 'Wow! I wish I had that much willpower!', 'You are so dedicated, how do you do it?' I would reply with some self-righteous remark about sticking to the routine, anyone can do it, it really is so easy once you know how! But truthfully, I was hooked. I was addicted to working out, and those comments just helped fuel me on further.

The addiction had started back in the anorexia days, sweating in secret and burning as many calories as I could every minute. I learned from that time that I could force my body to do just about anything. I could run silent laps of my house despite not having eaten for days. I could go up and down every staircase twice, three times, four times, as many as I could before someone started to notice. I could use movement to make my body what I needed it to be, and that one piece of knowledge was enough to fuel years of disorder.

I never really gave up the exercise addiction. I managed to suppress it for the times when I needed to gain weight, but it stayed. That constant buzzing feeling, a low vibration I could feel in my bones telling me move, run, jump, burn. I let it out of the cage again when enough time had passed and enough weight had been gained to kick off the dieting years.

No matter how restrictive the plan, the workouts were non-negotiable. Hours and hours every day, no rest, no excuses, no slowing down, not even for a minute. Every routine had to be the highest intensity I could find, every movement had to be perfectly executed. Everything I did and everywhere I went was a chance to burn more calories.

When I wasn't thinking about food I was thinking about exercise. Any social event that threatened my workout routine was immediately cancelled. Any injury that sprang up was ignored. My entire world revolved around eating less and burning more, and nobody questioned whether there was more going on in my mind than willpower.

There was so much more. And I didn't know how to turn it off. I wasn't just hooked on the movement, I was hooked on the feeling of superiority I got from being 'the fit one'. I was held up as a paradigm of health and dedication, I was proof that hard work pays off. I was also destroying my mental health in the process, but they didn't see that.

When I found the body positive community I met people who'd been dealing with the same level of exercise addiction as I had, and some of them didn't make it out unscathed. My friend Blair told me about some of the long-term effects she's still experiencing well into her recovery:

I would work out multiple times a day, non-stop for six-plus years. I thought I was being healthy; we never hear society or anyone talk about the negative effects of exercise and what it can do to your body.

The end of my freshmen year in college I finally got injured. I developed major knee pain, which I later got diagnosed as runner's knee in both of my knees. Did I stop? Did I listen to my body? No I didn't. 'No pain, no gain', right?

So I continued to work out even though my body said no. I pushed myself so hard to the point where I hurt my shoulders. It took a couple of years to figure out that I tore my labrum in both of my shoulders.

Eventually I got the surgeries to repair both of my labrums. You would think my body would be okay now, but it's not. I still have so much pain throughout my body, my shoulders still hurt. Everything hurts. I had no clue why; I went from doctor to doctor, and no one could figure it out. Finally, in 2016 I was diagnosed with fibromyalgia.

I am unable to exercise now; I can barely walk some days. I can barely get out of bed as well. I am a perfect example of what not to do – don't over-exercise.

Now Blair shares her experience online to help other people heal their relationship with exercise and find peace with their bodies, regardless of their fitness or physical ability:

Exercising is not meant to hurt, it is meant to be enjoyable, fun, and feel good. Society has an unhealthy obsession with over – exercising, don't fall for the trap; listen to your body, move in ways that are fun for you.

Oh, and it's perfectly fine if you are unable to work out; it's not meant for everyone. You're still worthy of love from yourself and others, you are enough even if you cannot work out or exercise.

It took me years to see exercise as anything other than a way to burn myself smaller. Making peace with movement was one of the biggest steps to take in truly recovering from my eating disorder. The messages teaching us that exercise should be a punishment for physical imperfection are so much more harmful than we realise.

If health is what our culture's obsession with fitness is really about, then we have to acknowledge how unhealthy, even dangerous that obsession can become. It's time to refocus our idea of health to include mental health and holistic well-being, not just how long a person can run or whether or not they have visible abs. As long as fitspo makes the rules about health, we're putting people at risk every day.

Thinspo in a sports bra

There is a fitspo phenomenon currently taking place in online eating disorder recovery communities. The message is that it's okay to gain weight in recovery from a restrictive eating disorder, as long as that weight is muscle.

Before and after pictures show a stereotypically emaciated figure transformed by daily workouts and high-protein meals into a strong, toned gym bunny. People in recovery are getting the message that extreme exercise regimes and 'clean' diets are the key to overcoming their illnesses. But if exercise addiction was part of their eating disorder in the first place, it's hard to see how encouraging it further will lead to recovery.

Every recovery is different. Recovered bodies will always look different. Some people might be able to incorporate exercise into their recovery in a healthy way, but a lot of people won't.

There are so many ways that fitpso is counter – intuitive to recovery from restrictive eating disorders. First of all, it doesn't get rid of any of the focus on your body and how it looks. It still prescribes an image of how your body should be, with just as much emphasis on weight and shape as before. Rather than freeing yourself from rules about how your body should look, you just adopt new, more muscular ones.

It's also still a numbers game. Even if the numbers aren't dropped pounds or skipped calories, they're still there in minutes run, weight lifted, repetitions completed. The need to control your world with numbers hasn't been addressed, it's just been shifted. Not to mention the fact that fitspo often comes with the same restrictive meal recommendations, rules and regulations that straight-up diet culture does; putting a sports bra on it doesn't change that. Fitness communities are also overflowing with competition and comparison, two things that are already all too prevalent in a disordered mind.

And perhaps most importantly, a recovery that only allows weight gain in the form of muscle does nothing to fight the fear of fat that takes hold in so many eating disorders. Until that gets addressed, then eating disorder sufferers who use fitspo to find their way out will only ever be able to hover in half recovery: allowed to gain weight, but only the right type, allowed to eat more, but only the right things, allowed to loosen the reins on weight loss, but not lose focus on how their body looks.

As Amalie Lee writes in her popular eating disorder recovery blog Lets Recover, 'the people I find the most inspiring are those who haven't gone from one obsession to another. I get inspired by free people. Brave people who embrace themselves and start a life that is not 90 per cent centred around food and body … Recovery is not about getting hot or #strongnotskinny, it is about freedom'.

In recovery we have to ask ourselves – is this helping me become free? Or is this tying me down in chains that look different but feel the same? If fitness helps you find your freedom, then by all means, sweat away. But for all of you who feel like you're 'recovering wrong' for not matching up to the fitspo version of recovery, there are a few things I want you to know:

You are allowed to be still. You are allowed to take time to rest and heal. I know that sometimes it feels like you'll explode if you don't move and burn, but you need to pay close attention to where that feeling is coming from. Remember: listen to your eating disorder, and then do exactly the opposite. If that voice is telling you that you need to work out every single day to stop your body from changing, then be still. It won't be easy. It won't be comfortable. But it will be worth it, I promise.

Let your body decide for itself. However recovery makes your body look is good enough. Whatever changes happen when you are the happiest, and the most mentally free, are supposed to happen. That might mean gaining more weight than you expected you would. It might mean looking nothing like the image in your mind of the perfect recovery body – let go of that image. Trust that your body knows its own set-point range, and its own happy weight better than the voice of your eating disorder does.

Your mental health is more important than having washboard abs. Or toned arms. Or a thigh gap. Or any other physical attribute. Mental health matters more than any idea of how you should look, any goal weight, or any fitspo ideal. And if you can't incorporate fitness into your life without compromising your mental health, then don't. If and when you're ready to bring physical activity back into your life in a healthier way ...

Be gentle with yourself. When I started to reincorporate exercise into my life I knew I had to go slowly. Otherwise I risked falling head first back into the all-or-nothing mindset that my exercise addiction thrived on. I'd spent so many years buying into the fitness messages that make us believe that anything less than 100mph isn't good enough – go hard or go home, better sore than sorry, sweat is weakness leaving the body, no excuses!

Those messages are bullshit. Listen to your body, go home if you want to, and you are not weak if you don't break a sweat.

My greatest exercise achievement wasn't in a record number of sit-ups or a highest weight lifted. It was finally being able to peacefully walk my dogs without it being about calories burned or speed achieved, but just plain joy. There is so much more to movement than what fitspo has led us to believe; let go of the rules, and start being kind to yourself instead.

No pain no gain

Has anyone else noticed how aggressive today's fitness culture is? It seems to be more about torture, pain and punishment than actual wellness. There's an overwhelming belief that if working out doesn't hurt then we're not doing it right, and I don't just mean the kind of ache that comes from vigorous, but enjoyable exercise, I mean full-scale pain.

Nothing captures the no-pain-no-gain attitude better than this quote from fitness tycoon Jillian Michaels – 'Unless You Puke, Faint, or Die, Keep Going!' ... And we wonder how people develop disordered relationships with exercise.

Just think about the language that's used in fitness articles. We're not allowed to just work hard, we have to kill our workout and crush each session. When it comes to fixing our 'flaws' with exercise things get even more brutal. How many times have you seen a workout designed to burn, blast or melt body fat away, as if the routine is one step away from taking a blowtorch to your abdomen? Our fat has to be eliminated, eradicated, annihilated, our bodies have to be blasted and shredded. Doesn't it all sound a bit ... violent?

When we buy into the fitspo rhetoric of pain being a positive thing we turn our bodies into the enemy. Instead of movement connecting us to all the amazing things our bodies can do, it alienates us from them even further. We start believing that exercise is the punishment we deserve for having bodies that disobey the ideal.

Working out becomes an issue of morality: we're good if we push ourselves to the point of pain; we're failures if we do anything less. And until we look like those images on the front of the fitness magazines, we'll never be good enough, and the punishment continues. If we miss a workout the punishment doubles the next time we hit the gym.

Laura Fraser wrote in *Losing It* that 'the goal of exercise, for many women, isn't to achieve good health, but a perfectly disciplined, slender body'. But why do our bodies need to be disciplined? You only discipline something when it's wrong, when it's broken the rules, when it needs to be taught a lesson. The fitspo image is providing us with one more way that we believe our bodies are wrong, they've broken the rules of what a fit body should look like and need to be taught, with punishing workout regimes, a lesson in how to conform. Haven't we punished our bodies enough already?

We've already been trained to deny our basic instincts and treat our appetites as enemies that need to be conquered. Try drinking a glass of water to stave off cravings, or do some crunches to reduce hunger pangs! (Or we could actually listen to our bodies telling us that we need more nutrients — radical, I know.) We've spent enough time ashamed of any pleasure that food might bring us, disciplining ourselves with restriction to account for the crime of eating (and, god forbid, enjoying it).

We've put our bodies through countless rounds of experimental starvation with the latest crash diet or extreme detox. Not to mention the methods of controlling our flesh from the outside – the corsets, waist-trainers and elastic bindings that range from the uncomfortable to the painful.

We've ingested unsafe chemicals, had our jaws wired shut, and even tried electric shocks to get our bodies to obey. When our own punishments don't work, we let surgeons with scalpels in to break our bones, slice us up, suction us out and perform any number of procedures in the hope that we'll win the battle against the bulge (read: the battle against our bodies).

Even the beauty rituals we think of as harmless come with a certain amount of hurt, our hair-removal procedures are never discomfort free, whether it's plucking, waxing or lasering. We wear undergarments that leave red welts on our skin and shoes that leave us unable to walk properly. I can hear those of you now saying 'oh it's not that painful', but why does it have to be painful at all? Why do the accepted beauty standards for anyone who identifies as female have to involve so much pain?

Why does beauty have to be pain? Are our bodies so disgusting for disobeying the fabricated rules of what's beautiful and what's not that they deserve to have this much hurt inflicted on them? All our bodies do each day is try their best to keep us alive. They strive to function as well as they can to let us live, and they have no idea that they're also supposed to be conforming to made-up aesthetic ideals.

Your stomach only knows its biological role as part of the digestive system; it doesn't know that it's also supposed to look as flat as possible at all times. Your body doesn't understand when it's deprived of nutrients so that it can fit into a smaller dress size; it just thinks it's being starved. Storing fat cells was once a sign that bodies were efficient and better equipped to survive times of famine. Nobody informed our metabolisms that times have changed and they can stop that pesky fat storing habit now – no famine! Just the Master Cleanse! Get with the programme! We are literally punishing our bodies for functioning how they are programmed to function for our survival.

In *The Beauty Myth*, Naomi Wolf wrote that 'for as far back as women could remember, something had hurt about being female … Today what hurts is beauty'. Fitspo has turned exercise into one more way that we're supposed to hurt ourselves in the name of beauty, rather than a way for us to feel better in the name of health. For so many of us it's just another ritual of punishing our bodies for not being good enough according to the beauty rules.

Let me say this loud and clear: WE DO NOT NEED TO PUNISH OUR BODIES. Not any more. We do not need to run until we're sick. We do not need to starve until we pass out. We do not need to keep breaking ourselves apart and trading in the pieces hoping to finally be good enough. Fuck beauty being pain. We've hurt enough.

We don't need to annihilate every ounce of our body fat to be fit. We don't need to blast our body parts into nothingness to benefit from physical activity. Intense pain is not weakness leaving the body, it's your body sending you a warning. And if you feel like you're going to puke, faint, or die, then stop.

It's time that we declared a truce with our bodies and reclaimed movement as a positive thing instead of a punishment. Whatever we choose to do with our bodies, those choices shouldn't be made out of hate and disgust. We deserve better than that.

Joyful movement

Maybe the most ironic part of fitspo culture is that it alien-ates people from taking part in physical activity. All those messages about sweat being our fat crying and pictures of glisten-ing muscles are supposed to motivate us to get moving, but they actually only serve to convince a lot of us that the spandex will never fit, so why try?

When we make fitness about achieving a certain body type, those of us who just can't attain that body type get left on the sidelines. Fitness becomes something for the elite, and anyone who enters fitness spaces without looking the part gets the message that they don't belong (ask any fat person about their experiences at the gym). As Marilyn Wann wrote in *Fat! So?* 'People don't go where they don't feel welcome ... If we don't fit in, we don't do fitness'.

Which means that a whole lot of us are missing out on the countless benefits of moving our bodies, simply because we've been taught that those benefits are reserved only for people whose bodies fit the bill. Because of the fitspo mentality, we've learned that when it comes to fitness it's all or nothing, and when we can't give the all that's required, we have to choose nothing.

Fitspo is sucking all of the fun out of movement. Teaching people that the primary purpose of exercise is to change their body is a sure-fire way to make them hate exercise. I remember a distinct shift in how I felt about exercise growing up. One year I was running and skipping and splashing and dancing with delight, taking pride in all the amazing things my body let me do. The next year it was all tainted by calorie-counting, body-sculpting, and all the knowledge of how I should look while doing it. I lost the joy.

Making exercise all about body-sculpting isn't just bad for our mental health, it's making us move less as well. Studies are showing that people whose motivation for exercise is changing their body shape (i.e. losing weight or getting washboard abs) are significantly less physically active than people whose motivation has nothing to do with their body shape.[90] Once more for the people in the back – that means that when we only use exercise as a way of forcing our bodies into a different shape, we are less likely to keep it up than if we were just moving for fun.

What if we could reclaim movement as joyful again? What if we could detach exercise from body-sculpting, remove the guilt, shame and punishment and still benefit physically? Remember Steven Blair's research showing that fitness is the key to physical health, no matter what size you are? I think it's time we took exercise back from fitpso and realised that we all deserve the mental and physical health benefits of regular movement, no matter how we look or what our level of ability is. Hanne Blank puts it perfectly in *The Unapologetic Fat Girl's Guide to Exercise and Other Incendiary Acts*:

> When we move our bodies for the sake of our own enjoyment and well-being, not because we're trying to look a certain way or as a way of paying for the 'sin' of being fat, it's a pretty serious form of rebellion.

Who's ready to rebel?

How? Let's start by forgetting every ridiculous rule about exercise being for the purpose of weight loss only. Forget the articles about which abdominal workouts burn the most fat. Forget those obnoxious charts that tell you how many miles you have to run to burn off a doughnut (the real answer is none, by the way, you are not required to burn off every single thing you eat). Forget picturing your 'dream body' while you force yourself through a workout that you actually hate. As long as diet culture is in charge of when, where, and how you move your body, the chances of you truly enjoying yourself are approximately zero.

Find an activity that you enjoy. I realise that's a strange concept if you've spent years seeing exercise as obligatory, painful and boring, but you'll be surprised where you can find joy if you go in with a different mindset.

You could try an activity that you used to love as a child, or find something completely new. How about swimming, aerobics, walking, hiking, Zumba, yoga, salsa, basketball, football, martial arts, jogging, gymnastics, kick-boxing, ballet, belly-dancing, tennis, cricket, volleyball, badminton, skiing, surfing, horse-riding, rowing, rugby or wrestling. The possibilities are endless. And it's okay if one thing just isn't for you, another thing might be.

While we're forgetting bullshit exercise rules, we can throw in that all-or-nothing fitspo mentality, too. You don't have to train like an Olympic athlete to benefit from physical activity. Remember, exercise isn't something we have to do to punish ourselves for how our bodies look. Which means there's no such thing as not going fast enough, whatever pace you're at is okay.

When I jumped off the fitspo train I decided to try yoga for the first time. It's something that I never let myself do before because I thought it was too slow and didn't burn enough calories to count. I'm by no means a masterful yogi, but when I do get on the mat I remind myself that I'm moving for me, carving out time for myself, and practising self-care. Sometimes I vinyasa so hard I wonder how I ever thought that yoga didn't count as exercise. Other times I take it slow and remind myself that there is no required pace. As long as I'm finding joy, it's enough.

On the other hand, I'll probably never enjoy an aerobic fitness DVD aimed to 'tone those glutes!' and 'burn that belly fat!' ever again. I've spent way too many years torturing myself with them to want to go back, in fact, I've probably spent entire weeks jumping up and down, staring at the same spot of wallpaper in my living room thinking about tomorrow's weigh-in. Sorry, Davina, Tracey and Jillian, I'm out. I'm done forcing my body to do things that make me miserable.

Take this as your permission slip: you are no longer obligated to move in ways that you don't want to.

In fact, if setting time aside for exercise just isn't your thing, or isn't an option, you can try what Linda Bacon calls 'active living' in *Health at Every Size*. She encourages people to find simple ways of incorporating more movement in their everyday lives, like parking in a further away spot and walking the distance, taking the stairs more often, playing more with your children or pets, or just getting up and moving around regularly if you have a sedentary job.

Not in an effort to lose weight or burn calories, but to reconnect with your body and get all the perks of movement. And if those options sound a bit tame you could always try having hot sex or dancing around the house in your underwear (#donthatetheshake).

The Association for Size Diversity and Health (ASDAH) list Life-Enhancing Movement as one of their five Health At Every Size® principles – 'physical activities that allow people of all sizes, abilities, and interests to engage in enjoyable movement, to the degree that they choose'.[91] Not a damn word about weight loss or working out to banish 'problem areas'. Just joyful movement on your terms.

And do you know the best thing about taking the fitspo out of fitness? There is zero guilt for missing a workout, not sticking to the plan, or going at a slower pace. Not being able to make it to your new dance class doesn't mean that you're a failure who should be banished from the class for all eternity.

Not being able to commit to regular activity doesn't mean that you have to shame yourself into feeling like a lazy slob. Any movement that you can do is great, and you don't have to beat yourself up over the things that you can't do. As soon as that guilt creeps in then we're exercising out of obligation, not for joy, so take a step back and remind yourself that movement is supposed to be fun.

If you've spent a lifetime forcing yourself to Feel The Burn! And Blitz That Belly Fat! then seeing movement in a different way is going to take a whole lot of unlearning. Be patient with yourself, and keep checking in with what your motivation is. If what you're doing stops being fun, then you don't have to do it any more. If it starts becoming an obsessive numbers game again, then stop, take as much time as you need to be still before you go back with a more body positive mindset.

HOW TO LEARN TO LOVE YOUR SWEATY SELF MORE

Anna, plus - size athlete and creator of @glitterandlazers
You don't need to meet the media's unrealistic expectation of a 'fit' body to enjoy movement. Here are three tips to make the gym your sanctuary, rather than another body war zone:

1. **Dress for success.** Treat the gym as a place you want to go. Instead of wearing your laundry-day leftovers, purchase an outfit that helps you feel confident and fierce while moving. Additionally, the right gear will actually make you feel better after a workout. Wearing the wrong gear can lead to chafing, unsupported movement, joint pain and body acne. So invest in

yourself by wearing gear you love to make movement more comfortable and frankly more fun. If you're unsure what you need for your first workout, I recommend getting a supportive athletic shoe, compression pants, a supportive sports bra, and moisture-wicking tank and socks.

2. **Start slow.** There's so much pressure in today's world to be the best right away. Often we approach movement similarly. Day one we push our bodies so hard that there never is a day two, because we hurt. Sure, a little soreness is normal, but if you're struggling to do day-to-day activities after a workout, you might need to step back and slow down. I started my journey with walking. It was simple, low impact, and easy to increase gradually. As I walked further and further, I found myself naturally challenging myself to do more. That natural progression is the ultimate goal: working out to be capable of more, rather than to have the 'perfect' body.

3. **Don't be embarrassed, be selfish.** Once I did something really weird after exercising. I asked a few random strangers if they had been watching me or seen me run. Each person looked at me as if I was a little loopy. People are naturally self-centred. This is just as true when being active. People on the track care more about their personal fitness goals, then they do about you. You should follow suit. Instead of wondering what others are thinking, check in on yourself. How is your breathing? Are you pacing yourself? How does your body feel? What can you do to keep challenging yourself? The initial steps of getting active are hard and you need to be your biggest cheerleader. You cannot do that unless you are 100 per cent focused on you. Don't be embarrassed, be selfish. You deserve it.

I realise this goes against every diet and fitness plan you've ever tried, but remember this: we are no longer sacrificing our mental health in the pursuit of a body type. Our mental health is more important than how we look.

Remember: if your level of physical ability means that exercise isn't an option for you, or if you just plain do not want to pursue physical fitness, you are still 100 per cent worthy of self-love. Exercise is not a moral imperative, and your physical health has no bearing on whether you deserve to feel good about yourself. You do, always.

FAQs

CAN I PURSUE FITNESS AND STILL BE BODY POSITIVE?

Of course you can! If exercise brings you joy (even the hardcore, limit-pushing, lung-exploding kind of exercise), then keep feeling the burn. Fitness only clashes with body positivity when we use body hatred as a motivator and move for the sole purpose of forcing our bodies into a different shape. As long as you're not working out as a punishment for how you look, then you can be a body positive fitness fanatic!

ARE YOU SAYING THAT GOING TO THE GYM IS BAD?

Nope, it's totally possible to go to the gym and not get sucked into the fitspo mentality. Your intentions behind going to the gym are the important part.

WHAT ABOUT PEOPLE WITH MUSCULAR BODIES? CAN THEY BE BODY POSITIVE?

Muscular bodies are beautiful, soft bodies are beautiful. Every body is worthy of self-love, there are no size limits or shape requirements.

I'M TOO SCARED TO TRY A NEW ACTIVITY, WHAT IF I LOOK WRONG?

You deserve to experience all the amazing things that your body can do, regardless of how you look. If the idea of trying something new alone makes you anxious, convince a friend to go with you, or get in touch with the organisers beforehand to break the tension.

Also, there is no such thing as a body that looks wrong. Our bodies are not wrong; how we've been taught to see them is wrong. One body type has dominated our idea of sport and fitness for far too long, so put your body positive boots on, and go break some boundaries.

WHAT IF PEOPLE MAKE FUN OF ME?

Unfortunately, most of the world hasn't got the message that it's not okay to body-shame people, so there may be arseholes who can't open their minds to all bodies being welcome in fitness spaces. Remember that they've been brainwashed by fitspo and diet culture, and you know better than that now.

Remind yourself that you are not there for them. Your body doesn't exist in public spaces to be visually pleasing to other people, and you certainly don't need their approval. You're there to have new experiences, to celebrate your body, and get the joy you deserve.

If you're dealing with persistent body-shamers, you could take it upon yourself to school them on body positivity and leave them stunned as you strut away in clouds of glitter and sass.

Or you could inform the management that you're being harassed and insist that they do something about it. If it continues, put your mental health first; you don't have to stay anywhere that is affecting you negatively. But be sure to speak up about your experiences and spread the word of any fitness establishments that think body-shaming is okay. If they don't respect your right to a shame-free space, they shouldn't get any of our business.

I CAN'T STOP SLIPPING BACK INTO FITSPO, HELP!

First of all: DO NOT BEAT YOURSELF UP ABOUT THIS. In fact, do not beat yourself up about slipping back on your body positivity, ever. You're trying to unlearn a lifetime of conditioning, while facing daily reinforcements of that conditioning in the form of diet culture, and that shit is hard. Feeling guilty for not being body positive 24/7 will only set you further back, you are incredible every day that you try to make peace with your body.

If obsession and guilt are creeping back into your movement, that's your cue to take a step back and allow yourself to be still. If you're starting to feel like everything will collapse and you're a terrible person for missing the gym, then challenge yourself not to go, and see what happens? Nothing. Nothing happens. Everything is okay and you are still worthy of self-love.

Remember that your mental health is more important than making it to the gym, and if you lose the joy, then what are you going for? Be honest about your motivations, and be gentle with yourself for slipping back. You're doing the best you can.

WHAT NOW?

A Step-by-Step Guide

'This self-love stuff is great for everyone else, but not for me'

– Me, 2014

If you've read this far then YOU ARE THE BEST AND I WANT TO HUG YOU RIGHT NOW! I hope by this point in the book you've learned some things that have helped you understand where your body-image issues have come from. I hope that you've started to question the lies we've all been taught about our bodies, and started to heal from the damage that's been done. However, you might also be feeling a little bit lost, since I've basically just dropped a whole load of ideas on to your lap that go against pretty much everything you've ever been told about bodies and beauty and worth. And that's a lot.

So you might still be wondering what you can do, right now, in this moment, to get your body positive journey started. Which is why I thought I'd fill this final chapter with a step-by-step guide of things that you can do today, things that you can work on this month, and things to keep practising always. So that when you close the final page you'll be ready to start growing into your new, unapologetic, body-lovin' self.

Before we dive in, it's really important for me to acknowledge something. I know that some of you will be feeling how I felt when I first found body positivity, which went something like this: all that self-love is great for them! I'll just lose some weight and then I'll try it. I'll just keep doing what I'm doing because it might work this time. I have to keep hating my body because if I stop I'll never change it enough to be happy. I'm the exception, everyone else deserves to love their bodies, but not me. Sound familiar? Read this next part very carefully:

You deserve it too.

No exceptions. No buts. No weight-loss clauses. You deserve this. You have spent far too much time hating your body, and now it's time for you to change that. It doesn't matter what you weigh – there's no size limit on body positivity. It doesn't matter how you've reached this point, whether you've struggled with eating disorders, bullying, yo-yo dieting, whether you've just started feeling bad about your reflection, or whether you've had a lifetime of never feeling good enough.

Body peace is for you. Every one of you. No matter your size or shape, the colour of your skin, how old you are, your gender, your sexual orientation, or your level of physical or mental ability. Regardless of anything about your body that you've been taught to see as shameful, you deserve this too.

Stop thinking that you're the only one who shouldn't make peace with their body. You should, and you can. I promise.

Things to do today

GET MAD

This is what separates the 'self-love is great for them but not me' people from the 'I fucking refuse to hate myself for a second longer' people. If you're a woman then you've probably been taught at some point that anger is not an attractive feminine quality. We're not supposed to get mad, we're supposed to be passive, quiet and polite at all times. But guess what? We are human beings with a full range of emotions, each one with the strength to move mountains. And the only reason that we're taught to keep our emotions small and contained is so that we never realise how truly powerful we can be once we tap into them. If there's one thing I'm sure of, it's that angry women will change the world.

If you're like me, then you probably started to get mad around the first chapter of this book. By the time you were finished with the diet-industry chapter, you were probably good and raging. Because at that point one thing will have become abundantly clear: we've been set up to hate our bodies from the start. As soon as we were born into a culture that's willing to sacrifice half the population's mental health in order to turn a profit, we were screwed. From day one. There was no way for us to escape the body-image issues that were waiting. I want you to really think about that, and how it makes you feel, so that you can channel that emotion into fighting back.

Get mad. Get mad about the first time you were ever made to feel bad about your body. Get mad about the fact that the average age for girls to start dieting is eight years old. Get mad about all that wasted time spent only half living. Get mad about not being able to turn on your TV, open a magazine, or walk down the street without being sold the idea that your body is wrong.

Get mad about all of the people starving themselves to death in a world that refuses to stop idolising the image they're killing themselves for. Get mad on behalf of all the extraordinary women you know who've never been able to see themselves clearly. Remember that none of us asked for this, and so many of us are still trapped believing the lies.

I want you to gather up all that anger, and all that pain, and refuse. Refuse to keep tearing yourself to pieces hoping to finally be good enough. Refuse to spend any more of your life believing that how you look is the most important thing about you. Channel that anger, and use it to decide that it's time to make a change.

SIGN THE DIET-FREE PLEDGE

Make a promise to yourself today to stop denying your body the nourishment it needs in an attempt to shrink it into a smaller size. Remember all of the things you now know about diets:

- They don't work.

- They're toxic for our mental health.

- They can be anywhere from damaging to dangerous for our physical health.

- They waste our money.

- They waste our time.

- They're the product of a multi-billion-dollar industry that profits from us hating ourselves.

- They keep us small, obsessed, and hungry.

- They stop us from thriving and being the unstoppable forces we know we are already.

If you need to go back and reread the Lose Weight For Good! (Only £29.99 a Month) chapter, go do that now. Then call a truce.

HAVE A DIET-CULTURE DETOX

This kind of detox actually works and you don't even have to drink any cayenne pepper! All you have to do is go through your life, and throw out anything that makes you feel like you're not good enough. Think of it as a self-esteem spring clean.

- Go into your drawers and fish out that old 'cellulite reduction' cream that never worked. Find that expensive serum that promised to boost your cleavage in 10 days. Search out all of the snake oil you've bought over the years that did nothing but raise your hopes and drain your bank account. Then throw those suckers away.

- Go into the kitchen and blitz every last diet-food product that you hate but force yourself to eat (when I did this I found a three-year-old zero-calorie pancake syrup. You know what kind of food has zero calories? None. I'm not even sure if it should even be allowed to call itself food). Of course, you can keep any traditional 'diet' foods that you really do like, there's no shame in your cottage cheese game! This is just about no longer making yourself eat things that you don't enjoy as a punishment for your size. You don't need to do that any more.

- If there are any old diet pills rattling around or sachets of detox tea, throw them the hell away. You can always pop to the chemist for some plain old laxatives when you have digestive issues that require them.

- Next stop, the bookshelf. How many diet books do you own that all promised to be the miracle answer to your weight-loss struggles? Were they? (Hint, if you lost weight at first then gained it back, you didn't fail, the diet plan did, remember?). Ditch the diet books. Then head for the magazines.

- If you can read women's magazines without wanting to burn your entire life down afterwards, then keep them! But beware of the ones that only ever show one body type with a token size 12 thrown in for 'diversity' every six months. Maybe switch to a feminist, body positive magazine instead? They're harder to find, but the effect on your self-esteem will be worth it.

- Now for your phone. If you currently have any apps down-loaded that track your calories, send you diet plans, or generally encourage you to see your body as a work in prog-ress - get rid of them. Because you're already a masterpiece. All those apps do is alienate you from your internal hunger signals and make you obsess over the numbers. Now that you know how to start practising intuitive eating, you can let go of the numbers.

This is the best part: your social-media feeds. It's time to culti-vate a safe online space where you can log on and feel celebrated! Be ruthless, and get ready to tap that unfollow button. Start with that Facebook friend who keeps trying to sell you Herbalife; they can go. Then unfollow those fitspo models who post 'what's your excuse?' quotes – you don't need an excuse to accept yourself as you are. Next up, that celebrity you're following as 'body goals' inspiration; you don't need that any more, you are your own body goals.

Then check those lifestyle pages you're following that post pictures of sunsets and acai bowls, do they also only ever post thin, white, young, able bodies? Because that's a problem. After you're done there, feel free to unfriend that person you haven't spoken to in seven years who keeps posting about their weight-loss progress and saying that if they can do it, anyone can!

Detox everything that's a source of negative comparison for you. If none of the above ever make you doubt yourself and your own body, then they don't have to go, these are just things that I personally had to detox from. But be honest about how the things you expose yourself to every day online make you feel. Remember that having a safe space for your mental well-being is more important than being polite to a near stranger by keeping them on your friend list.

If the source of the diet-culture messages is a closer friend, you can try to let them know that sometimes what they post can be damaging to your self-esteem, and ask them to consider that in the future. If that seems like too much confrontation, you can always create a new online account reserved for positivity to go to when you need it. Which brings us to ...

CREATE A BODY-POSITIVE SOCIAL-MEDIA FEED

Now that you've got a blank slate to work with, it's time to fill it up with real diversity. We might not be able to control all the images of the ideal body we're exposed to in the outside world, but we can curate our social media feeds, and take charge of what we see online.

Follow people of all different shapes and sizes. Follow body positive and fat-acceptance activists, read their words and learn from them. Make sure that your feed is diverse in skin colour as well as size, and varied in ages. Follow people in the disabled community, and listen to them. Follow people who break the gender binary. Follow all the people we never get to see positively represented in mainstream media. Because those people are living proof that you can lead a full, vibrant, stylish, meaningful and HAPPY life no matter how you look.

What we see every day teaches us how to see ourselves. The more different body types you see and recognise as beautiful, valuable, and worthy, the easier it will become for you to recognise that you are those things as well.

Things to do this month

HAVE A WARDROBE CLEAR OUT

How many items of clothing do you own that don't fit you? Yep, I'm talking about those 'When I Lose Ten Pounds' jeans. That 'Well, It Fit Me Five Years Ago' jacket. That one dress you've never worn but pull out every once in a while as proof of how hideous you are because you still can't get it on. It's time to let those clothes go. Because all they are are reminders of your insecurities that you see every single time you get dressed.

Once upon a time I had a black fitted jumpsuit that made me feel like I'd just stepped out of a music video. The problem was the only time it had ever fit comfortably was after a week-long stomach flu I had one year over Christmas. Every time I tried it on after that it either left dents in my skin and gave me the mother of all camel toes, or just plain refused to zip up.

But I kept it for a long time, it was my 'When I Fit Back Into That I'll Be Okay' outfit. In fact, about half my wardrobe was made up of things that were one, two, or even three sizes too small. I just couldn't bring myself to let them go; that would feel too much like giving up on myself.

I didn't realise that every time I stuffed myself into a too-small pair of trousers or a shirt that I couldn't even lift my arms in, I was reinforcing a belief that my comfort didn't matter until I was a smaller size. That I did not deserve to feel comfortable because I was too big. But we all deserve to feel comfortable in our clothes. How we feel every day when we get dressed matters. And our self-esteem is worth way more than the number on a lifeless bit of fabric ever could be.

So blast your favourite music, ask a friend to come round for emotional support if it'll help, and get rid of the ghosts of dress sizes past. You can sell them online and put the proceeds towards some new threads, or donate them! You'll be amazed at how much lighter you feel without those bits of material staring at you accusingly whenever you open your wardrobe.

BELLY LOVE TIP #4

STOP HIDING

Wear the clothes that you love, and not just the ones that disguise the shape of your belly. When a camera comes out, don't try to twist and turn your body to make your tummy look as flat as possible; let the world see you as you are. Catch yourself whenever you're sucking it in; take a deep breath and let it go. You don't need to be ashamed of having your belly on show. Remember that there's nothing wrong with the size or shape of your stomach; the only thing that's wrong is how you've been taught to see it.

SHOUT BACK AGAINST NEGATIVE SELF-TALK

Do you remember that statistic in the very first chapter about women having an average of 13 negative body thoughts every day? How many do you have? How do they sound? Do you tell yourself that you're disgusting? Ugly? Worthless? How the hell are you supposed to feel anything positive about yourself with someone being so mean to you all the time?

The next time that critical voice pops up and starts trying to tear you down, I want you to challenge it. If it calls you fat, tell it that fat isn't a bad word, and that you're valuable regardless of how much fat you have. If it tells you that no one will ever find you attractive, tell it that you're no longer placing your worth in how visually appealing you are to others. If it unleashes a tirade of body shame on you whenever you look in the mirror, shout back. Speak over it. Speak out loud and let it know who's really in charge.

Slowly but surely, you're going to replace the negative self-talk with positive affirmations instead. If you can't think of anything positive to say about your body yet, here are some that you can try on for size:

- I might not be okay with my body yet but I'm fighting to be, and I'm proud of myself for that.

- I'm grateful for everything that my body allows me to do in the world, and all the ways it works to take care of me.

- I am hotter than the inside of a poptart in this outfit!

- There's no such thing as a problem area, my body is not a problem to be fixed!

- My softness is beautiful.

- My belly is cute.

- My cellulite clusters are constellations mapped across my thighs and I am magical.

- I deserve the space I take up in the world.

- I am good enough.

- My body is not the enemy.

The affirmation that I find the most comforting is this: my body is exactly how it's supposed to be. When you're constantly being bombarded from all directions by things telling you how you should look, there is strength is saying no, this is how I should look, in this moment my body is exactly how it's supposed to be. After all, your body isn't supposed to look like anyone else's, your body is yours and yours alone.

In time, you'll be able to cut that critical voice short. Eventually, you'll be ready to fight it off before it even starts. It might never disappear completely; negative self-talk creeps up even on the most body positive people when they're feeling vulnerable. What's important is having the weapons ready to fight back. Positive affirmations are your weapons, and even though you might not believe the things you're saying at first, every time you say them you'll believe them a little bit more. Try it right now, say something nice about your body. Out loud. I dare you.

GET READING!

There are so many incredible body positive books out there, I definitely couldn't have written this one without them. I've included a reading list at the back with some of my favourites — go soak up that body positive wisdom!

SAY GOODBYE TO THE SCALE

If reading that made your insides flip over, hear me out. I know how scary the idea of letting the scales go can be. How can you let go of that number? How do you say goodbye to something that's been such a vital measure of your worth for so long? I get that.

When you wake up every day and jump on the scales before you have breakfast, you can end up getting addicted to that feeling. That rush of seeing a number that's lower than the day before, how proud you get to feel all day long. I also know how easily that feeling shatters when the number isn't what you want it to be. Suddenly instead of pride, you feel shame.

All your clothes somehow feel tighter than they did yesterday. You're so sure that everyone around you can see the difference. You spend the whole day drowning in negative self-talk, feeling guilty for everything that passes your lips, and praying for a better result tomorrow. That daily weigh-in can make you or break you. And that's the problem.

Every time we step on to the scale hoping to see that magic number, we're handing our happiness over to a hunk of metal, plastic and glass. We're letting whatever digits pop up dictate how we feel about ourselves for the whole day. We're buying into the idea that the number the hand settles on defines us. Which is why the scale has to go. Because your happiness is more important than that number, and always will be.

From now on, instead of relying on an inanimate object to tell us our value, we're going to decide it for ourselves. And instead of forcing our bodies to match a certain number that we think will make us better, we're going to start trusting our bodies' set-point weights, and accepting that fluctuations are normal. We're going to stop giving our power away to the scale.*

*Note: if you're currently in recovery from an eating disorder and you've been told that weight restoration is necessary, you probably won't be able to say goodbye to the scales just yet. But you can limit your usage of them to when it's medically necessary for you to be weighed, and try your best to let go of the numbers outside of that. Once you're weight – restored and in a better place mentally, you'll be able to banish them from your life, so keep going.

Here are a few options of what you can do with your current scale: hide it out of sight. Throw it away. Give it a weight neutral make-over (search for Marilyn Wann's Yay! Scale on Google; it's a scale made body positive by replacing all the numbers with words like 'hot' and 'perfect' instead). Or, my personal favourite, take a sledgehammer to it! Channel all that anger about being made to hate yourself for so long, and go to town on that scale. Make sure you're wearing the appropriate protective gear! Safety first, even when smashing diet culture.

Things to practise always

INTUITIVE EATING AND JOYFUL MOVEMENT

Go back to the Dessert Every Damn Day and #BODYGOALS chapters anytime you need to refocus on ways to heal your relationship with food and exercise. Remember that you deserve to eat without guilt, your body deserves nourishment and you deserve to find joy in movement. Also remember that if your physical movement is limited, if you don't have resources available to you, or you're just not interested in intuitive eating or exercise, you are still worthy of self-love. You are invited to the body positive party no matter what.

STAND UP FOR YOURSELF AGAINST BODY-SHAMING

I'm willing to bet that every single one of us has been body-shamed. Maybe it was a stranger in the street. Maybe it was a backhanded compliment from a friend. Maybe it was that one family member who's always berating you about your body. Maybe it was a plain old Internet troll. Whoever it came from and whatever they said, body-shaming is never okay. So it's time for you to stand up for yourself and shut it down.

WHEN IT'S FROM A STRANGER

Fact: anyone who feels the need to attack a complete stranger's appearance – online or in person – is not happy with themselves. Often those people believe that tearing you down will boost their self-esteem. Sometimes they're pissed off that they've spent their lives striving for happiness through attaining the ideal body, and you daring to exist visibly in a body that isn't societally ideal devalues their efforts (they'll be extra pissed off if you're daring to be happy in that body, too!). Or maybe this person is simply a grade-A wanker who needs to step back, drink a glass of water, and re-evaluate their life choices.

But do you notice something that all these instances have in common? YOU ARE NOT THE PROBLEM. In fact, it isn't even about you. It's about them and all the poisonous ways they've been taught to think about other people's bodies. They are the problem, and their words say a whole lot more about who they are, than who you are. With that in mind, you can choose how to react:

- You can decide not to waste your precious energy by giving them any kind of attention. Remind yourself that nobody else has the power to decide how you get to feel about yourself, only you can decide that. Move on, ignore, block etc.

- Or, if you're feeling feisty, you might want to ask that person to explain to you exactly how your body is their business (answer: it's not, ever, no matter how hard they might try to convince you that it is).

- If they try the most common form of body-shaming and spew out some variation of 'you're fat', catch them off guard by replying with 'I know! Isn't it great?'. Since we've reclaimed the F-word, they're going to have to do a lot better than 'you're fat' to bring you down.

- If none of the above appeal to you, simply telling them to go and eat a whole bag of dicks can work wonders.

WHEN IT'S FROM A FRIEND

Sometimes a friendship turns toxic without us realising, it can start to feel like a competition, back-handed compliments pop up out of nowhere, and body-shaming becomes the norm. This can be especially common among groups of female friends, since we've been trained to see each other as competition (more on how to escape that in a bit).

When you witness body-shaming among your friends, whether it's about you or anyone else, call it out. Let them know how much damage their comments could do. Tell them that it's hard enough being okay with your body without your friends picking on your insecurities as well. If they really are friends, they'll be apologetic as hell and they'll stop doing it. If they carry on, then it might be time to admit that they're not worthy of your friendship. You deserve friends who lift you up and make you feel like royalty, and nothing less.

WHEN IT'S FROM FAMILY

This is, without a doubt, the question that I get asked the most. What do you do when a family member won't stop criticising your body? How do you make them see the effect that those comments have, without causing arguments or family divides? Especially if you live with that family member and see them every day.

Here's something I want you to know first of all: as difficult as it might be for them to understand, not even your family gets to dictate what you should do with your body and how you should look. You shouldn't have to be around someone who chips away at your self-esteem whenever you see them. Here's a way for you to stand up for yourself.

- Step 1: When it happens, ask if you could talk to the person privately. Explain that you're trying really hard to work on building a more positive body image, and when they make those comments about your body, it hurts. If they insist that they're only concerned about you or trying to help, assure them that the best thing for you, mentally and physically, would be to feel better about your body. And in order to do that, you need them to stop commenting negatively on how you look. As uncomfortable as that conversation might be, hold your ground and remember that you are entitled to a body-shame-free home.

- Step 2: If criticising your appearance has been a long-standing habit of theirs, you'll probably have to remind them that you're not putting up with that shit any more. Be firm, try something like: 'Could you please not comment negatively on my body?'/'Remember I asked if you could stop saying things like that?'/'Hey, we've talked about this, please don't say those things to me any more, they upset me.' It's completely up to you how many times you're willing to remind them. If it's just not working, then move on to the next step.

- Step 3: Walk away from those conversations. You are allowed to set boundaries and prioritise your own mental health. If you've made it clear and they're still unwilling to respect your feelings, you do not have to stick around for the body-shame show. Leave the conversation. Leave the room. Leave the house. Get some space, set your boundaries, and remember your worth. In case you've forgotten already – you are worth the world exactly as you are.

QUIT DIET TALK

There will be a time in the near future when you're around friends/family/colleagues, and the conversation turns to how much weight everyone wants to lose. Or how bad someone was for *gasp* ordering dessert! Or what the best way to prepare broccoli is to harness the mystical fat burning powers within the stalk (I'm just waiting for this to be the next big miracle diet method, the book would be called *Stalk Your Way to Your Best Brocco-Life Yet!*).

My point is, diet talk is unavoidable. It's our socially conditioned go-to small talk topic. But if you're just starting to break free from diet culture, or if you're in recovery from an eating disorder, those conversations can be toxic for your mental health, and you're not required to listen to them. If you don't feel like you can just back away and leave those people to their group self-deprecation, you could shift the conversation instead. Depending on your relationship to the person speaking, try one of these:

- I'm not sure if you know about my experience with eating disorders/body-image issues, but I'm trying really hard to focus on recovery/building a more healthy body image and this kind of talk can be really damaging. I'd appreciate it if you could be aware of that when I'm around.

- Isn't it such a shame that when a group of badass, intelligent women come together we still can't stop talking about our bodies? Seriously, what we ate today is not the most interesting thing about us.

- Have you heard about body positivity? It's a way of accepting yourself as you are and not being so obsessed about food, calories and weight. It's really helping me, and I'd love to get you involved in it if you want.

- God diet talk is so boring, what do you guys think is going to happen on *Orange is the New Black* this season?

- Person: I was so bad this weekend, I ate like 3,000 calories. You: Why do you think the number of calories you ate has anything to do with your moral value? You're not a bad person for eating what you want, stop beating yourself up.

STOP THE COMPARISON

We have been conditioned to see each other as competition. Since there's only one kind of beauty, according to the ideal body rules, we must always rank ourselves against one another to see who gets the prize. When we see someone who we think is beautiful, our mind immediately reminds us that they must be more beautiful than we are. Their hair is glossier than ours, their skin is smoother, their legs are more toned, their smile is brighter. Before we know it we've been swept away on a wave of negative comparison.

Suddenly the complete stranger with the glossy hair is our fiercest competitor, and we go home plotting how we can improve ourselves to outrank them. Not only does this alienate us from connecting positively with other people, it means that every time we go out we're expending huge amounts of mental energy rating ourselves against everyone we see. It's exhausting, and it doesn't need to be that way.

The next time that you see a beautiful person, instead of listing all the ways that you fall short against them, I want you to try something different. I want you to consider that no matter how perfect this person looks to you on the outside, they might be drowning in just as many body-image issues as you are.

The parts of their body that you've compared to your own might be their greatest insecurities. While you've been wishing away your features and coveting theirs, they might have been doing exactly the same thing to someone else. No matter how perfect you think that their body is, there's an overwhelming chance that they don't see what you're seeing when they look in the mirror.

The truth is that you have no idea how that person feels about their body. They could be struggling with an eating disorder, they could be obsessively dieting and over-exercising, they could have body dysmorphic disorder. To you, they might be flawless, but there's a big fat chance that they're still not happy with their body.

So instead of seeing them as competition, try to see them as someone who's up against the same unrealistic beauty standards, and the same fatphobic diet-culture bullshit that we all are. Instead of ranking ourselves against one another, it's about time we realised that there is room for all of us. Another person's beauty is not the absence of your own.

One more thing ...

Before I go, I want to leave you with my favourite quote, written by Naomi Wolf in *The Beauty Myth*:

'The woman wins who calls herself beautiful, and challenges the world to change to truly see her'

So get out there my loves, challenge the world to change, and remember that you are more powerful than you will ever know.

NOTES

Get Thin or Die Trying

1. www.pacey.org.uk/news-and-views/news/children-as-young-as-3-unhappy-with-their-bodies/
2. www.glamour.com/story/shocking-body-image-news-97-percent-of-women-will-be-cruel-to-their-bodies-today
3. http://news.bbc.co.uk/1/hi/health/2402363.stm
4. www.bbc.co.uk/news/health-16430142
5. Laura Fraser, **Losing It, America's Obsession with Weight and the Industry that Feeds On It** (USA, Dutton, 1997) [pg. 47]
6. www.dosomething.org/us/facts/11-facts-about-body-image
7. Henriks, Alexandra "Examining the effects of hegemonic depictions of female bodies on television: a call for theory and programmatic research" *Critical Studies in Media Communication*, 9 November 2010
8. www.refinery29.uk/2016/07/117341/victoria-secret-photoshopping-tricks-interview
9. www.isaps.org/Media/Default/global-statistics/2014%20ISAPS%20Global%20Stat%20Results.pdf
10. http://jezebel.com/5335022/self-editors-explain-covers-arent-supposed-to-look-realistic
11. www.sciencedaily.com/releases/2009/03/090302115755.htm
12. www.livestrong.com/article/287441-is-it-normal-to-have-a-flat-stomach/
13. www.smithsonianmag.com/history/why-footbinding-persisted-china-millennium-180953971/?page=1
14. https://en.wikipedia.org/wiki/Foot_binding
15. Laura Fraser, **Losing It, America's Obsession with Weight and the Industry that Feeds on it** (USA, Dutton, 1997)

16. Becker, Anne E., Burwell, Rebecca A., Gilman, Stephen E, Herzog, David B, Hamberg, Paul "Eating Behaviours and Attitudes Following Prolonged Exposure to Television Among Ethnic Fijian Adolescent Girls", 2002

17. http://news.bbc.co.uk/1/hi/health/347637.stm

Lose Weight for Good! (Only £29.99 a month)

18. www.bbc.co.uk/news/magazine-35670446

19. www.slate.com/blogs/xx_factor/2016/01/28/little_girls_reactions_to_curvy_barbie_prove_why_we_need_curvy_barbie.html

20. www.mintel.com/press-centre/social-and-lifestyle/dieting-in-2014-you-are-not-alone

21. Glenn A. Gaesser, **Big Fat Lies, The Truth About Your Weight and Your Health** (USA, Ballantine Books, 1996) [pg. 29]

22. https://i-d.vice.com/en_us/article/how-the-fashion-industry-affects-the-bodies-of-young-women

23. www.refinery29.com/2015/01/81288/children-dieting-body-image

24. The U.S. Weight Loss Market: 2014 Status Report & Forecast, www.marketresearch.com/Marketdata-Enterprises-Inc-v416/Weight-Loss-Status-Forecast-8016030/.

25. www.marketsandmarkets.com/PressReleases/weight-loss-obesity-management.asp

26. Laura Fraser, **Losing It, America's Obsession with Weight and the Industry that Feeds on it** (USA, Dutton, 1997)

27. **Vogue**, July 1, 1918.

28. American Medical Association Adult Weight Conference, 1926, New York, Flappers had "mastered the art of eating their cake and yet not having it. Inducing regurgitation, after a plentiful meal, either by drugs or mechanical means".

29. Terry Poulton, **No Fat Chicks, How Women are Brainwashed to Hate Their Bodies and Spend Their Money** (Canada, Key Porter Books, 1996) [pg. 38]

30. Laura Fraser, **Losing It, America's Obsession with Weight and the Industry that Feeds on it**

31. Roberta Pollack Seid, **Never Too Thin: Why Women Are at War With Their Bodies** (New York, Prentice Hall Press, 1989) [pg. 168]

32. www.sec.gov/Archives/edgar/data/105319/000119312514069945/d644264d10k.htm,

33. David M. Garner, "Ineffectiveness of Weight Loss and the Exaggeration of Health Risks Associated with Obesity", 1990.
34. http://nymag.com/scienceofus/2015/10/why-weight-watchers-doesnt-work.html
35. www.allianceforeatingdisorders.com/portal/laxatives
36. www.dietpillswatchdog.com/skinny-mint/
37. http://metro.co.uk/2014/03/24/the-detox-myth-trust-your-body-and-stop-wasting-money-on-juices-4675501/
38. Gina Kolata, **Rethinking Thin, The New Science of Weight Loss – and the Myths and Realities of Dieting** (New York, Farrar, Straus and Giroux, 2007) [pg. 24]
39. www.dietpillswatchdog.com/xls-medical-fat-binder/
40. https://authoritynutrition.com/do-raspberry-ketones-work/
41. http://newsroom.ucla.edu/releases/Dieting-Does-Not-Work-UCLA-Researchers-7832
42. Traci Mann, et al. "Medicare's Search for Obesity Treatments: Diets Are Not The Answer," *American Psychologist* 62, 2007. Glenn A. Gaesser, **Big Fat Lies, The Truth About Your Weight and Your Health.**
43. www.nationaleatingdisorders.org/get-facts-eating-disorders
44. Laura Fraser, **Losing It, America's Obsession with Weight and the Industry that Feeds on it** (USA, Dutton, 1997)
45. http://jn.nutrition.org/content/135/6/1347.full, Em Farrell, **A is for Anorexia, Anorexia Nervosa Explained** (London, Process Press Ltd., 2015) [pg. 30]

Dessert Every Damn Day

46. Roberta Pollack Seid, **Too "Close to the Bone": The Historical Context for Women's Obsession with Slenderness, Feminist Perspectives on Eating Disorders**, (New York, The Guilford Press, 1994) [pg. 4]
47. Susan Bordo, **Unbearable Weight, Feminism, Western Culture, and the Body** (California, University of California Press, 1993) [pg. 112]
48. Laura Fraser, **Losing It, America's Obsession with Weight and the Industry that Feeds on it** (USA, Dutton, 1997)
49. Linda Bacon, **Health at Every Size, The Surprising Truth About Your Weight** (Texas, Benbella Books, 2010)

50. Traci Mann, **Secrets from the Eating Lab:The Science of Weight Loss, the Myth of Willpower, and Why You Should Never Diet Again** (USA, Harper Collins, 2015)
51. Hallberg, Leif et al., "Iron Absorption from Southeast Asian Diets, II. Role of Various Factors That Might Explain Low Absorption," *American Journal of Clinical Nutrition 30, no.4*, 1977, Linda Bacon, **Health at Every Size.**

I'll Do It 10 Pounds From Now

52. www.zionmarketresearch.com/news/global-anti-aging-market

Not Sick Enough

53. www.anorexiabulimiacare.org.uk/about/statistics
54. www.b-eat.co.uk/about-beat/media-centre/information-and-statistics-about-eating-disorders
55. www.anorexiabulimiacare.org.uk/about/statistics
56. www.nationaleatingdisorders.org/get-facts-eating-disorders
57. www.eatingdisorders.org.au/key-research-a-statistics#4
58. Susan Bordo, **Unbearable Weight, Feminism, Western Culture, and the Body** (California, University of California Press, 1993)
59. www.b-eat.co.uk/about-beat/media-centre/information-and-statistics-about-eating-disorders
60. www.nice.org.uk/guidance/cg9/evidence/full-guideline-243824221

'Being Overweight is just as Unhealthy as Being Anorexic'

61. Kitta MacPherson, Edward R. Silverman, 'Fat's Overlap, Many of the experts who decide you need to shed pounds work for the industry that profit from their declarations,' (**The Star-Ledger**, 1997)
62. Laura Fraser, **Losing It, America's Obsession with Weight and the Industry that Feeds on it** (USA, Dutton, 1997)
63. Kate Harding, Marianne Kirby, **Lessons From The Fat-O-Sphere, Quit Dieting and Declare a Truce with your Body** (USA, Perigee, 2009) [pg. 170]
64. Pat Lyons, **Prescription for Harm, The Fat Studies Reader** (New York, New York University Press, 2009) [pg. 80]

65. Harriet Brown, **Body of Truth, How Science, History and Culture Drive our Obsession with Weight – and What We Can Do about It** (USA, De Capo Press, 2015) [pg.102]

66. www.consumerfreedom.com/2005/03/2768-life-expectancy-another-obesity-myth-debunked/ It's important to note that the CCF is not a source without conflicts of interest – the organisation is funded by the restaurant industry, meaning they have a vested interest in lowering concerns about the health risks of obesity so that people continue to eat out.

67. www.scientificamerican.com/article/obesity-an-overblown-epidemic-2006-12/

68. www.bmj.com/content/342/bmj.d772

69. www.washingtonpost.com/wp-dyn/content/article/2005/03/26/AR2005032601561.html

70. www.cbsnews.com/news/obesity-bigger-threat-than-terrorism/

71. Cathryn M. Delude, **Time to Take a Vacation from Television as School Ends, Keep Kids Healthy by Limiting TV Time**, (Boston Globe, 2003)

72. Flegal, KM et al. "Association of all-cause mortality with overweight and obesity using standard body mass index categories: A systemic review and meta-analysis". (JAMA 2013)

73. Dr. Reubin Andres the clinical director of the National Institute on Aging and discovered a similar U-shaped curve when researching obesity and mortality in relation to age. He found that weight gain with age resulted in lower mortality rates.

74. www.nature.com/news/the-big-fat-truth-1.13039#/obesity

75. http://exerciseiq.com.au/fit-vs-fat-an-expert-opinion/

76. Linda Bacon, **Health at Every Size, The Surprising Truth About Your Weight** (Texas, Benbella Books, 2010)

77. One of the most heart-warming stories of internet fat shaming is that of Sean O'Brien, a man who was bullied online for dancing in public because of his size, and the post went viral in 2015. The internet took a stand against the blatant fat shaming, rallying to organise a celebrity filled dance party in LA to celebrate dancing freely no matter how you look. Sean turned into an internet sensation, and is now known as 'Dancing Man'.

78. For more on this search for **Flying While Fat**, a short animated documentary by Stacy Bias.

79. R. Puhl, K.D. Brownell, "Bias Discrimination and Obesity", (Obesity Research Vol. 9, 2001)
www.telegraph.co.uk/finance/jobs/11522021/Nearly-half-of-employers-unlikely-to-hire-overweight-workers.html

80. T.A. Judge, D.M. Cable, "When It Comes to Pay, Do the Thin Win? The Effect of Weight on Pay for Men and Women", (Journal of Applied Psychology, 2010)

81. L. Angrisani et al. "Bariatric Surgery Worldwide 2013", (Obesity Surgery, 2015)

82. American Society for Metabolic and Bariatric Surgery, "Gastric Bypass and Laparoscopic Gastric Bypass." Linda Bacon, **Health at Every Size, The Surprising Truth About Your Weight** (Texas, Benbella Books, 2010)

83. https://fathealth.wordpress.com/

84. http://friskyfairy.com/wp/blog/2015/06/24/my-cancer-pt-ii-medical-fat-shaming-could-have-killed-me/

85. N. K. Amy et al., "Barriers to Routine Gynecological Cancer Screening for White and African-American Obese Women", (**International Journal of Obesity**, 2006)

86. www.theguardian.com/society/2012/apr/28/doctors-treatment-denial-smokers-obese

87. Rebecca Puhl, Chelsea A. Heuer, "The Stigma of Obesity: A Review and Update", (Obesity, 2009)

88. National Association of Anorexia Nervosa and Eating Disorders (ANAD), "Eating Disorder Statistics"

#Bodygoals

89. www.educationworld.com/a_news/report-social-media-blame-low-self-esteem-young-women-2903645

90. Segar et al, "Go Figure? Body Shape Motives are Associated with Decreased Physical Activity Participation Among Midlife Women", (Sex Roles, 2006)

91. www.sizediversityandhealth.org/content.asp?id=76

READING LIST

Naomi Wolf, **The Beauty Myth: How Images of Beauty are Used Against Women** (Great Britain, Chatto & Windus, 1990)

Marilyn Wann, **Fat! So?: Because You Don't Have to Apologize for Your Size** (USA, Ten Speed Press, 1998)

Jes Baker, **Things No One Will Tell Fat Girls: A Handbook for Unapologetic Living** (USA, Seal Press, 2015)

Laura Fraser, **Losing It, America's Obsession with Weight and the Industry that Feeds On It** (USA, Dutton, 1997)

Linda Bacon, **Health at Every Size, The Surprising Truth About Your Weight** (Texas, Benbella Books, 2010)

Harriet Brown, **Body of Truth, How Science, History and Culture Drive our Obsession with Weight – and What We Can Do about It** (USA, De Capo Press, 2015)

Kate Harding and Marianne Kirby, **Lessons From The Fat-O-Sphere, Quit Dieting and Declare a Truce with your Body** (USA, Perigee, 2009)

Evelyn Tribole and Elyse Resch, **Intuitive Eating: A Revolutionary Programme that Works** (USA, St. Martin's Griffin, 1995)

Terry Poulton, **No Fat Chicks, How Women are Brainwashed to Hate Their Bodies and Spend Their Money** (Canada, Key Porter Books, 1996)

Paul F. Campos, **The Diet Myth: Why America's Obsession with Weight is Hazardous to Your Health** (USA, Gotham Books, 2004)

Summer Innanen, **Body Image Remix: Embrace Your Body and Unleash the Fierce, Confident Woman Within** (Canada, Archangel Ink, 2015)

Cyndi Tebbel, **The Body Snatchers: How the Media Shapes Women** (Australia, Finch Publishing Pty Limited, 2000)

Susan Bordo, **Unbearable Weight, Feminism, Western Culture, and the Body** (California, University of California Press, 1993)

Esther Rothblum and Sondra Solovay [ed.] **The Fat Studies Reader**, (New York, New York University Press, 2009)

Abigail C. Saguy **What's Wrong With Fat?** (UK, Oxford University Press, 2013)

Linda Bacon and Lucy Aphramor **Body Respect, What Conventional Health Books Get Wrong, Leave Out, and Just Plain Fail to Understand about Weight** (USA, Benbella Books, 2014)

Amy Erdman Farrell, **Fat Shame:Stigma and the Fat Body in American Culture** (New York, New York University Press, 2011)

Susan Greenhalgh, **Fat-Talk Nation: The Human Costs of America's War on Fat** (USA, Cornell University Press, 2015)

Glenn A. Gaesser, **Big Fat Lies, The Truth About Your Weight and Your Health** (USA, Ballantine Books, 1996)

Kim Chernin, **The Obsession: Reflections on the Tyranny of Slenderness** (USA, Harper & Row Publishers, 1981)

ACKNOWLEDGEMENTS

I'm not sure if there are enough 'thank you's in the entire world to express how grateful I am to have had the chance to write this book, but I'll share a few anyway.

First of all thank you to my wonderful editor Morwenna, for believing that this was possible, being eternally patient and kind, and sending me pictures of baby animals throughout. Thank you to the whole team at Ebury for working so hard to help make this book happen, especially to Josie and Clarissa, and to Kelly Bastow for your awesome illustrations.

Thank you to every person in the body positive community who welcomed me, taught me a whole new way of seeing the world and myself, and who continues to fight for every body to be celebrated and valued. Thank you to all of the writers, researchers, activists and unapologetic women who've inspired me beyond words, and shaped me into who I am now.

Thank you to all of the friends who've stuck by me and cheered me on the loudest, and to the vagaggles for being my soul sisters.

Thank you to my family for being the best support system that I could ask for. To my sister, for being a brilliant role model. To my brother, for being the best human I've ever known. To my mum, for looking after me in the millions of ways you still do. To my dad, for teaching me everything and always being there to pick me up. To Topsy, Marli and Bella, for endless hugs and happiness. And to Ben, for all of the love. I couldn't have written this book, or be anywhere near where I am today without you all.

I _____, hereby pledge to stop dieting.

I promise to stop counting every bite and obsessing over the numbers.
I promise to stop letting my scales tell me how beautiful, valuable, or loved I am.
I promise to stop buying miracle weight-loss cures that don't work.
I promise to stop giving my money to companies that rely on me feeling like my body is wrong.
I promise to respect my body's hunger.
I promise that I will no longer use exercise as punishment for what I've eaten.
I promise to stop taking part in self-deprecating diet talk.
I promise to try my best to unlearn all the toxic lessons about my body that diet culture has taught me.
I promise to stop dieting, and start living instead.

Signed: _____